D0741925

Praise for *Sharing Hidden Know-How*

"The next generation of leadership effectiveness is about conversation and reflective facilitation, not just texts and tweets. *Sharing Hidden Know-How* makes the case for intentional, conversation-based leadership, and provides the practice model to pull it off. Viewed from above, this important book is itself a conversation between Kate Pugh's basic propositions and those of a diverse group of other thinkers, all woven into a unified whole. Viewed on the ground, it is an intellectual joyride, coherent, insightful, promisingly pragmatic, and with just the right measure of the personal to fully reveal a fruitful mind in motion."
—David Kantor, director, Kantor Institute, author, *Reading the Room* (Jossey-Bass)

"Knowledge is indeed power. But capturing knowledge is not enough. Organizations must have ways to engage those who know with those who need to know in a context-building process that produces real business results. With the Knowledge Jam, Kate Pugh shows you how."
—Michael Wilkinson, author, *The Secrets of Facilitation* (Jossey-Bass), managing director, Leadership Strategies

"One of the key ingredients for building capability in diverse, distributed and virtual teams is sharing know-how. Kate Pugh was my partner and advisor as I built that capability for my teams in offshore locations such as Bangalore and Chennai by using the Knowledge Jam process. This book will be an asset for all those who manage or work in virtual teams."
—Neeraj Wadhera, VP, head of Global Operations, Security and Fraud for a Fortune 100 Financial Services Company

"Organizations today are dealing increasing pressure to accomplish their objectives more effectively, more efficiently, and with fewer resources. Managers are rethinking all aspects of their business strategies to optimize the way they work, including how people connect to people and to information. *Sharing Hidden Know-How* highlights key issues for managers to tackle and practical strategies for innovative, smarter work."
—Suzanne Livingston, IBM Social Software, senior product manager, Lotus Connections

"What a fantastic replacement for the long dormant and never used lessons-learned repository! A great book for anyone who doesn't want their organization to make the same mistake twice. This book provides well documented and effective tools for really learning from your organization. As our business continues to go through transformational change, I hope to make good use of the Knowledge Jam to guarantee our success and make that transformation efficient."
—Sheryl Skifstad, MBA, MFA, MM, BSEE, senior director, Supply Chain IT at a Fortune 100 company

SHARING HIDDEN KNOW-HOW

How Managers Solve Thorny Problems with the Knowledge Jam

Katrina B. Pugh

JOSSEY-BASS
A Wiley Imprint
www.josseybass.com

Published by Jossey-Bass
A Wiley Imprint
989 Market Street, San Francisco, CA 94103-1741—www.josseybass.com

Readers should be aware that Internet Web sites offered as citations and/or sources for further information may have changed or disappeared between the time this was written and when it is read.

Limit of Liability/Disclaimer of Warranty: While the publisher and author have used their best efforts in preparing this book, they make no representations or warranties with respect to the accuracy or completeness of the contents of this book and specifically disclaim any implied warranties of merchantability or fitness for a particular purpose. No warranty may be created or extended by sales representatives or written sales materials. The advice and strategies contained herein may not be suitable for your situation. You should consult with a professional where appropriate. Neither the publisher nor author shall be liable for any loss of profit or any other commercial damages, including but not limited to special, incidental, consequential, or other damages.

Jossey-Bass books and products are available through most bookstores. To contact Jossey-Bass directly call our Customer Care Department within the U.S. at 800-956-7739, outside the U.S. at 317-572-3986, or fax 317-572-4002.

Jossey-Bass also publishes its books in a variety of electronic formats. Some content that appears in print may not be available in electronic books.

The opening quote in Chapter 11 is from "At the Cliff Edge of Life," from CROSSING THE UNKNOWN SEA copyright © 2001 by David Whyte. Used by permission of Riverhead Books, an imprint of Penguin Group (USA) Inc.

Library of Congress Cataloging-in-Publication Data
Pugh, Katrina.
    Sharing hidden know-how : how managers solve thorny problems with the knowledge jam / Katrina Pugh.
        p. cm. – (J-b us non-franchise leadership; 387)
    Includes bibliographical references and index.
    ISBN 978-0-470-87681-7 (hardback)
    1. Knowledge management.   2. Organizational learning.   3. Organizational learning Management.   I. Title.
    HD30.2.P84 2011
    658.4'038--dc22

                                                            2010052164

Printed in the United States of America
FIRST EDITION

HB Printing   10 9 8 7 6 5 4 3 2 1
PB Printing   10 9 8 7 6 5 4 3 2 1

CONTENTS

FOREWORD

Sharing Hidden Know-How offers the opportunity for the reader to rethink the idea of lessons learned so that what is learned is an active exchange between those who have just gained important knowledge from a project and co-workers who want to improve the way they are working on a similar topic. The process is not limiting us to a look backward but to regard the process as an act of *discovering, with the help of colleagues, what can be drawn from a recent experience.*

Any organization must have the ability to learn from its own experience if that organization wants to change and innovate. Unfortunately "lessons learned" has earned a negative reputation in many organizations. And the reality is that such efforts have often been ineffective. However, a new way for organizations to learn from their successes and failures is provided in this book.

Kate Pugh invented the very interactive process that became "Knowledge Jam" while working at Intel and then carried it with her to Fidelity and finally to her own consulting practice. I've had the opportunity to work with Kate on a number of Knowledge Jams so I know that the process works. I've seen it draw out knowledge that an originating team would not have mentioned without process having stimulated their thinking. And I have even seen the members of the originating team come to a new understanding spurred by a provocative question asked during the Knowledge Jam.

The most difficult aspect of lessons learned has always been moving what has been learned into practice. Knowledge Jam addresses this issue by bringing brokers (representatives of the seeker organization) in to ask questions and to be responsible for implementing what they just learned in their own parts of the organization. Brokers are selected from those groups that are most likely to be able to make use of the knowledge that the originating team has gained through their work. When brokers leave the Knowledge Jam, they do so with specific implementation intentions and are measured as they complete those. The formality of the broker role solves the long-standing impediment to the implementation of lessons learned.

Knowledge Jam is an interesting combination of *push* and *pull*. Push happens when I tell you what I think you need to know. Pull happens when you ask a question based on your own need to know.

Knowledge Jam employs push when a manager decides that what has been learned by a project team needs to be shared. Targeted and limited push is the most effective way to push knowledge. Pull happens in the Knowledge Jam through the questions that brokers ask to pull knowledge from the originating team. The questions they ask arise out of their own curiosity and the answers they receive help them implement the lessons learned in their own units.

Knowledge Jam is a conversational process. Conversation remains the most effective way to exchange tacit ("hidden") knowledge. Explicit knowledge can be shared through documents, but tacit knowledge requires the give and take of conversation, which clarifies meaning, explores alternatives, expands the context, and creates *new* meaning.

Knowledge management (KM) is badly in need of more processes like the Knowledge Jam. Now, after nearly fifteen years, we have learned that the transfer of tacit knowledge requires conversation, not just documentation, no matter how exhaustively that documentation is written.

The reason why documentation is not the answer lies not in the inadequacy of technology but in how our brains store knowledge. Everything is stored, not in whole chunks, but in bits and pieces of experience. What we think of as tacit knowledge is really the human ability to draw on our past experiences to respond to new problems or questions. My friend Nick Milton tells a story about teaching his daughter to drive. His daughter asked, "When changing gear going down a steep hill, do I put my foot on the clutch before I put it on the brake, or do I brake first?" To answer that question, Nick had to get into the car and put himself "in the situation" in order to draw on his tacit knowledge.

That is what happens in a Knowledge Jam. The originators are asked questions that put them "in the situation" of the brokers. In order to answer the questions, the originators put together bits and pieces from different parts of what was probably a year-long experience. Knowledge that was tacit until the originator heard the question now comes together in the moment of responding. Originators do not "know" the response until faced with the need for it. Karl Weick, the well-known organizational theorist, is fond of saying, "How do I know what I think until I hear what I say?"

If knowledge management wants to meet the challenge of making use of the tacit knowledge, it will have to use processes like the Knowledge Jam, which bring the seeker and the originator into conversation with each other. Knowledge Jam is leading the way!

Nancy M. Dixon, Ph.D., principal, Common Knowledge Associates, and author of *Common Knowledge: How Companies Thrive by Sharing What They Know* and the "Conversation Matters" blog (nancydixonblog.com).

INTRODUCTION

At a new production facility of a major computer hardware manufacturer, performance appeared relatively stable during the first month of operation. Yet, when veteran operators (who had been "on-loan" to the new facility) departed, yields dropped and outages skyrocketed. Senior management couldn't comprehend why this could occur. Traditional knowledge-transfer methods, such as veterans' painstakingly recording procedures and one-on-one job-shadowing, failed to sufficiently engage operators in their future roles and failed to draw out the range of things that could go wrong when all parts of the factory were up and running.

In order to accelerate knowledge transfer between consultants, a leading strategy consulting firm decided to produce video recordings of veteran consultants. After hours of recording time, preparation, tagging, uploading, and promotion, the fifteen-minute videos were not looked at by new project teams, even when those new project teams were doing follow-on work at the same clients as the consultants in the videos. The follow-on teams didn't find that watching videos "fit" with their road-warrior schedules and provided little value over and above simply reading PowerPoints. They continued to interact directly with the veteran consultants to sound them out about how historical lessons learned would play out in the future projects.

When NGOs tried to introduce fertilizer application procedures to African farmers, initially the uptake was poor. The fertilizer process didn't fit in with the farmers' planting routine or the credit structures already in place for seed purchases. Unfortunately, fertilization didn't fit with the production methods or the local customs either. Until the community could be included in the process, farmers felt their new methods and values were in conflict.[1]

Sound familiar?

Managers have tried to deal with the failure to spread knowledge across organizations and groups by investing in process, people, and technology. Twenty years ago, it was "intelligence acquisition." Fifteen years ago, we tried "organizational learning." Ten years ago we tried "collaboration tools." Today, we put great hope in Web 2.0 or Enterprise 2.0.[2] And throughout these periods we applied dozens of knowledge-elicitation strategies like after action reviews. These practices each addressed only part of the problem.

I lived this first-hand. In my twenties as a strategy consultant I joined the intelligence acquisition crowd, and spent many long nights and weekends collecting information and designing data-structures for mining. After business school in the 1990s, I immersed myself in organizational learning. I memorized "action inquiry" phrases, scrawled systems thinking loops across walls of butcher paper, and sat in many dialogue circles. As collaboration technologies evolved, I trumpeted knowledge-portals and groupware tools. Today, I've become a zealot for Web 2.0 tools and Enterprise 2.0[3] tools—"Enterprise Social Software Platforms" or ESSPs—which tie people and knowledge together across companies and continents "frictionlessly."

Through that journey each business practice targeted symptoms of the times (info glut, change-resistance, globalization), but, taken independently, none has given managers consistent insight into how our experts or teams think about complex problems, and how to expose and apply that hidden know-how. Nor have those practices enabled us to consistently mobilize ourselves apace with markets and competitors, let alone to avert threats to our global climate or national security. How can we get better at sensing and responding (or, as President Obama's chief technology officer, Aneesh Chopra, puts it "How can we best contain, bob, and weave?"[4])? (See Figure I.1.)

THE ORIGIN OF THE KNOWLEDGE JAM

People have told me that I'm good at this bobbing and weaving thing. They tell me I've a knack for "reinventing" myself. I'm flattered, but that's not exactly how I see it. I think it's actually because I'm a packrat. Unlike my friends who collect cars and gadgets, I hoard yellow-highlighted grad school readings, worn running shoes, decades-old computer disks, and annotated spreadsheets of people I know. At first, when I counted the boxes of paper (twelve), the CDs (forty-eight),

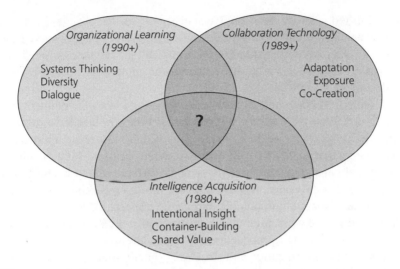

Figure I.1. *Historical Competences for Managing Knowledge*

loosely organized contacts (893), the pairs of running shoes (nine). I asked myself (rather sheepishly), "With all the great knowledge out there on the web, aren't I supposed to be clutter-free? The shining example of efficiency?"

But then, I saw my own method here: my things are imprinted with my experience. I find these useful because they are *accessible* and they are wrapped in layer of visible—and, surprisingly, practical—*context*. For the packrat like me, just as for the organization, context bridges to the useful from the random and arms me for what may come.

This I saw when working for Intel Solution Services, a small IT consultancy that was a division of Intel Corporation.[5] We lived in a sea of complexity—our clients had huge data-center optimization challenges, pressured to expand capacity and speed, while reducing costs and power consumption. Meanwhile, we had to generate both service revenue (happy clients) and chip revenue (Intel design wins).

We had a few highly successful consultants who had solved some of these problems in separate engagements across disparate industries and geographies. Management felt that brilliant ideas were not getting around the firm fast enough. Time-worn knowledge "capture" approaches—such as "post-mortems," "after action reviews," and "lessons learned"—seemed to fail because the knowledge captured had only limited value or shelf life. Even energetic idea exchanges in "town halls" had a short half-life, as only few intrepid associates absorbed the shared "best known methods." Nor did blogs or Innovation Jams produce high-quality, relevant, or enduring content without considerable effort.

Thinking about context, it occurred to me that we were doing things backward. We were pushing, not pulling. People who needed to use the knowledge should drive the conversation, as they were more likely draw out context that would make applying knowledge easier. But we couldn't completely abandon structure—we still needed coordination and a way to ensure that the concepts were relevant to our consulting service and sales goals. Nor could we underestimate the importance of collaboration technology—we were, after all, in seven countries and four time zones.

Ever a packrat, I proposed we bring in the three practice experiences. That is, the intention and structure ("Facilitation") of Intelligence Acquisition, the participation and social interaction ("Conversation") of Organizational Learning, and the idea mobility and integration ("Translation") of Collaboration Technology.

Here's how it worked: After some planning with management, I would bring together a team of project veterans, or the team of *knowledge originators*,[6] into conversation with seeker, or receiving, groups' representatives or *knowledge brokers*. This ninety-minute real-time exchange I facilitated virtually, typing into a Word document shared via a live-capture web tool, Microsoft LiveMeeting, where everyone could correct and comment on what was said. Afterwards, the brokers would recast, in their own formats, knowledge they had helped to collect (frequently with a few post-meeting clarifications from the originators). The collected ideas showed up in project plans, marketing documents, job aids, and process maps.

The "Knowledge Jam" term and jazz metaphor (both of which I adopted later) nicely capture how the brokers and knowledge originators "riffed" during the session. As they built on each other's ideas, originators' recollections became more specific and they added context ("Here's why we did that *then* and not before. ..."). Context made the knowledge more relevant to the brokers, as they were intent on discerning the portability of the ideas to *their* new contexts. Improvisation continued: our Knowledge Jam notes and diagrams not only were fed into process documents as planned, but they also fed MS SharePoint sites and forums, where other consultants found new ways to both leverage the

Jam content and to Jam further, with the now-famous Knowledge Jam participants.

THREE STURDY DISCIPLINES

In the years since, the three disciplines—Facilitation, Conversation, and Translation—came to be the sturdy legs of a Knowledge Jam stool. What appeared to be critical to the Knowledge Jam was that balance of coordination, improvisation, and a pragmatic "pull" of knowledge into its future uses around the organization. Unlike other attempts at knowledge transfer, this collaborative approach moved things along more efficiently and with more of a sense of ownership.

And closure. Originators knew their know-how was getting put to use, brokers felt that they had a hand in getting out "the good stuff," and managers felt dollars were not going into a sort of knowledge repository "black hole."

You'll be learning more about how these three disciplines flow through the Jam process, where they came from, and how, as culture and behaviors, they may become part of any dynamic knowledge-work culture (see Figure I.2). For now, let's get acquainted with them because they are the lead characters in the story:

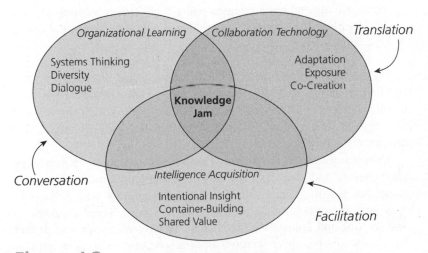

Figure I.2. *Knowledge Jam Disciplines for Managing Knowledge*

1. *Facilitation:* A facilitator helps select, plan, and coordinate the Knowledge Jam process, organizing the early structuring of the concepts (or "agenda"), providing quality control, aligning Jams to business objectives, and, most importantly, setting a tone of curiosity and respect for the Jam—a tone that fuels conversation which, in turn, yields unique and reusable insight. Facilitators model and reward respectful, open inquiry and discourage defensive, criticizing or protective attitudes.

2. *Conversation:* Knowledge Jam invites the curiosity of those who will use (or transmit) the knowledge. An open conversation between the knowledge brokers and originators/originator teams surfaces the conditions around the facts (How did you decide to do *that*?). It can also surface connections between events, outcomes, people, and the industry or markets that we hadn't considered. Drawing out context in this manner makes captured know-how more translatable from context to context.

3. *Translation:* Involvement gives the knowledge brokers a sense of ownership. Later, the brokers (and their cyber allies) efficiently translate and transmit the context-rich knowledge re-mixed within their world and reformatted for action. New vehicles suit the knowledge seekers, those who are embarking on a decision, product innovation, process revision, or outreach program. Brokers use change management strategies and collaboration technology like ESSPs to ensure Jammed knowledge is used and doesn't stagnate in a repository.

Facilitation, Conversation, and Translation are threaded into the Knowledge Jam's five-step cycle: Select, Plan, Discover/Capture, Broker, and Reuse. That cycle runs from targeting what (and whose) know-how is needed through eliciting it, translating it, reusing it, and measuring its impact.

In *Sharing Hidden Know-How* I start by describing the Knowledge Jam process, and then explain how facilitation maintains the tone throughout the five steps—involving the originators and brokers in know-how discovery and its remixing for new uses. Then, chapters on Conversation and Translation focus on the Discover/Capture and Broker steps, respectively, where relationships emerge, and so do new applications for the knowledge, enabled by collaboration tools, social media, and other technologies. Figure I.3 shows the steps.

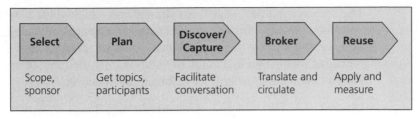

Figure I.3. *Knowledge Jam Steps*

What You'll See in This Book

■ Chapter 1: "Knowledge Jam Rationale," describes three thorny knowledge-work problems—"knowledge blind spots," "knowledge mismatches," and "knowledge jails." Knowledge Jam responds to these by insisting on more intentional prioritization and planning, by involving knowledge seekers in choosing and surfacing knowledge relevant to them, and by having a "put-knowledge-to-work" step (not just a repository). I'll teach you the Knowledge Jam process in Chapter 2, and then expand on Knowledge Jam's three disciplines in Chapters 3 through 5; then in Chapter 6 I'll see where Knowledge Jam rejuvenates the manager plagued by thorny problems into a "Bespeckled, Married, Emancipated" hero.

■ Chapter 2, "Knowledge Jam Basics," describes the five steps of the Knowledge Jam cycle. That is, how we choose, prepare, execute, and get value from the Knowledge Jam. We'll discuss how each step reveals Knowledge Jam's uniquely collaborative spirit and its dogged focus on applying—not just collecting—know-how. You will learn how the five-step process makes up Knowledge Jam's essential *mechanics*, while the disciplines of Facilitation, Conversation, and Translation (detailed in the chapters that follow) make up its *ecology*.

■ Chapters 3 through 6 explore the key differentiators of Knowledge Jam and why it is uniquely suited to solve those thorny problems that drag efficiency, innovation, and job satisfaction:

  ■ Chapter 3, "Discipline 1: Facilitation," explains how facilitators bring intention, tone, and a value-orientation to the Knowledge Jam. They play the roles of process consultant, project manager, change agent, cheerleader, and networker.

Their responsibilities range from strategizing a high-value Jam "portfolio" to adjusting the subtle chemistry of each conversation. In this chapter we also discuss some of the finer techniques of facilitation that come in handy during the Jam cycle, such as maintaining energy or diffusing dysfunction.

■ Chapter 4, "Discipline 2: Conversation," shows how the "posture of openness," the "pursuit of diversity," and the "practices of dialogue" make collaborative knowledge elicitation possible. Bringing a diverse, widened perspective to respectful interactions results in more generative conversation. That, in turn, helps us to generate more useful know-how. Conversation also fuels a lasting rapport between originators and brokers from which we all can benefit as we take on the task of putting know-how work.

■ Chapter 5, "Discipline 3: Translation," provides a how-to for Brokering, that is, knowing and representing the knowledge-customer or "seeker," remixing content for reuse, promoting and modeling reuse, and capitalizing on the relationships triggered in the Knowledge Jam to help refine ideas. Here I also describe how social media best broadcast and integrate know-how, improve originator-seeker networking, and extend knowledge velocity and durability.

■ Chapter 6, "Bespeckled, Married, and Emancipated," revisits the "blind spots," "mismatches," and "jail"—thorny problems from Chapter 1—and recaps how the Knowledge Jam's boundary-spanning (Facilitation discipline), participative knowledge-elicitation (Conversation discipline), and stewardship (Translation discipline) are a viable combination for overcoming those hazards.

■ Chapters 7 and 8 explore where Knowledge Jam came from and where it might be extended into the planning and managing of change in the organization:

■ Chapter 7, "Knowledge Jam Heritage: Prequel to the Three Disciplines," shows how the disciplines of Knowledge Jam (Facilitation, Conversation, and Translation) derive, respectively, from three business practices developed over the last twenty years: intelligence acquisition, organizational learning, and collaboration technology. Rooted in those business practices, Knowledge Jam may also be in for an exciting ride, as those practices are not standing still. They evolve as work becomes more wired, more globalized, and more interdependent. Knowledge Jam as a practice will also evolve, but it won't forget its origins.

- Chapter 8, "Comparing Knowledge Jam to Other Knowledge-Capture Methods," proposes a model for looking at Knowledge Jam's properties alongside other knowledge capture/transfer methods. Many managers have asked, "What's new here?" To help you answer that question, I provide a side-by-side comparison so that you can consider when Knowledge Jam might replace or complement other methods that you are currently using to bring out and share know-how. Knowledge Jam is in good company, but it is the only practice that scores high on all three method components: structure and intention (Facilitation), sense-making (Conversation), and knowledge pull and integration (Translation).

- Chapters 9 through 11 and the Appendices help you to take action:

  - Chapter 9, "Building a Knowledge Jam Practice," shows how to define, sell, staff, launch, and evaluate a Knowledge Jam program. You'll also find frameworks to model your Knowledge Jam business case. I invite you to explore how to integrate Knowledge Jam into a larger KM or innovation strategy. And I propose Knowledge Jam facilitation—with its strategizing, planning, eliciting, and motivating—as a leadership developmental opportunity.

  - Chapter 10, "Knowledge Jam for Leading Change and Leveraging Social Media," explores Knowledge Jam as a practice that can be used in making strategy—and "making it stick." Knowledge Jam brings about a culture of change—intention, openness, and stewardship—and brings that culture into today's tools of change, such as formalized strategic planning and transformational technology implementations. In this chapter, Knowledge Jam and social media switch roles: Social media efforts are not simply Knowledge Jam's enablers, but they can be enabled by it, resulting in better content quality, interaction quality, and velocity for ideas.

- Chapter 11, "An Invitation," considers how current events and collaboration technology developments could mean new uses of Knowledge Jam and new forms of "Jamming." It also issues an invitation to the reader to participate in a community of "Jammers Without Boarders."

- The Appendices provide a glossary, templates, case studies, and FAQs, as well as deep dives on Knowledge Types.

Knowledge Jam improves how many actors inside and outside the organization adapt to the thorny problems in knowledge work in our marketplaces, institutions, and nations. It does this by building on what we know (even when we didn't know we knew) and by putting hidden know-how into action. I'm writing this book for several of you actors.

- For the business, IT, or HR manager (who might be a Knowledge Jam sponsor and underwrite the business case for Knowledge Jam), I describe Knowledge Jam's rationale, program steps, and its surprisingly lean use of resources.

- For the process facilitator (who plays the drumbeat of the Jam), I help you lead through each of the steps and learn to set a tone of common curiosity.

- For the participants (knowledge originators and brokers), I help you to listen, probe, and reflect out loud on your own experiences, and discern how to remix the know-how (and its context) for new processes, products, strategies, and organizational structures.

- Finally, for change agents (doing projects, innovating products, and improving your operations and functions), I offer improvements in knowledge absorption into your planning, and change absorption into your organization. You realize these when you put Knowledge Jam's process and disciplines "inside," and Knowledge Jammers capitalize on collaboration tools such as wikis, blogs, microblogs, and teamspaces.

In a way, I'm *your* broker, too. Most of the chapters are practical how-tos with examples and my lessons from others who have been my knowledge originators for this book. I will share stories and references I've found useful as I've played facilitator, sponsor, broker, and champion myself.

Just a note on terminology: I use the terms "knowledge," "know-how," and "insight" interchangeably, and I don't get hung up on whether his *wisdom* is her *data*, so long as it all makes us more productive and resourceful. I *do* make the distinction between explicit knowledge (written, documented) and tacit knowledge (unwritten, hidden). For Knowledge Jam, we care most about the latter. Also, I use the term "organization" generously. It applies as much to the incorporated or registered company as to the non-profit group, the government agency, and the loose network of affiliated practitioners.

Knowledge Jam improves the organization's resilience by drawing in practices from the best of intelligence acquisition (Facilitation), organizational learning (conversation), and collaboration (Translation). I hope you'll come to see that a Knowledge Jam culture of intention, openness, and stewardship can extend beyond the Knowledge Jam cycle (Select-Plan-Discover/Capture-Broker-Reuse) and into the fiber of your organization. I invite you to join me in a practice that's more authentic, efficient, and, ultimately, more rewarding than traditional means of process improvement, change planning, and innovation. Just grab your tambourine and join the jazz ensemble!

CHAPTER

KNOWLEDGE JAM RATIONALE: SOLVING THORNY PROBLEMS

"Knowledge Jam Rationale," describes three thorny knowledge-work problems—"knowledge blind spots," "knowledge mismatches," and "knowledge jails." Knowledge Jam responds to these by insisting on more intentional prioritization and planning, by involving knowledge seekers in choosing and surfacing knowledge relevant to them, and by having a "put-knowledge-to-work" step (not just a repository). I'll teach you the Knowledge Jam process in Chapter 2, and then expand on Knowledge Jam's three disciplines in Chapters 3 through 5; then in Chapter 6 I'll see where Knowledge Jam rejuvenates the manager plagued by thorny problems into a "Bespeckled, Married, Emancipated" hero.

"I could speak volumes about the inhuman perversity of the New England weather, but I will give but a single specimen. I like to hear rain on a tin roof. So I covered part of my roof with tin, with an eye to that luxury. Well, sir, do you think it ever rains on that tin? No, sir; skips every time."

SAMUEL CLEMENS (MARK TWAIN), AT THE NEW ENGLAND SOCIETY'S SEVENTY-FIRST ANNUAL DINNER, NEW YORK CITY[1]

Being able to leverage and quickly act on knowledge is the key to your competitiveness—whether you are a for-profit business, a non-profit organization, a nation, or a network. Insights into better manufacturing processes could improve cycle times and position the organization for cost leadership. Marketing insights could point to creative strategies or product attributes that could help to differentiate the brand. Engineering know-how resulting from solving yield problems in one part of your organization could improve manufacturing efficiencies in your other divisions.

But these nuggets only contribute to competitive advantage when there is some effective mechanism for transferring the knowledge. More, such nuggets contribute to *sustainable* competitive advantage only when we can put know-how to work across the organization just in time. That's when the process and culture are in place. Then we're fit to pivot and respond to opportunities, while anticipating change. Many organizations fail to take advantage of their employees' knowledge or that of the groups with which they collaborate (their networks). Consider these lost opportunities:

Markets

Savvy customers with ever more accessible price and product information negotiate down our margins and demand rapid product enhancement. Even though we know that timely innovation correlates with corporate profits, we often don't make sense of the new product, market, or channel information that streams across our customer interactions. We realize that insight resides in those of our employees or partners most involved with customers, but only the most agile companies tap it before the market or the competition makes sense of it before we do. For example, airline phone reps may observe that harried flyers changing flights anger because agents ask the same questions each time they change a flight. If only website designers could craft a form that could eliminate the first ninety seconds of the call, flyers would not complain or leave, and millions in service costs could be saved.

Processes

Organizations face price pressure from competitors with lower labor, materials, capital, and transactions costs. For example, engineers tell us that spreading best practice procurement and production processes reduces operations costs. However, we struggle to discern what the best practices are. Seasoned managers are increasingly scarce (due to retirements, layoffs, transfers, and simply overextension). Meanwhile, bits of process knowledge are diffused among many distributed team members, scattered across the organization's divisions or functions—or even across the supply chain.

Networks

Organizations are interdependent (for example, in expanding markets, cleaning rivers, restoring fish stocks, or reducing carbon emissions). We sense that problems can only be solved collectively, that is, with diverse departments, diverse companies, diverse communities, or diverse nations. However, interpreting multi-organizational problems is often like swimming in brackish water—we can't see the weeds until we are in them. We feel the presence of other players or policies that obstruct or amplify our actions, but only after time has passed. We struggle to navigate through this murky mix, to understand who's acting, when, and how the whole system behaves.

In short, as employees, market players, and citizens, we need more timely and efficient approaches to take in and make use of know-how.

WHAT'S NOT WORKING?

Time-worn knowledge "capture" programs—such as "post-mortems," after action reviews, "lessons learned," or automated "document-authoring"—often fail because the know-how captured is not representative of experience, is incomplete (or complete at the wrong detail level), or doesn't get into the right hands. In the rare cases when a capture "event" results in an idea hand-off and a document, the "lessons-learned" fail to inform other teams or divisions without heroic efforts by motivated networkers or by desperate learners.

For example, a team that built a series of four department websites in just six weeks did a post-mortem on the remarkably accelerated process. They spent fifteen person-hours filling a spreadsheet with best-known-methods ("BKMs"). But the spreadsheet failed to inform any other web team (and, ironically, the originating team, themselves). It was difficult to find the final version in the repository, and even when anyone did, he would find that it was labeled with a specific technology version that was being phased out. You'd have to be pretty curious to open it up and dig for the more enduring messages.

Some claim technology, like crawlers and recommendation engines, can solve this thorny problem. But many a KM manager will attest that simply installing technology to bind together people doesn't guarantee knowledge quality, relevance, or durability. Our tools may very well make us stupid. With ever more abundant technology (like social media, which I'll be redeeming later!), people are less and less inclined to reflect on and document know-how except in the provincial ways, without considering novel future applications. In modern collaboration-rich environments, we run the risk of operating under the fallacy that all useful truths will float to the "top of the feed" in the course of our blogging, Yammer-ing, or online conversations.

Why are none of these approaches working? After more than a decade of trying, most organizations have two troublesome knowledge issues unresolved.

1. They fail to surface *usable* know-how.

2. They fail to *circulate* what they have to those who need it, where they need it, when they need it.

This was Prusak and Jacobson's premise in 2006 when, at Babson College, they studied knowledge transaction costs for 200 knowledge-workers at US Defense Intelligence Agency, Battelle, Educational Testing Service, and Novartis.[2] The researchers measured the entire knowledge-transaction process, starting from the knowledge-seeker's initial search for experts, then to their negotiating time with those sources, next to their asking or eliciting knowledge, and, finally, to their actually adapting that knowledge to a new problem.

Tellingly, they found that 38 percent of the seeker's time, on average, was spent drawing knowledge out of experts. Then another 46 percent of the time was spent figuring out how to make use of knowledge in a new setting. The remaining 16 percent—a small share of the knowledge transaction time—was identifying and getting to the experts. Figure 1.1 captures this as a timeline.

In one study I conducted for a financial services company doing information technology projects, knowledge transaction costs for U.S. employees working in the United States were in the range of fifteen hours (approximately two person-days per knowledge-seeking event) across the spectrum from searching, through negotiating, through asking, and through translating/adapting. That number went up to two and one-half weeks (thirteen person-days) for India employees working in India on U.S.-based IT projects. Consistent with Prusak and

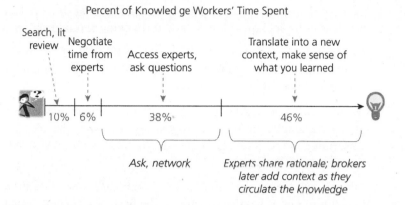

Figure 1.1. *Knowledge Transaction Time Breakdown*

Data reprinted by permission of *Harvard Business Review*. Percentage of Knowledge Workers' Time Spent from "The Cost of Knowledge" by Al Jacobson and Laurence Prusak, *Harvard Business Review*, November 2006, reprint F0611H. Copyright © 2006 by the Harvard Business School Publishing Corporation; all rights reserved.

Jacobson's study, the gap was due largely to the fact that India employees found it difficult to efficiently inquire with their virtual colleagues (for example, about product specifications or code modules), and they had a tough time applying the Americans' ideas to their unique situation in India. For example, U.S. teams referred frequently to a large U.S. initiative that had been cancelled, and for which few had good documentation. Indian knowledge-recipients would have to seek out the often overworked, beleaguered developer who knew about the dependencies between the initiatives and who could articulate the impacts today. Then the Indian teams would have to figure out what code might be impacted locally back in Bangalore.

Such an analysis is concerning. Why are we putting a lot of our time and energy into not-so-productive interactions? From Prusak and Jacobson and my own experience, it appears that organizations fail to share "hidden" know-how because they start with three faulty assumptions:

1. Managers think they know where the knowledge with the highest economic value resides. They believe that simply pointing

knowledge-capture resources (tools, interviewers) at smart people or teams will yield good know-how for solving future problems;

2. Knowledge-originators (experts or teams) think they can accurately predict what subjects or topics or context will be important to potential knowledge-seekers; and,

3. Managers assume that knowledge-seekers are known, or in-waiting (for example, trolling the repository, perusing the blog, or subscribing to the system), and would voluntarily take the time to seek that knowledge out.

From my experience with hundreds of companies, none of these assumptions turn out to be truly accurate. The system needs more than isolated knowledge-originators' time, knowledge stores, search tools, and faith in seekers' curiosity. It takes process and participation.

To sense what's missing, think about these problems as "knowledge blind spots," "knowledge mismatches," and "knowledge jails."

BLIND SPOTS

"Knowledge blind spots" are gaps in our understanding about where knowledge resides or gaps in our awareness that pieces of a puzzle might be spread out among unexpected sources. For most organizations, blind spots are not a concern during business as usual. Subject-matter experts, or SMEs, and their teams are humming along, delivering projects and managing operations. But then, when reorganizations, outages, retirements, or market mishaps occur, our blind spots are exposed. Then managers make a wild dash to identify "who knows" and "what they know."

Blind Spot 1: Knowledge Flight

Our most common blind spots concern our at-risk employees or teams. In many industries and government agencies, experienced employees are retiring or being downsized, taking their valuable expertise out the door. Meanwhile, experienced teams are routinely disbanding with incomplete knowledge handoffs:

■ *Retirees* leave behind a large gap between themselves and the relatively inexperienced thirty-somethings who comprise the next hump in the demographic camel. Organizations are rightly anxious about losing so much experience, if not the people themselves.

Having tried everything from exit interviews to bringing retirees back in consulting roles, they have had relatively little success in retaining useful knowledge or in getting the thirty-somethings to bother accessing the expert knowledge that has carefully been collected for their benefit.

- *RIF'd (reduction-in-force) employees* may have been targeted because of their span of control (de-layering), their failure to conform to corporate culture, or their unfortunate assignment to non-essential products or services. A friend recounted her recent layoff due to de-layering. A ten-year project manager, she was the human glue for several multi-million-dollar programs. With her departure, out walked the tacit knowledge about how the team worked, who knew what, and who knew whom.

- *Transferred employees* leave behind a gap, even when their movement is predicted. Much knowledge has lived in the interactions they routinely had with co-workers. For example, they never thought to write down how they learned to collaborate with a demanding boss, a siloed function, or mistrusting supplier or how they managed to persuade leadership to take a risk on a local project. Or it may be that the success that won them the new positions spawns a bit of competition with their previous departments. (A bit more sinister is the transferred employee's tendency to hoard knowledge and contacts to justify her uniqueness in the new role.)

- *Consultants and contractors* are often mocked as merely "reading your watch to you" and not providing unique insights. In my experience, this is not usually the case; clients can get a lot of insight out of those temporary employees. They often synthesize a vast store of knowledge about such things as how departments interact, how systems work, how the market influences decisions, and who (at the client, in the industry) knows what piece of all this. Rapid, intense sense-making is both the luxury and curse of that profession. (Yes, consultants do lack work/life balance!) Rarely do clients formally capitalize on this knowledge store.

- *Project teams* often disband with little awareness of their collective knowledge. Despite the attempts at after action reviews, postmortems, and process documentation, many teams never write down or speak out enough about what they have learned as a *collective.* For example, before disbanding, a corporate legal team failed to assemble a collective picture of how they built a legal defense, how they came to negotiate their respective roles, how they dealt with subpoenas, or how they successfully (or unsuccessfully) interacted with external legal counsel.

Blind Spot 2: Separated Puzzle Pieces

A second blind spot is this very issue that the legal team faced: where the knowledge is fragmented across members of a team, organization, or network, and not in one place. At least not enough to make sense of it as a whole picture. This know-how, what Nancy Dixon calls "Common Knowledge,"[3] is remarkably useful once seen in the composite. When combined, different insights may refine or amplify each other. Consider this example from a former oil company engineer:

> *"Many of the examples that first come to my mind are situations where we had problems that originated across org boundaries. For example, while I was at [Oil Company] the process engineers designed a piping system to integrate two new crude tanks into the refinery feed network, and they had it all spec'd out before sending it out to the instrumentation and control group (my group). But when we saw the design we noted that there was a lack of degrees of freedom in the control network which would result in oscillatory and unstable control. So we demanded that they change the whole design, which caused major re-dos on the design and so we wasted a lot of time.*
>
> *"Issues like this happen all the time in construction projects: process engineers design it one way, the control guys say it has to change, then the civil guys say the required foundations are too expensive, then the piping guys say that the pipe runs are too long, the environmental guys say we need spill protection everywhere, the safety guys say we need redundant everything, and it goes around and around in iterations. To some extent I think that the iterations are inevitable, because as each group digs deeper into details they always find new issues that affect everything, but eventually, and somewhat miraculously to me, it all comes together. And of course, sometimes it results in failures and valve blowouts like in the Gulf."*

So how do you know where complementary knowledge lives? Social network analysis (SNA) is one reputable tool for identifying knowledge concentrations (for example, clusters of subject-matter experts) and people who connect them ("hubs"). SNA is a means of mapping the existence and strength of interactions among knowledge workers. It entails identifying and mapping the network—pathways, nodes, and hubs of knowledge exchange—and assessing the frequency or volume of exchange at various parts of the map. Based on data culled from a survey or email (or social media activity) tracking tool, SNA gives a point-in-time picture of the flow of knowledge. It might, in the future, be helpful in predicting how cognitive diversity, brought together in *cross*-network conversation, could enable contributors to solve complex problems. (More to come in Chapter 4 on this type of diversity!)

The trick is actually getting discrepant ideas to flow across networks, once they (the ideas and the network) are discovered.

And then to do it again and again.

MISMATCHES

The second knowledge transfer issue after "blind spots" is "mismatch." That is, our failure to get out the knowledge that is the most valuable to the organization or to *make it valuable* by framing it in a way that makes it usable across time, place, or culture.

In some cases, we're simply piling up knowledge with the hope that people will use it, without regard to the relevancy, comprehensibility, or quality. (Just like the application developers' post-mortem earlier in this chapter—an example of "If you pile it, they will come.") Or, in other cases, we're inadvertently rewarding people for innovation at the expense of efficiency (reuse). In both cases we've built in a mismatch between the knowledge-capture program and people's incentives to use it. And finally, mismatches result from our failure to really grasp where and when knowledge seekers could apply knowledge in their work. So, even if they were had the incentive to reuse knowledge, the good stuff is hard to find. (Another dreaded epithet: "Too much of my effort, too late.")

Here is some more color on these mismatch types:

Mismatch 1: Lack of Context

Often a knowledge artifact, such as a PowerPoint presentation, is very specific to a given project or problem and reflects many unwritten assumptions. Assumptions could include previous projects, related problems (solved and unsolved), political or economic currents, and localized use of terms or acronyms. For example, a final report for a factory feasibility study might take for granted that the company already has built several facilities of the same size in a given state. So permitting issues may be omitted from the final feasibility report, even while such issues could potentially be a showstopper elsewhere.

Where context about the knowledge is thin, knowledge seekers will have to come to their own conclusions about how to adapt the knowledge to their new application. This takes effort, and in some cases, seekers make mistakes.[4] In other cases, the mismatch in context results in seekers' disregarding potential gems. For example, a Chicago-based creative agency might find French ad copy with attractive artwork from their subsidiary in Paris. If none of the Chicagoans spoke French and saw that the artwork was tremendously effective for selling widgets, the team might not know that they had a reusable gem in hand.

Mismatch 2: Mixed Incentives

Knowledge originators often face mixed incentives. Many KM programs jump-start their knowledge-bases by having all employees submit content. Though much of what originators share can be very useful, many times junk is mixed with gem.[5] The incentive may have rewarded contribution at the expense of quality. Matched with a second incentive to reuse what's in there, you see knowledge-seekers earnestly searching—and getting frustrated—as they find that the search effort doesn't pay off.

Another mixed incentive pits reusing knowledge up against "original thought" incentives (or "intellectual capital contribution" performance measures, as we called it in my consulting days). Knowledge seekers are less inclined to seek other examples of ideas when they are incentivized to "invent." Meanwhile, originators might hold back, fearing they might not "get credit" before someone else capitalizes on their good ideas. For example, if our creative agency were rated for originality, not efficiency, they might not seek out existing digital assets like photos and copy that could save their client money.

Mismatch 3: Wrong Place

Many knowledge managers assume that knowledge seekers will "just find it." This puts a burden on the seekers. They need to know about a body of knowledge on a topic, understand its relevance to the their situation, and either search or "put themselves into knowledge's way." That is, they need to be connected to the right people or on all the right alert-streams to receive notifications of relevant content.

To do this, such seekers have to understand how to be in many places at once. They need to know how to use the search tools, how to navigate repositories, and how to navigate the organization. For a newbie, non-headquarters employee, or an employee working where there isn't much investment in search or document tagging, that effort can be feckless.

One of my clients exclaimed (railing against a flotilla of SharePoint team sites):

"I don't expect to find useful knowledge serendipitously. I have to have some trust in the source or author, and some curiosity to dig further. That doesn't happen easily with so much [expletive] out there."

Coming back to our agency example, if Paris knew that Chicago was simply "pitching" a visual concept to the client, they could have pushed that French piece out to them. No trolling required.

KNOWLEDGE JAILS

In many KM programs, a third knowledge transfer issue, reuse, is tremendously elusive. By reuse, I mean motivating new teams to consider existing knowledge, to adapt it to their own world, and to put it to work.[6] Knowledge gets caught in jail—that is, into a format, location, or association that makes it invisible or inaccessible to seekers. Knowledge capture may produce volumes of knowledge, but finding the useful stuff may be like trying to find the dog that ate your school lunch by following the lead "Has fur." Or, alternatively, it could be like listening to a teenager's monosyllabic response. Either there's so much *content* there that it's hard to discern what might be applicable, or there isn't enough *context* to make sense of the few precious syllables. Here are some typical knowledge jails:

Jail 1: Info Glut

According to 2010 statistics, 107 trillion emails were sent each day, of which only 12 trillion were believed to be legitimate (non-spam). On top of this, 152 million blogs were on the Internet.[7] Such information overload has been shown to reduce morale and increase anxiety, as people fear that they are missing information they need, and spend more time than they wish weeding through clutter:

"Prolonged exposure to information overload produces so called information fatigue syndrome. Symptoms include paralysis of analytical capacity, increased anxiety, greater self-doubt, and a tendency to blame others. Long exposure produces symptoms similar to post-traumatic stress syndrome and in milder form is intrinsically connected with demoralization and burnout."[8]

Product-centric organizations or project-centric organizations, for all of their efficiency, are particularly prone to the "glut" variety of knowledge jails.

- *In project-centered organizations*, project teams pour lessons, project reports, and after-action reviews into knowledge bases. (For example, one of my former consulting employers did not do final expense reimbursement until we posted the project's knowledge assets.) However, there is frequently no incentive to upload content that might have unique reuse value. Depositors may be largely unaware of (and indifferent to) what could make others succeed.

- *In operations,* teams may be encouraged to submit new ideas into an idea bank. Without a sense of the "market" for the ideas, workers either submit volumes or withhold what seems obvious them.

Jail 2: Language Barriers

We often assume others know as much as we do or, simply, that only those who know our discipline or field will consume what we produce. As a result, we often record what we know in a cryptic way. We assume that we don't need to elaborate on certain elements of the context that seem normal to us.

We're so often like the Rogers couple in *Amelia Bedelia*. As a young girl I loved this book. Amelia was hired as a maid. When leaving for the afternoon, her new clients left her a list of various things to do while they were gone. They thought she knew what it meant to "draw" the drapes and "measure" the rice. Had Amelia had a cell phone back in the Sixties, rather than "trimming" the beef with ribbons and "changing" the towels with shears, she might have called her employer and asked for some context. A cell phone might, too, have preempted a marital spat upon her employers' arrival home. That is, Mr. Rogers' taking sides with Amelia, while a distraught Mrs. Rogers wailed over her talcum-"dusted" furniture.[9]

Jail 3: Prose Erosion

As the use of prose in our communication erodes, so, too, do meaning and sense-making. Many users of social media and text messages seem to unlearn their writing skills. We write in motifs. This is not only because of the awkward Barbie-sized-keyboard (say, on an iPhone), but also because we often consider our recipient's knowledge as filler for what we don't write. Storytelling experts argue that frequent texters and Twitter users often omit the very parts of the story that most enable us to generate shared meaning and sense-making. Such communication is transactional and rarely expansive or generative. Sadly, this trend is overflowing into our (lack of) documentation for projects, products, and operations.

The blog, on the other hand, is a communication technology that easily affords prose—and lots of it. Indeed, in this age of reduced editorial budgets at news media, some of our best prose can be found on blogs. However, what blogs gain in language, they lose in interaction. The blog interaction doesn't achieve what a dialogue could, had the commenter been able to stop the blogger's flow of thought and ask clarifying questions three hundred words earlier. All too frequently, commentators on blogs complement or react, and rarely expand or illuminate, except occasionally in other blogs on other sites. The reader becomes lost in all this.

A third modern communication technology, the Wiki, holds more promise as a defense against prose-erosion, as I discuss in Appendix F. When knowledge originators and knowledge seekers interleave ideas or questions (and write in prose), we can recapture some of the generative quality of conversation. This is not a substitute for meaningful real-time inquiry. Yet, even if it's not a release from jail, maybe it's a furlough worth taking.

■ ■ ■

The weather forecast for knowledge-sharing using typical tools and methods is not fair: mostly cloudy, with showers and occasional drought. We often fail to recognize our valuable knowledge, we rarely get out the knowledge that could have an impact, and we get it to those who need it too late, not at all, or as indecipherable deluge.

In Chapters 2 through 5 you'll learn about the Knowledge Jam process—a process that actually addresses those thorny problems face-on. It does so by putting into practice three disciplines:

■ *Facilitation* calls on us to intentionally scan the environment for what's useful, so it is the relevant knowledge that comes into the open (clearing Blind Spots).

- *Conversation* calls on us to draw out the meaningful context to better understand and better apply knowledge (reducing Mismatches). and

- *Translation* calls on us to explicitly involve knowledge-seekers in the knowledge elicitation and transfer, while using change management (springing knowledge from Jail) to smooth its introduction and adoption into new contexts.

SIDEBAR: CONTRASTING THE EFFECTS OF NON-PARTICIPATIVE VERSUS COLLECTIVE CAPTURE

Contrast the following excerpts. One is from the U.S. Chemical Safety Board, where experts collected knowledge, did investigations, and wrote reports. In the write-up below, they conclude that "considerable effort would then be required" to put the knowledge to work, as they hand off their findings to hapless readers who did not participate in the knowledge-capture. The second excerpt is from a Knowledge Jam conducted with a Chinese project team (originators) joined by brokers who successfully learned from the Jam. Brokers could re-apply the "cost of ownership" methodology in subsequent projects because they asked questions of the originators and drew out relevant context.

Excerpt from Chemical Safety Board (CSB) Mission Statement

"Over a course of several months, investigators sift through evidence, consult with board members, and review regulations and industry practices before drafting key findings, root causes, and recommendations. During the process, investigators may confer with plant managers, workers, labor groups, and other government authorities. The investigative process generally takes six to twelve months to complete, and a draft report is then submitted to the board for consideration. Reports may be adopted through a written vote of the board or in a formal public meeting near the incident site or in Washington, D.C.

"In addition to investigations of specific accidents, the board is authorized to conduct investigations of more general chemical accident hazards, whether or not an accident has already occurred. In 2002, the board's first hazard investigation on reac-

In Chapter 6, "Bespeckled, Married, and Emancipated," I'll revisit blind spots, mismatches, and jails, and show how the Knowledge Jam weatherman has, in the end, brought us sunny skies. In Chapter 8 ("Comparing") you will see Knowledge Jam in the context of complementary KM practices, and in Chapter 9 ("Building") find tools to build your Knowledge Jam practice. You will be well on your way toward "sharing hidden know-how" for productivity, innovation, and job satisfaction.

tive chemicals reviewed more than 150 serious accidents involving uncontrolled chemical reactions in industry. This investigation led to new recommendations to OSHA and EPA for regulatory changes. A second hazard investigation on combustible dusts is now in progress.

"Both accident investigations and hazard investigations lead to new safety recommendations, which are the board's principal tool for achieving positive change. Recommendations are issued to government agencies, companies, trade associations, labor unions, and other groups. Implementation of each safety recommendation is tracked and monitored *by CSB staff. When recommended actions have been completed satisfactorily, the recommendation may be closed by a board vote.*

"While some recommendations may be adopted immediately, *others require extensive effort and advocacy to achieve implementation. Board members and staff work to promote safety actions based on CSB recommendations. In many cases, the lessons from CSB investigations are applicable to many organizations beyond the company investigated. Many CSB recommendations have been implemented in industry, leading to safer plants, workers, and communities." (www.csb.gov/about/mission.aspx)*

Notice how much passive voice shows up above. It doesn't say who made the recommendations, or who's to take action now. Knowledge captured without participation from seeker organizations faces adoption challenges. It's not clear anyone could easily do something even with lots of advocacy and plenty of money. As this was not collaborative (apparently no brokers identified upfront) it requires advocacy to advance, thereby leaving reuse to hazard.

(Continued)

Excerpt from Knowledge Jam Conducted in Shenyang, China (Please Pardon the Chinese-English)

Originator: The total cost of ownership (TCO) should consider the unique environment, especially country by country situations. For example, in [client's] project, we considered local salaries, the hiring situation in Shenyang, vendor support availability for migration, vendor pricing strategy, and their local maintenance cost calculations. These items will contribute to the final TCO result, and vary considerably across the locations. Since it was a [technology] migration project, these elements were added to the TCO methodology, instead of relying on the general SAP cost analysis. We tailored the SAP TCO modeling by removing application development cost areas (since SAP development is same on all platforms), while adding costs such as migration planning and migration deployment.

Broker: We can use this methodology for enterprise planning in our region! While we will use your improved in the TCO analysis, we would recommend also adding employee turnover rate as a TCO factor, since there are high IT turnover rates where we are. They bring risk and cost to the equation, too.

Knowledge captured via this energetic participation from a seeker organization caused the originator to frame her description in a manner more conducive to reuse. She acknowledged that there were choices—she was sensitive to unique needs of different regions of China. We also see that knowledge starts to get translated here on the spot, as the broker informs the originator about employee turnover in his environment and how he'll supplement the methodology.

As we will see in the following chapters, the Knowledge Jam is collaborative, context-revealing, and directed toward reuse. Participants bring in the interests of far-flung or future project teams and ask questions about suitability of carrying over the conclusions to other projects.

CHAPTER

KNOWLEDGE JAM BASICS

"Knowledge Jam Basics" describes the five steps of the Knowledge Jam cycle. That is, how we choose, prepare, execute, and get value from the Knowledge Jam. We'll discuss how each step reveals Knowledge Jam's uniquely collaborative spirit and its dogged focus on applying—not just collecting—know-how. You will learn how the five-step process makes up Knowledge Jam's essential *mechanics*, while the disciplines of Facilitation, Conversation, and Translation (detailed in the chapters that follow) make up its *ecology*.

"Lights come up.
Drums romp.
Double bass hums.
Trumpets wail a motif.
A beckoning.
Then sax declares the melody,
Like a bold claim,
Challenging each to propel forward."

KATE PUGH

While running outside in the spring air, I picked up a shiny bottle top. As I discarded it, I remembered, as a kid, picking up things like bottle caps, shards of sea glass, and rings of plastic. My parents looked on with horror as I filled the kitchen sink with "art materials" from my wanderings and cleaned them for their next act. I'd imagine them as my future Barbie mirror, collage, or puzzle. I often stared, mystified, turning an o-ring in my hand, wondering whom I could ask about why it had a fine grove or ragged edge from its *last* act. I didn't see myself as a pure "collector"—I was connecting the found object with some art project or new game. And I felt a certain urgency to understand where it came from, to connect its new purpose with its past.

Knowledge Jam shares that sense of intention and curiosity. Deciphering the origins of know-how is an essential part of making it reusable. By having *conversation* among knowers and seekers, and not just doing serial transfer (for example, through expert interviews or documents), we decipher the originator's know-how and the context for that know-how. Conversation allows new contexts for re-applying the knowledge to be explored and managed. So ideas arrive at their next act appropriately costumed and rehearsed.

These benefits come at a surprisingly low price tag. Practically speaking, Knowledge Jams take between nine and sixteen total person-days across all participants, with the facilitator investing the bulk of those hours (60 to 80 percent). So Knowledge Jam is highly leveraged: time-starved originators and brokers[1] typically invest only 15 to 25 percent of the hours.[2] This is partly because of facilitators' work behind the scenes. What's more is that Jam conversations, what we will call "discover/capture events" below, are not marathons; they are generally one to two hours of highly efficient facilitated interaction. Jam cycles can take a few days or be spread out over a few months, depending on the perishability of the knowledge (such as reassignment or retirement of the originators) or upon the urgency of the seekers (such as the moment of the receiving-projects' development cycle).

Knowledge Jam is both a *process* and a unique way of *engaging* with others and with shared ideas. In this chapter I focus on just the process—the mechanics—but I will explain the larger ecology of the Jam in greater detail in Chapter 3, "Facilitation," Chapter 4, "Conversation," and Chapter 5, "Translation." In addition, in Appendix C you will find a glossary of terms to help you review the concepts.

A Knowledge Jam cycle involves identifying and selecting content, planning and conducting knowledge-capture activities, and working as a continuous partnership between facilitators, originators, brokers, and seekers to drive knowledge reuse in a way that improves efficiency, innovation, revenue, and job satisfaction. The Knowledge Jam cycle has five steps:

1. ***Select.*** *Identifying and prioritizing Knowledge Jam subjects, beneficiaries, and sponsors.* Selection involves sponsors, knowledge originators, and those who will steward the knowledge forward, or brokers. Selection is a continuous process. As attractive Knowledge Jam subjects emerge throughout the organization, such as process or product innovations, we add to, and periodically reprioritize, a Knowledge Jam "portfolio" or "pipeline."

2. ***Plan.*** *Planning each Knowledge Jam cycle as a "project."* Facilitators, sponsors, and representatives from the participants do agenda-setting (decomposing subjects into topics), identifying participants, orchestrating knowledge-capture events, and planning vehicles and promotional activities for putting the know-how into use.

3. ***Discover/Capture.*** *Engaging knowledge originators and brokers in a real-time event, or "conversation."* In conversation, participants collectively draw out and make sense of a (sometimes incoherent) set of ideas and their context.

4. ***Broker.*** *Translating the Jammed know-how for reuse.* Led by brokers, but with facilitator help, Brokering entails applying the appropriate vehicles, the appropriate framing, and appropriate change management strategies so that know-how gets to the seekers who can use it.

5. ***Reuse.*** *Applying the Jammed knowledge to improve efficiency, innovation, revenue, and job satisfaction.* Knowledge-seekers might capitalize on knowledge just in time, through an originator's "warm transfer," or through more extensive translation activities as the brokers as seekers consume Jammed knowledge in a new process or product, analogous task, or similar context.

Figure 2.1 summarizes the mechanics of each Knowledge Jam step.

Knowledge Jams can be spread over days or months, depending on the availability of participants, the urgency of the seekers or the perishability of the knowledge. (Chapter 9 includes estimates of time investment and calendar time.) Periodically across the Knowledge Jam cycle,

FIGURE 2.1. *Summary of Knowledge Jam Steps*

facilitators perform a health check—an evaluation of overall progress, participants' comprehension and satisfaction, the completeness of the Jammed content, and time investment. Chapter 3 describes the process-facilitation activities that keep the five steps purring along.

In the next section we detail what goes on during each of the five steps.

STEP 1: SELECT

A key difference between a Knowledge Jam and typical knowledge capture processes similar to after-action reviews or journalistic interviews is that Knowledge Jams are tremendously selective in what topics are focused on. There are two reasons for being selective. One is simply pragmatic: up-front evaluation of alternative subjects increases the likelihood that the most useful know-how is chosen and is brought out in the precious available time. The second reason is psychological. It's the principle of "effort justification": people come to commit to an idea or a change when they have a hand in directing it. This is certainly my experience. Participants in a knowledge process are more committed to knowledge reuse if they have supported it from the outset.

Knowledge Jam facilitators coordinating the Select step have a bit of a balancing act. Participants in the step include the originating organizations, receiving organizations, and, sometimes even a separate sponsoring organization. Originators will want their particular areas of expertise to be selected, while seekers will want the Jam to focus on the topics they believe will be most useful for their upcoming projects. Meanwhile, sponsors and management from all groups will be watching the expenditure of time.

At Intel Solution Services, a consultancy focused on data centers, mobile computing, and digital health, we convened our division's senior leadership quarterly to review the Knowledge Jam subject portfolio, to reassess Knowledge Jam priorities, and to identify upcoming demands on participants' time. We also used this regular interaction to remind sponsors to advocate for the Knowledge Jam.

A Knowledge Jam portfolio is generally a listing and description of Knowledge Jam subjects so that we can prioritize them according to shared criteria. For example, a hotel might consider subjects such as "staffing up for local sporting event crowds," "cultivating repeat customers," or "shielding finicky business travelers from unruly conference groups." A typical Knowledge Jam portfolio balances impact and feasibility.

- *Impact* relates to the value of putting the elicited knowledge into practice, for example, to improve efficiency, innovation, and job satisfaction. In a short, contribution to *competitiveness.*

- *Feasibility* relates to ease of getting the Knowledge Jam done, for example, coordinating the five to twenty hours each of the knowledge originators and brokers, securing appropriate patent or confidentiality protections, and surfacing the perishable knowledge before everyone moves on and forgets or receiving organizations simply reinvent the wheel.

Sponsor engagement merits some emphasis as we talk about feasibility. All business process change books call for executive sponsorship "to inspire a shared vision," "to model the way," etc. With Knowledge Jam, it is even more important, as different divisions or functions may be engaged, and great (and sometimes conflicting) expectations are placed on the brokers and knowledge originators. These expectations can't be offloaded to the facilitator alone. Complicating matters more, either group may need to "save face."

For example, the Knowledge Jam could focus on learning from failure (so, Originators would risk being shamed). Or the seeking organizations may desire to be perceived as original-thinkers, and would risk being called copy-cats.

Characterizing the Select process as "portfolio management" on par with other project and program evaluation processes (part of a routine sponsor-interaction) can go a long way to increasing Sponsor engagement and ensuring that we avoid the blind spots we contemplated in the first chapter, "Rationale."

STEP 2: PLAN

Knowledge Jam planning has a lot in common with project planning —there are roles, topics, events, deliverables, risks and even performance metrics. Yet there is one major difference between Knowledge Jam planning and project planning: The central Knowledge Jam event is actually a conversation. There is a limit to how much you can *plan* a conversation. Content will emerge. No matter how intensely you plan, you cannot fully predict what will happen. In the Conversation chapter (Chapter 2) I contend that you can create the conditions for *productive* conversation. And, before the conversation, you can set the stage for having the right people together, focusing on the right topics, with the right commitment to putting knowledge to work.

The first action in the Plan step is for the facilitator and sponsor to solidify Knowledge Jam roles. Here's the typical cast of characters:

- *Facilitator:* Person who guides the organization through the five steps of the Knowledge Jam cycle and who facilitates the conversations around and including the Discover/Capture event.

- *Knowledge Originators:* Subject-matter experts, project veterans, or teams whose knowledge is to be captured.

- *Knowledge Brokers:* Seekers accountable for representing their seeker-organization by helping to surface knowledge during the Jam and by translating it into their new processes, products, training, etc.

- *Sponsor:* Person who selects Knowledge Jam subjects, funds the Knowledge Jam, advocates for Knowledge Jam steps (especially Broker and Reuse, which sometimes need an energy boost).

■ *Champion:* Person who plays on-the-ground coordinator, maintains participant attention, manages logistics, helps get out communications, and makes sure that the Knowledge Jam is informed by current organizational events. (Champion roles are optimal where facilitator is not familiar with the originating or seeking organizations.)[3]

Planning means not only getting the participants committed to their roles, but also establishing a tone for the whole Knowledge Jam as the cycle begins. During Planning, the facilitator fosters the sense of "common curiosity." Facilitators do this through a variety of means. They conduct interviews with several participants. They secure the brokers' commitment to participating and translating the knowledge into their knowledge products (such as process templates, training, designs, or job definitions). And they organize a formal planning event, during which representatives from the knowledge originators, knowledge brokers, and sponsoring organization start with the Knowledge Jam "subject" and draw up a list of topics (or agenda), for the upcoming Discover/Capture event. (In Chapter 3, "Facilitation," is a template that you can use for recording the Planning event.) Planning can also be expanded with greater input and potentially valuable refinements by using social media, such as the discussion forum or wiki, as I relate in Chapter 5, "Translation."

Like a project manager, the facilitator estimates and communicates participants' time commitment. For example, for the originator, approximately ninety minutes in the Discover/Capture event, with other preparatory and follow-up interactions. (See Chapter 9, "Building," for more estimations.) Facilitators get approval from the originators' organizations and brokers' organizations, and they prepare event logistics, templates, and web-conference technology. As appropriate, facilitators will also work with brokers to set up collaboration or social media tools that can be used to help with the translation and circulation of captured knowledge.

STEP 3: DISCOVER/CAPTURE

The Discover/Capture event is the centerpiece of the Knowledge Jam. This is the real-time meet-up (in person or virtual) between originators and brokers. It typically lasts from ninety minutes to two hours. The originators assemble in a "panel" (or metaphorical panel) with the brokers "before" them in a sort of master class format. A circle is generally the best configuration (with the originators together), so that everyone can see each other.

The facilitator or sponsor starts the Discover/Capture event by describing why the Knowledge Jam is happening, what subjects concern the organization, which ones will be addressed in the ninety or so minutes, and *why now*. Next, the facilitator recaps the outcomes of the Planning event. She describes the agenda (topics) and position herself and the brokers as "stewards" but not "owners" of the knowledge that will be discovered and captured. She advises that the conversation will likely evolve beyond agenda topics, and she agrees to consult with the group on course correction if the shared insights are tugging the group into a new direction.

The facilitator also sets the tone and shares ground rules for conversation. Discover/Capture ground rules can be very explicit, if the organization doesn't typically have meeting etiquette standards, or very general, when they do. Typical ground rules relate to paying attention, using shared data (not simply taking positions), driving for clarity, and speaking one's truth. Echoing the Planning event, facilitators underscore that the most important ground rule is the principle of "common curiosity." No one is an observer; everyone should consider the group's learning and strive to inquire and to push collective insight.

With common curiosity come other practices that facilitators may add to the ground rules. For example, being open to surprise or challenge, granting respect, asking the group for permission to digress or probe, and committing to a "parking lot." The parking lot may lead to possible extended Jams or other originator-broker discussions, for example, for the purpose of filling in details. In Chapter 4 I will describe the whole group's conversation responsibilities (posture of openness, pursuit of diversity, and practices of dialogue) and how the facilitator models and encourages those responsibilities. It is everyone's responsibility to uphold *curiosity as a heartfelt value.*

Essential to the Knowledge Jam is transparency. During the Discover/Capture event, transparency means recording visibly for all to see. Know-how that surfaces during the event becomes the common property of the participants. Using an overhead projector, and, as appropriate for remote participants, a shared-desktop tool, such as Microsoft LiveMeeting, IBM Lotus Sametime, Google Docs or Cisco WebEx, the facilitator creates a shared real-time, visible narrative of the event. As the facilitator is typing while the conversation occurs, the participants can see what they have contributed, and they can make on-the-fly editing recommendations or seek clarifications in each other's presence. It's generally impossible and not effective for the facilitator to capture everything verbatim, so this transparency enables all present to confirm that the capture is reasonable and sufficient for future reference.

In Chapter 3 ("Facilitation") and in Appendix B are templates for capturing the Discover/Capture event. The three-column format enables participants to see how they are tracking to the topics on the agenda (left-most column), to see what is being said, by whom (wide central column), and to see what it means (far-right column). In my experience, in the fast-paced conversation of the Discover/Capture event, it is difficult to put a meaningful summary into the far-right column. It requires standing back and seeing the big picture, a luxury in a ninety-minute Jam. Tidying up the "what it means" column is generally done after the Discover/Capture event.

In addition to the "raw" Knowledge Jam template, post-event the facilitator drafts an executive summary (often with the help of participants). This often starts with the themes in the far-right column of the template. Executive summary documents may be as much prescriptive (about how the know-how will be translated and used) as it is descriptive.

STEP 4: BROKER

The starring actor in the Broker step is, not surprisingly, the brokers, those representatives of the knowledge-seeking organizations who participated in the Jam. Immediately after the Discover/Capture event is over, formal brokering starts. (*Informal* brokering may have already started if a broker tweets during a Discover/Capture event, at least within the ground rules set by the group.) Brokers begin by working with the facilitator to extend the executive summary for their specific organization. The summary document is more suitable as a Knowledge Jam "calling card" than the "raw" Knowledge Jam notes. On the other hand, because any summary necessarily represents a subjective cut of the detail, it is generally not a sufficient data source for the seeking organizations to put the knowledge into action.

The brokers' goal is to discern how ideas that have been captured could be applied by their organization. For example, brokers from the Forest Bioproducts Research Initiative felt they were bringing home insights on engaging non-university partners such as investors. Yet, ninety minutes of interaction didn't fully round out a new stakeholder plan, so brokers set up immediate follow-on meetings with the knowledge originators. Relationships seeded in the room (or conference call) during the Discover/Capture event later bore fruit.

"Translation" is the term I use for what the brokers do next: they size up their audiences, re-mix, transmit, and promote. In effect, translation entails taking the knowledge originators' and brokers' conversation and crafting it into something of value. Here are some examples of valuable broker translations:

- New sales work aids, for example, for promoting certain product features

- Improved desktop procedures, for example, for making optimal use of an analytical tool

- Re-factored technology development steps

- Expanded research protocols

- More effective fund raising call techniques

- More timely new employee on-boarding resources

- More efficient Army recruit training

- Simplified framework for "gelling" of multi-functional teams

Good brokers are also change agents. They know that "experts'" ideas can be met with mixed reactions. Some recipients feel resentful ("Just because the grey-haired guy said it, doesn't mean that it's right!") Other recipients feel unworthy. ("They could do that, but we can't. We don't have [name] on our team or the [name of tool].") Brokers need to craft "translation" strategies to handle both reactions.

Translation is not a solitary act. In effect, translation of know-how into a usable form in the broker's homeland requires its own set of conversations, its own gives-and-takes. It can entail lengthy in-person and online iterations with seeker teams. Happily, the message bearer is one of their own who was vested with the responsibility of surfacing knowledge on their behalf. As we'll learn in Chapter 5 ("Translation"), this sincerity of purpose gives brokers a competitive advantage in the market for improvement ideas.

. In an ongoing collaboration between brokers and knowledge originators, Jammed knowledge may go through many re-mixings. Knowledge originators may host field trips or weigh in to the seeking teams' online forums. In Chapter 5 we'll explore the nature of the extended online conversation that helps put Jammed knowledge to work.

STEP 5: REUSE

Reuse starts when a motivated individual comes across the Jammed know-how, for example:

- In a repository
- In a Yammer discussion
- On a collaboration site
- In a communication directly from a broker, facilitator, or originator
- Embedded in a vehicle downstream from the Knowledge Jam, such as a sales aid developed by an instructional designer

Reuse yields value when we put that know-how to work in solving a new problem.

In theory, Reuse is a follow-on to the broker's translating efforts. In practice, Reuse is not a distinct step; Reuse can occur whenever anyone participating in the Jam takes action on something he learned. So counting reuses is elusive. Where the Broker step does involve publishing or inclusion of the knowledge in some vehicle (for example, the sales aid), we generally can *count* each time it's accessed, even though we need make judgments about (or give "haircuts") where not all accesses constitute a bona fide Reuse.

The Reuse step's most difficult measurement is the actual value of knowledge once we've done that "counting." Counting value is even more elusive than counting reuses. Knowledge reuse valuation has plagued managers for many years. The value of the knowledge is difficult to separate from other things in its new incarnation. Imagine trying to isolate a newly added phrase about how to promote a third new product feature in an lengthy sales aid, and then trying to measure its impact on the selling process. It's difficult to attribute value directly, and even if you could, that attribution effort might be more costly than the value realized. Also, the incremental cost of including the new phrase could be equally hard to discern in a credible way. Perhaps the sales aid would have been created, even without a Knowledge Jam to inform it. And, as a knowledge-product, adding a new phrase ends up forcing us to rewrite other phrases or scrap them altogether. For this reason, I encourage Jam facilitators to team up with brokers and their translating partners to establish a total value of the Jammed knowledge plus other content in the translated format, and compare all of the new investments to all of the incremental benefits. The net amounts to a shared benefit, triggered by the Jam, but not uniquely attributed to the Jam. Valuation takes care. I attempt to shed some light on this "hybrid" knowledge process valuation in Chapter 9 ("Building").

Five Steps. Five Roles. Three Disciplines. Knowledge Jam seems like a walk in the park, right? My experience is that knowing the steps and disciplines *and* doing them with efficiency and authenticity are harder than they seem. It's like the difference between reading a screenplay and directing it. As director, you have the actors, their staging, their expressions, their attractions, and also an audience who brings their very real-life experiences and ambitions. If I don't make you into the next Hollywood millionaire, I do hope to equip you with some lessons learned from my own practice. The following three chapters spell out what I consider my profoundest lessons learned in doing Knowledge Jams. They describe Knowledge Jam's three disciplines: Facilitation, Conversation, and Translation, an ecology that makes those five steps hold together and propel know-how into our businesses, nations, and institutions. The disciplines bring out the magic of coordination, the alchemy of innovation, and the pride of productive collaboration. Let's Jam!

CHAPTER

DISCIPLINE 1: FACILITATION

"Discipline 1: Facilitation" explains how facilitators bring intention, tone, and a value-orientation to the Knowledge Jam. They play the roles of process consultant, project manager, change agent, cheerleader, and networker. Their responsibilities range from strategizing a high-value Jam "portfolio" to adjusting the subtle chemistry of each conversation. In this chapter we also discuss some of the finer techniques of facilitation that come in handy during the Jam cycle, such as maintaining energy or diffusing dysfunction.

"A leader is best when people barely know he exists.
When his work is done, his aim fulfilled,
they will say: 'We did it ourselves.' "

LAO TZU (CHINESE TAOIST PHILOSOPHER, 600–531 BC)[1]

A few years ago I took an introductory course in facilitation.[2] Having managed projects and meetings for a decade, I could count a few notable successes and far more failures than I wanted to admit. When I watched other facilitators at work it seemed second-nature for them, but certainly not for me. They made the "plate-spinning" of content, personalities, and logistics seem effortless. I wanted to do that. I wanted to understand the facilitator mystique. What I learned in the course (and in many hours of trial and error since) was that facilitation takes an immense amount of *planning*, *personal strength*, and *collaboration*.

Planning I expected. But, to my surprise, I found that planning the "content" of the event or meeting was a mere third of the effort. The second third was working ahead of time to improve people's receptivity to ideas and directions. The last third of planning was physical. That is, participants' comfort, attention, and sensory experience. I also learned, to my surprise, that while facilitation feels to the novice like the "facilitator show," when done right, it's the "participant show." Facilitators filter and channel the insights, passions, and intent of the participants. They direct, but don't wear, the limelight.

So it is with Knowledge Jam. While the facilitator is the central mover in the Knowledge Jam and the catalyst for knowledge exchange, it is the participants who are on stage. The facilitator builds the conditions for bringing out originators' tacit knowledge, helps brokers to drill down on ideas so that they can translate the knowledge to new contexts, and shepherds the whole Knowledge Jam process along.

This is where the *personal strength* comes in. Knowledge Jam facilitation is much more than conducting a brilliant Discover/Capture event. In Chapter 2 ("Basics"), I described the five steps of the Knowledge Jam process. The facilitator is responsible for managing that process, recording the knowledge (or managing the recording of knowledge), and stimulating productive, sustaining relationships among the participants. That takes both personal strength and stamina. (Not surprisingly, this chapter is the longest in this book. Bear with me. It's worth the read.)

Fortunately, the facilitator is not working alone. This is where *collaboration* comes in. Collaboration is essential to the process. Facilitators share responsibility for the Knowledge Jam's success. Just as the stand-up comedian becomes entertainment only in partnership with the audience, facilitators partner as both audience and director. For example, the sponsor is prominent during the Select step. The champion, during the Plan step. The originators during the Discover/Capture step. And the brokers during the Broker step. The facilitator is at times the director and at times audience, ready to deflect attention onto those participants who know or want to know. Facilitators amplify and help others take action on newfound know-how.

THE FACILITATOR'S MANDATE

Figure 3.1 is a recap of the image shown in the last chapter, but with the facilitator's specific responsibilities spelled out by step. This figure also provides an outline of this chapter.

It's helpful to represent the Knowledge Jam as a series of facilitated interactions. Consider Figure 3.2. These are the gatherings of the participants, during which knowledge topics are defined, tacit knowledge comes to the surface, brokering decisions are made, and knowledge is translated into practical future uses. In the following section I will narrate this trek and describe what the facilitator does to convene productive conversions among originators and brokers. Done skillfully, such convening results in know-how accumulating, becoming ever more useful, and being put to work.

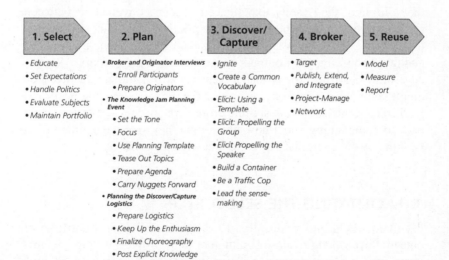

FIGURE 3.1. *Facilitator's Role in Knowledge Jam*

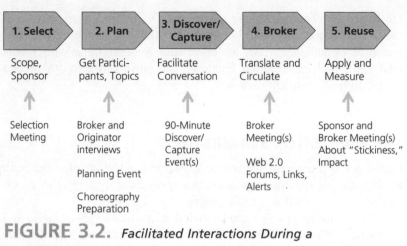

FIGURE 3.2. *Facilitated Interactions During a Knowledge Jam*

In one of my workplaces a few years ago, a manager tried to phase out the role of the Knowledge Jam facilitator. She asserted that "self-managed" Knowledge Jams were just as good. That phase-out effort had marginal results at best. Teams Jammed less frequently, and, when they did Jam, they rarely experienced a deep conversation between knowledge originators and brokers. The poorly fleshed-out, poorly contextualized knowledge wasn't readily picked up by knowledge seekers, and the Knowledge Jam outputs became stale in the corporate knowledge base. Start-up project teams went back to complaining that they didn't know what was going on around the organization; engineers and marketers went back to designing from scratch; and old-timers went back to complaining about how much time they spent explaining (that is, *if* they were even discovered by knowledge-seekers).

1. FACILITATING THE SELECT STEP

Facilitators help the organization to assess the value of a portfolio of potential Knowledge Jams. Facilitators help provide a "big picture" view: tracking, winnowing, and reminding the organization of how Knowledge Jam supports strategic priorities.

Facilitators' responsibilities include:

1. *Educate.* Prior to defining potential Knowledge Jam topics, facilitators do some education. All too often managers operate under the assumption that everyone understands and agrees with the value of a knowledge-transfer process. Frequently that isn't the case. Some people assume that the Knowledge Jam is just a knowledge dump from an exiting team or employee or that the Knowledge Jam is like a peer assist (a collaborative design process with the knowledge originators primarily playing the role of "coaches," not storytellers). During the Select step (and continuing thereafter), the facilitator communicates the Knowledge Jam outcomes (productivity, product innovation, job satisfaction), describes differentiating disciplines (Facilitation, Conversation, Translation), and frames the five steps. Selling is not as difficult as some fear. In Chapter 9 ("Building") we will talk about developing and selling a Knowledge Jam practice with some pillars for your business case.

2. *Set Expectations.* Facilitators jointly establish the expectations (process, roles, and outcomes) for the Knowledge Jam with the sponsor, knowledge originators, brokers, and other stakeholders, such as various managers of those players. Facilitators work with managers to secure participants' time commitments to the Knowledge Jam. Facilitators gain the confidence and trust from the sponsor, as the facilitator will serve as a sort of guardian for knowledge and participants' egos.

3. *Handle Politics.* With the sponsors' help, facilitators identify and defuse the political minefields, sown, for example, by fears of power loss (when one shares know-how) or fears of a copy-cat reputation (when one reuses know-how), or simply fears of looking failure in the face (when one shares mistakes). In a more mechanical sense, where employees have utilization targets, facilitators secure billing or time-charge codes.

4. *Evaluate Subjects.* Facilitators manage the Knowledge Jam subject selection, helping to evaluate potential Knowledge Jams based on *impact* and *feasibility.* See the box on the next page for some sample questions.

Knowledge Jam Selection Criteria: Knowledge Impact and Knowledge Jam Feasibility

Knowledge Impact

Evaluate Knowledge Jam subjects according to their potential to improve process efficiency, product innovation, or job satisfaction. Recognize perishability, that is, the degree to which knowledge originators or originating teams are at risk of leaving or being reassigned:

1. Is this an area critical to our competitiveness? For example, are we investing in product line extensions? Are we trying to drive out costs here?
2. Is there a risk of not having knowledge? For example, if customers' use of the product or system is increasing, could this stress the system, increasing support or supply pressures?
3. Is this a mission-critical operation, and are there single points of failure?
4. Is this an important operation, and are our knowledge originators moving or retiring?
5. Are there other operations that are vulnerable to repeating the same mistakes or vulnerable to reinventing the wheel?
6. Is there a regulatory process challenge or a regulatory concern about the adequacy of operational knowledge, for example, Sarbanes Oxley or OSHA considerations?
7. Is there a significant success or failure that the organization wants to repeat or avert?

Knowledge Jam Feasibility

Determine whether the participants of the Knowledge Jam are available and ready to participate and whether relevant knowledge is accessible:

1. Can we gain the knowledge originators' time and commitment?

2. Can we gain the brokers' time and commitment?
3. Are our sponsors committed (for example, will they advocate for their staff's time investment in this activity over others)?
4. Are the facilitator(s) available?
5. Are legal issues contained, such as intellectual property, confidentiality, non-disclosure, or privacy?
6. If we'll need to transfer the knowledge to distant (and/or, as of yet unnamed) seekers, do we have the right brokers and knowledge-transfer vehicles available?
7. What's the knowledge-absorption rate of the organization for topics under consideration? Typical Knowledge Jams take one to three months from initiation through brokering (time elapsed, not time invested), so it may make sense to have concurrent, staggered Knowledge Jam cycles.

An example of selection criteria is shown in Figure 3.3.

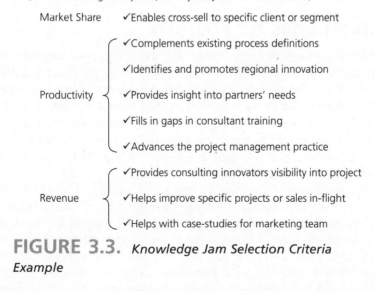

(Tech Consulting Example: Quarterly Subject Selection Criteria)

Market Share   ✓Enables cross-sell to specific client or segment

Productivity
- ✓Complements existing process definitions
- ✓Identifies and promotes regional innovation
- ✓Provides insight into partners' needs
- ✓Fills in gaps in consultant training
- ✓Advances the project management practice

Revenue
- ✓Provides consulting innovators visibility into project
- ✓Helps improve specific projects or sales in-flight
- ✓Helps with case-studies for marketing team

FIGURE 3.3. *Knowledge Jam Selection Criteria Example*

These criteria are just illustrative. Each organization will have a unique set of criteria, and that set will change over time. As a facilitator at Intel Solution Services, a consultancy focused on data centers, mobile computing, and digital health, I met with the product leaders once a quarter to review a portfolio of candidate Knowledge Jams. Our criteria resembled those in Figure 3.3. As the organization grew and became more global, it was increasingly critical for us to codify and spread our best delivery processes. As part of the larger organization, it was also important to improve the likelihood that clients would choose Intel microprocessors and to channel insights to our sales and marketing group.

5. *Maintain Portfolio.* Facilitators record the history of decisions and publish the portfolio of potential Knowledge Jams. Typically, the inventory is a list of the Knowledge Jam subjects, participants, time frames or triggers, and names of advocates or sponsors for a Knowledge Jam.

With my Intel Solution Services sponsors, I compiled these criteria and updated them monthly. I then used the criteria to rank and discuss thirty to forty candidate Knowledge Jam subjects at each quarterly meeting.

2. FACILITATING THE PLAN STEP

The Discover/Capture event is only effective if concepts, attitudes, and time commitments are aligned beforehand. Facilitators start planning by initiating contact with brokers and originators. After this initial contact comes, preparatory interviews, and planning workshops that ultimately give brokers and originators a clear picture of how they will contribute and benefit. Conscientious planning is important the first time the organization goes through a Knowledge Jam cycle so that the Discover/Capture event is a home run.

The outcomes of the Plan step are a topic outline for the Discover/Capture event(s); sponsor, originator, and broker commitments; Discover/Capture event logistics and dates; and strategies for the facilitator to handle derailments of time, topic, and temper during the Discover/Capture event. In addition, in partnership with the brokers, the facilitator may set up collaboration tools or configure existing ones to help with planning and resource-sharing. Plan components include:

- Broker and originator interviews
- Planning event
- Choreography preparation

Broker and Originator Interviews

Facilitators' responsibilities for broker and originator interviews include:

1. *Enroll Participants.* In the Planning step the facilitator identifies the knowledge originators and brokers to participate in the Discover/Capture event. Sometimes brokers may not initially realize the nature and importance of their role. The sponsor can rouse interest and commitment, but the facilitator needs to engage the originators and brokers to help build a sense of ownership in the process.

   Enrollment begins here, and it begins with conversation. Enrollment usually takes the form of one-on-ones or email exchanges. All participants learn that they will be active contributors in the Knowledge Jam, collectively responsible for the success of the Plan and Discover/Capture events. All too frequently, non-owners of meetings do not expect to contribute and tend to sit back (or do their email) while others work. Facilitators build the case that the Knowledge Jam will bring together people who might not have interacted (at least not in a facilitated, focused way). In addition, they point out that the Discover/Capture event promises to be a safe haven for topic exploration.

   Most critically, the facilitator makes sure that the brokers and originators agree to the benefits of the Knowledge Jam (translating intuition to action that lifts the bottom line) and to their roles:

   - *Knowledge originators* will share insights they or their teams have gained in the course of work. Prior to the Planning event they informally review (alone or with their teams) the sequence of events or decision pathways they have experienced. The Knowledge Jam benefits for the knowledge originators are the prospect of fewer random questions from seekers or an opportunity to teach (and learn from) others in safety. In highly competitive environments, aligned incentives are critical. Originators need to know they will receive recognition even though they don't have to spend hours typing. And originators need to know that they will receive a form of amnesty from criticism if they chronicle a trail of events or decisions leading to failure.

- *Knowledge brokers* will interact with originators and help surface tacit (unwritten) know-how. In a well-facilitated setting they may be able to interact with originators whom they either did not know/ know of, could not access, or perhaps did not trust. They will also save time: the Discover/ Capture event brings originators into the room (or virtual room) with the brokers and takes a big bite out of those knowledge transaction costs that we saw in Chapter 1 ("Basics").

- *Champions* help navigate all of the logistical elements of the Knowledge Jam, particularly when the facilitator is not familiar with the group or the equipment. They also keep the Knowledge Jam high on the radar screen of the participants, especially when there is a time lapse between Planning and Discover/Capture events. Champions are most helpful when facilitators are outsiders.

2. *Prepare Originators.* In some cases, prior to the Planning and Discover/Capture events the knowledge originator team may need the facilitator's assistance to help better prepare. Karl Weick notes that individuals may need to step through three levels of agreement about their joint experience, prior to sharing their know-how with others:[3]

- Agreement on which concepts best abstract their joint experience (for example, "We created barriers to market entry for our competitors, so competition was minimal.")

- Consensus on relations among these concepts (for example, "Those barriers to entry were because we invested heavily in branding and formal contracts with the channel). These it difficult to for competitors enter our market.

- Consensus on how these related concepts affect each party (for example, "Marketing and Distribution had to work together to get this right, despite our initial differences of opinion. We are both 'heroes' here and we both deserve recognition.")

When originator teams see these mental models Knowledge Jam efficiency improves. The Discover/Capture event will be an exploration of how the system works, rather a debate about who has the best model of the system (or who's the hero).

Weick's first agreement is surprisingly elusive. A team member can work six months on a project and never really know what is going on in another part of the project or precisely how it interfaces with his or her contribution. To understand how to repeat a positive outcome (or avoid a negative one), the team itself has to come to that understanding. Without that sense-making, anything they communicate as an originating team will be superficial.

Nancy Dixon (Common Knowledge Associates) and I saw this first-hand when we facilitated a workshop on Knowledge Jam in the fall of 2007 for knowledge managers. We divided the group into four teams of five and asked each team to construct a tower in ten minutes. They had only eight extra-long straws, eight flip-chart pages, eight tongue depressors, and eight foot-long pieces of tape. After twenty minutes of frenetic building, bending, and taping, the tallest tower won the role of knowledge originators and others played the roles of marketing-brokers, process-brokers, finance-brokers, new project-brokers, and so forth. A lively Knowledge Jam ensued. At one point an originating team member was asked how he constructed the tower base. He described an ingenious reinforcing mesh of tongue depressors. Another originating team member piped in and said, "You did that? I stood only a foot away from you and didn't even know you were so clever." The reflection by the originating team taught them about each other's actions, formerly missed during their intense tower-building efforts. With sense-making like this, the whole project team saw how the system of parts came together.

Weick's first agreement, which concepts best describe experience, is a necessary starting point to sharing knowledge. On the other hand, Weick's second agreement (on cause and effect) is not always necessary or helpful for insight generation. As I will explain further in Chapter 4 ("Conversation"), research shows that diversity in perspectives and heuristics can stimulate new discussion among all Knowledge Jam participants and lead to richer sense-making. Moreover, differences in mental models among knowledge originators may actually expand the possibilities for brokers to imagine translating knowledge into new uses. Where originators' mental models are more dispersed, there may very well be a greater possibility of overlap between originators' mental models with those of different brokers and the organizations they represent.

In my illustration above for the second Weick agreement, one originator may believe that it was patents and trademarks—not branding or channel dominance—that resulted in competitors' staying away from the target segment. A broker carrying forward the idea of "barriers to market entry" could try on both pairs of causes as they translate into their division or product area.

The Planning Event

The climax of the Plan step is the Planning event. Engaging representatives from each stakeholder group—originators, brokers, and sponsors—the Planning event fleshes the "subject" (chosen during the Select step) out into "topics" or an "agenda" around which the Discover/Capture event can be organized.

Facilitator actions during the Knowledge Jam Planning event include:

1. *Set the Tone.* The facilitator sets the tone in the Planning event just as she will set the tone in the Discover/Capture event. She models the attitude of common curiosity and welcomes each person's authentic voice—steering away from one-sided topic monopoly, veiled accusation, or unfettered praise.

2. *Focus.* In establishing the goals of the Planning event, the facilitator emphasizes that the focal point for Knowledge Jam will be gaps in "tacit knowledge" (trapped in people's heads), as opposed to "explicit knowledge" (in documents, often trapped in hard-drive "jail").

   I know personally that not explaining this ahead can cost time and even cause embarrassment. A year ago, during the first few minutes of a Discover/Capture event in academia one of the originators exclaimed, "Oh, I thought we were going to spend our time talking about the papers we've written." Even after receiving the event description ("surfacing tacit [unwritten] knowledge from the initiative") and the agenda, some participants still expected to use the time to discuss documents!

3. *Use Planning Template.* The Planning event's logistics are effectively a rehearsal for the Discover/Capture event. The Planning event is best done in a room with a projector or online where all

participants can see the typing by the facilitator. Exhibit 3.1 is an example of a Planning event template used for the Forest Bioproducts Research Initiative Knowledge Jam, for which there is a case study in Appendix D. The "seed" knowledge topics are intended to get the originators and brokers to begin to describe knowledge they have or seek, respectively.

4. *Tease Out Topics.* In the Planning event, facilitators help originators and brokers parse the knowledge "subject" into "topics." The goal is to have topics that reflect the tacit knowledge gaps that could help the organization's processes, products, or professional development. These topics will become the agenda for the Discover/Capture event.

Having a "seed" topic outline like the one on the far left column of template above is helpful, particularly for keeping the group focused on the Planning meeting goal and for helping participants unfamiliar with the Knowledge Jam concept. With the outline, the facilitator can draw an initial boundary around the subject. I typically start with a sweeping question like, "Are we trying to operate better or change how we compete?" Or, if the subject is known to be related to competitive strategy, I might ask, "What have we learned about where we compete, how we win, or how we sustain competitive advantage?" This is an example of scaffolding on which we begin hanging what we know or don't know.

Here are typical scaffolding concepts that could lead to Jammable topics that more quickly yield insight relevant for future use:

- *For product knowledge:* Product or product feature change, product upgrade, a change in product interface (to another application, complementary product, data, or partner product). Products could be anything from door knobs to drug development software.

- *For process (procedure), project, or functional knowledge:* Scaling up or scaling down, cycle time compression, project/ process/function scope, stakeholder or team member change, working with outsiders/contractors, working with virtual participants, introducing new measurements, or adapting to new controls or regulations.

EXHIBIT 3.1. Knowledge Jam Planning Event Template from Forest Bioproducts Research Initiative Knowledge Jam

Step 1: Complete Knowledge Jam information

Knowledge Jam Title:					
Project Manager/Sponsor:					
Knowledge Planning Participants:					
Planning Session Date:					
Last Updated:					

Step 2: Document knowledge planning session(s) in the table below.

Knowledge Topic	Description, Themes, Related Documents, Off-Line Considerations	Jam Event Date	Estimated Time for Topic	Knowledge Originator Names	Knowledge Broker Names
1. How do we build multi-disciplinary organizations effectively? Is there a deliberate process that we can derive from our experience with FBRI?					
2. How do we integrate with commercialization opportunities? What learning can we take forward?					
3. Are we pushing the science envelope? New knowledge encourages academic pursuit. How do we know whether it is differentiated enough to be a magnet for researchers and funders?					

- *For competitive or market strategy knowledge:*[4] Anticipating or responding to new entrants, to changes in competitors' features or pricing, to changes in customer or segment preferences, to changes in customer or supplier concentration, to changes in supplier reliability, or to changes in ability to control bargaining (for example, through control of resources or channels).

You can imagine other scaffolding themes outside traditional business contexts—variants of Product, Process, and Market—for contexts such as humanitarian services, fund raising, and international trade strategy.

Here's an interesting "scaffolding" anecdote. With the Cambridge, Massachusetts-based healthcare improvement non-profit Institute for Healthcare Improvement (IHI), the selected subject was the multi-hospital "perinatal" community of about one hundred doctors, nurses, technicians, administrators, and project managers who had been working with IHI for two years to improve labor and delivery care by using IHI's evidence-based methods. IHI knew that it would be launching several more improvement communities in other care areas, and the organization felt it could learn a great deal from this group. During the Planning meeting we considered two options for topics:

- How did hospitals become ready to consistently adopt IHI's practices. In a word, how did diverse hospital quality teams "gel" and become a force for change within their organizations?

- What can we learn from the current perinatal community members about what activities and online content make a multi-hospital improvement community effective and attractive to them?

After much discussion, we decided that the first was critical to IHI's success as they planned to roll out other mostly virtual communities beyond the perinatal area, and future communities would have only a year for hospital member-teams to form and storm. We realized that, in tapping the know-how of diverse hospital teams from around the country, the Jam could explore the processes that each quality team undertook to become "functional."

The second topic, though also valuable, did not need a Knowledge Jam. Data could be pulled together from surveys, interviews, and usage patterns for IHI's existing perinatal community knowledge-sharing platform.

IHI's dilemma is the "process versus content" dilemma. With the second option, we get a list of items and opinions from the Jam. With the first we'd use the Jam to explore the experience of forming a team, and use the discussion to draw out what teams did to shift process, mindset, and power structures. When I framed it as "process versus content," it was an easy choice for the IHI leaders. They saw this as a unique opportunity to tap into deeper knowledge patterns: "How the participants came to know what they knew in the broader context of their history and their surroundings." This contrast between process and content is similar to how Larry Todd Wilson classifies knowledge into "social" and "systemic," on the one hand, and "declarative" and "procedural" on the other.[5] (Wilson's Knowledge Types are described in Appendix A.)

5. *Prepare Agenda.* Once the draft topics are defined, during or just after the Planning event, facilitators and representative brokers, originators, and sponsors jointly prepare the topic sequence or agenda for the Discover/Capture event. The agenda is bounded and specific, including schedule and estimated time investment by topic. The goal of sequencing topics is either to allow them to build on each other cumulatively or to expand from the innocuous topics to the more divisive. (It can help to have the group share a sense of victory as they step up into more controversial territory.) Time allotment should reflect each topic's value, give or take minutes needed to explain a topic or rationale for topics to follow one another. A rule of thumb: Leave time for some conversation meandering and the inherent improvisation of a Jam. As we will see in the next chapter, topics may be emergent; they will evoke others.

6. *Carry Nuggets Forward.* Invariably, participants start Jamming right there in the planning event, so, in addition to synthesizing an agenda out of the Planning discussion, it is essential to capture those initial ideas and be prepared to put them back in front of the group during the Discover/Capture event. (Facilitators must guard against knowledge originators' having to repeat themselves or feeling they were not heard.)

Choreography Preparation

The steps for planning the Discover/Capture choreography include:

7. *Prepare Logistics.* Once the topics are sequenced, and any additional brokers or originators identified, facilitators map out the logistics of the Discover/Capture event:

   - Timing

   - Participants (including originators, brokers, champions, sponsors, or observers)

   - Format (live or Lotus Sametime, Microsoft Live Meeting, Cisco WebEx, GoToMeeting)

   - Projector and phone/microphone placement

   - Contingencies

   - Invitations

   - Recording

   Even when many participants will be joining on the phone from different locations, such as their homes, it's always preferable to have at least one broker sharing a room with an originator. The facilitator can parlay their casual interaction into to more interaction with the larger group.

   I generally only take an audio recording if I have a very large number of originators representing separate teams or if the sponsor or originators have asked to collect verbatim quotes. Recording can inhibit contribution, so in most cases I stay to the typed (and displayed) word which the group sees and agrees upon as we go. (See Appendix E for more discussion on recording.)

8. *Keep Up the Enthusiasm.* If the time gap between Planning and Discover/Capture is several weeks, email or phone check-ins with participants may be important for continuity. These keep up the enthusiasm for, and commitment to, the Knowledge Jam and the upcoming Discover/Capture event.

9. *Finalize Choreography.* Discover/Capture event "choreography" planning can be very beneficial. Transitions and handoffs between sponsors, facilitators, and champions can be rehearsed. During these final moments, political or organizational changes could

derail the calm of participants. Knowing about these beforehand and having a plan about how to deal with them, we start out the Discover/Capture event on sure footing.

10.   *Post Explicit Knowledge.* As a result of the Planning event, the facilitator may recommend posting explicit knowledge that was alluded to during the Discover/Capture event. This may be a radical step for some organizations—a planned document harvest. As mentioned in the scene with the embarrassed Jam participant above when that academic hoped the Jam would be reviewing papers, such an effort would not go unrecognized. As I said in Chapter 1 ("Basics"), much know-how is jailed in hard drives.

3. FACILITATING THE DISCOVER/CAPTURE STEP

Facilitators chair the Discover/Capture event and set the tone. They encourage participants to engage in common curiosity: to speak concretely, avoid blame, withhold judgment, and ground their statements in shared meaning. In effect, they create a climate of safety that, in turn, sustains the type of conversation that results in surfacing valued tacit knowledge. Facilitators apply hard skills, such as information-gathering and mapping, and softer skills, such as hearing what is not being said, unleashing participants' energy, and managing dysfunctions.

During Discover/Capture event, facilitators' responsibilities are to ignite, elicit, provoke, agree to vocabulary, build "containers," be traffic cops, and lead the sense-making process. We'll talk about these in turn.

Ignite

Facilitators start the session by orienting the group to the Knowledge Jam process (what it entails, what it yields), defining roles (Originator, Broker, Facilitator, Sponsor, Champion), recapping specific logistics, explaining the recording method (for example, the Knowledge Jam template), explaining the ground rules, and presenting the agenda for the event.

Below is a list of typical Discover/Capture event ground rules.

1.   Be responsible for inquiring/pushing the collective thinking (show "common curiosity").

2.   Use data (illuminate points of view or positions).

3.   Drive for clarity with questions, but not judgments.

4.   Speak one's truth.

5.   Ask the group for permission to digress or probe (use a "parking lot" liberally).

6.   Pay respect/don't interrupt.

7.   Pay attention (laptops, mobile devices off).

8.   Share outside the "room" only as agreed on by the group.

The facilitator positions the knowledge originators as a "panel." If possible, they arrange the room with originators together, with the rest of the participants completing the circle. If the event is virtual, it is still helpful to introduce the originators as a panel.

Despite the panel metaphor, the facilitator notes that brokers, champions, and even observers will contribute plenty of original insights during the course of the conversation.

At this point, as facilitator, I have participants introduce themselves (name, affiliation, experience with Knowledge Jam), and thank the planning subgroup who came up with the agenda. I also lighten the atmosphere, perhaps by ribbing someone about a favorite sports team or complaining about local weather. (In virtual Discover/Capture events, someone always wins the weather contest.)

Despite all of the intensive preparations during the Plan step, the facilitator will inevitably have people in the event who wonder why they are there. They could be concerned about safety, confidentiality, relevance, or even about wasting time. A process for building up knowledge benefits at the organization level is in Chapter 9 ("Building"). Table 3.1 also shows some benefits-discussion ideas that can help get over any "what's in it for me" delays that can happen during the Discover/Capture event. (This table can be a good aid for the facilitator during the planning interviews as well.)

Create a Common Vocabulary

When the facilitator requires participants to agree to a common vocabulary, it forces them to reflect on how concepts interrelate. It can also have a profound effect on the group: giving participants a platform of agreement from which to build.

I saw this in our Forest Bioproducts Research Initiative Discover/Capture event. The word "multidisciplinary" was a throw-away word, typed into a list of topics late the night before the Planning meeting

TABLE 3.1. Answers to Participant Concerns

Concerns of Participants	Facilitator's Answer
"What's in it for me?"	Originators can "offload" knowledge to reduce frequent interruptions by seekers (and get kudos for being an expert). Originators may also benefit from sense-making with people outside their working area.
	Brokers have access to the right originators in a sanctioned/sponsored forum.
	For the organization, the Knowledge Jam (facilitated, collaborative, with knowledge translated) is much more effective than other forms of capture.
"What if the topic is confidential or threatening to me individually or to our group?"	Ask for commitment from group to confidentiality parameters, for example, "What's said here, stays here, unless the group agrees to share it." (Facilitator should work out major confidentiality issues ahead with the sponsor. In some instances, where patents are critical, participants may opt to write up patentable ideas before joining a Jam.)
"What if I look bad in front of others on the call or in the room?"	Work to maintain an atmosphere of safety and common curiosity. For example, "No questions are stupid, but some may receive lower priority, given the need to use time effectively."
"What if the immediate topic doesn't seem to pertain to me?"	Where a topic is far off the agenda, facilitator will ask the group whether a topic should move to the parking lot.
	Facilitators remind the group about virtual team etiquette, such as saying one's name before speaking, muting background noise, staying brief, and closing email.

without paying much attention to the academic convention of using the word *"interdisciplinary."* During the Discover/Capture event, multidisciplinary raised people's curiosity. After some colorful discussion, it stuck. In fact, participants felt passionate about the distinction between "multidisciplinary" and "interdisciplinary." "Multi" felt more collaborative and inclusive. And, because it was unconventional, it was more notable. Participants seemed to feel a sort of team victory having created this shared definition for their work.

Elicit: Using a Template

The Knowledge Jam purpose can seem nebulous to the participants at the outset, particularly those who did not participate in the planning event and who have not had exposure to tacit knowledge capture approaches such as after action reviews. Participants generally begin to feel grounded when the facilitator walks through the Discover/Capture template, which contains the topics from the Planning event. An example is shown in Exhibit 3.2.

The facilitator fills most of page 1 out in advance. Listing participants prominently and summarizing the Planning event gives the Discover/Capture event a sense of momentum and gives those who have already participated an early sense of ownership. The facilitator acknowledges and summarizes themes that have started to emerge.

The facilitator projects the template on an overhead projector and across the network using a tool like Lotus Sametime, Microsoft Live Meeting, Cisco WebEx, or GoToMeeting, so that remote participants can track (and add to) what is said.

The facilitator types into page 2, a table for recording ideas that come out during the conversation, as seen in the exhibit.

The table has three columns: Topic (as defined during the planning meeting), Comments (where participants' comments are recorded), and Summary/Implications. Alternative headings for this third column could be "Lessons Learned," "Best Practices," "Gems," or "Best-Known Methods."

Each row represents one topic from the agenda. Before the Discover/ Capture event, the facilitator notates time estimates for each row. The Comments column should also include preliminary thoughts from the Planning event (set off in color or italics to emphasize that they pre-date the Discover/Capture event).

The facilitator (or a facilitators) fills out the template during the discussion. Generally, in a typical ninety-minute event the I focus on the middle column. In my experience, it is challenging to capture comments (middle), and effectively type the Summary/Implications column (right). Collecting links (left), is equally difficult. Participants and I tend to summarize themes out loud as we move from topic to topic and at the end of the discussion. I complete the Summary/Implications after the event.

Agenda revisions are common, as knowledge evolves during the Discover/Capture event. In addition, it's not uncommon for the facilitator to type in a row ahead or jump back rows as the conversation unfolds.

The narrative is projected overhead and/or online so that all participants can see it and agree to the language. By capturing the conversation and making it available across space (and after the event, across time), the group has a vivid, yet structured recording of what was said. Exhibit 3.3 is an example of a completed page 2 of the template. A team of engineers with Intel Solution Services did a proof of concept for the first Wi-Fi installation on commuter trains in August 2006.

While typing in the middle column, the facilitator captures speakers' initials before comments so that, during the editing, the facilitator can request participants' clarification for comments, and participants can re-create the Jam in their minds as they edit. (In general, speakers' names are removed when Jam outcomes got to people outside of the participant group, as I have done in the Wi-fi installation sample Jam.)

The facilitator captures as much verbatim as possible and asks approval if summarization becomes necessary. In effect, the knowledge needs to be seen as the property of the group, not of the facilitator. When it's too time-consuming (or too confusing for the group) to capture speakers' exact words or write out acronyms, the facilitator asks for permission to paraphrase or edit.

A "parking lot" at the base of the document is where the facilitator records questions, ideas for other Knowledge Jams, or reminders to participants to retrieve or share related documents. I make liberal use of the parking lot.

Unlike other types of knowledge acquisition, the surfacing (or "eliciting") of tacit knowledge during Knowledge Jam is most effective when it's not the facilitator who is probing, but the knowledge brokers. They are motivated to dig into the topics so that, at the other end,

EXHIBIT 3.2. Knowledge Jam Discover/Capture Event Template

Date:

Revision:

Format: (Conference call, in person, asynchronous collaboration)

Next Meeting:

Scribe:

Distribution: (Participants only or participants, plus who?)

Participants:

Name				Originator			Broker	

Table of Contents

Planning Event Background

Program Overview	
Team Composition	
Project Time Frame	
Planning Meeting Notes	

Discover/Capture Event Notes

Topic	Comments	Summary/Implications
Topic 1	Name: Comment	
Topic 2		
Topic 3		
Topic 4		
Topic 5		
Topic 6		

EXHIBIT 3.3. Sample Completed Page 2 of Template

Topic	Comments	Summary/Implications
What we planned in the technical design (compare to what we got/ surprises)	*Originator 1*: The project goal was to do wireless backhaul for all of the proof of concept, but we found out that the 40-ft. masts were not usable. (Can't hang equipment from them.) We had to use other assets. We added some separate poles.	**Available pole structure for Wireless Backhaul may be limited.**
	Originator 2: Design goal was to have each rail car using Wi-Fi. A stretch goal was overlapping coverage, so that riders could have access from adjacent cars if signal was disrupted. The BOM cars were ok, but the Galley cars (mostly metal) were not ok.	**Overlapping Wi-Fi coverage is limited by train construction.**
What are installation considerations (physical, power, thermal)?	*Originator 1*: Installation is a lot more complex than client execs thought: (1) on train: need adequate space; (2) within car: used AC power for the proof of concept, but would normally use DC (cleaner power). We grabbed power off of a lighting circuit; (3) to the trackside: trackside backhaul to the network operating center (NOC).	**Help client appreciate installation complexity.**
	Originator 2: Airflow and temperature are important in the train.	**Airflow and temperature**
	Originator 1: Antennas have to be rugged: This is a harsh environment (antenna lie flat on a metal roof in the hottest part of CA).	**Antenna ruggedness**
	Originator 1: Vibration is a big issue on trains. Things come loose. More along the right of way, ground moves with other passing vehicles.	**Vibration tolerance**
	Originator 2: Support cannot be required: There's no one on the train who can support this. The system needs to be self-diagnosing.	**"Self-healing" requirement**
	Originator 1: Installation is a true "construction project." We barely scratched the surface during the proof of concept. It's much more regulated in real life.	**Construction regulations**

their organization can put that know-how to work. Brokers will be accountable for stewarding the know-how going forward, so it is in their self-interest to understand and to see the words captured. At times, brokers may be restrained because they are "out of their league," or they may have seen different approaches under different circumstances and they don't have the skills to debate those differences. It is the facilitator's role to draw out the broker and the originator, while maintaining a climate of respect and common curiosity. (Without a doubt, derailments of time, topic, and temper will happen. Be prepared for this.)

Elicit: Propelling the Group

The facilitator can help propel the conversation by starting with the clear agenda, and by using some basic information-gathering strategies. I tend to start with provocative questions, or what I call "structuring moves." Three primary structuring moves are scaffolding, topic probing, and context probing.

- *Scaffolding* requires using a readily available, commonly understood model or structure to start digging into a problem. Already a great deal of scaffolding exists from the Planning event, and I described some scaffolding strategies above. New concepts will emerge during the Discover/Capture event and facilitators may need to do scaffolding on the fly. Sometimes it can be as simple as, "What are the pros and cons of those options?" or "If this were a project, what would you say was the scope?" If a group has a common basis of marketing experience, I might use something like "How did you define the target market?"

- *Topic probing* means diving into and exploring a topic, once it is agreed on. Topic probing does two things. First, it tries to put some boundaries around the topic. For example, I might look for definitions ("What did you mean by 'multidisciplinary'?" or "What does it mean for a team to 'gel'?") Next, topic probing takes the topic down a level to discern how much we know and why it matters. When I do this, I draw out knowledge originators' and brokers' passions by going straight for the victories or pain points. For example:
    - "What made you say, 'Eureka'?"
    - "Tell me about a never-again moment."

- "What were examples of time-savers and time-wasters?"
- "What did you see that led you to know that it was going well? Not well?"

Topic probing may also reveal that a great deal of detail merits further discussion, but that would extend the Discover/Capture event by hours or days. This is when we schedule the next Knowledge Jam or encourage participants to set up their own follow-ups.

- *Context probing* means discerning what were the conditions under which the knowledge originators made a decision, took action, or got results, for example, "Which capacity utilization tests would you study now that you knew that the client was planning to build a whole new data center?" or "Would you have marketed the decongestant using athlete-actors if you were not on the same TV network as the Olympics?" Context probing is not only critical for the facilitator to start the discussion, but is also a critical skill for the brokers to have. It can help to remind brokers to consider simple context questions like "When?" "Why?" "How?" and "What if?"

The excerpt from a Jam below is a great example of where context mattered and had an enormous impact on the decision making by originators. The presence of the healthcare providers union in Germany constrained the way the team could measure physicians. Drawing out the role of the union was an important clarification for the U.S. brokers where doctors' unions are a rarity.

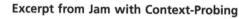

Excerpt from Jam with Context-Probing

Broker: Why was the electronic physician tagging excluded in the Digital Health Operating Room and Emergency Room implementations?

Originator 1: The first release of the dashboards excluded patient and physician tracking. We saw that patient flow and room throughput were the quick wins.

Originator 2: There are also considerable change management issues associated with tagging physicians and staff, particularly as the Workers' Council [union] forbids data collection that could be interpreted as judging workers' performance.

Elicit: Propelling the Speaker

Sometimes helping people to interact in conversations doesn't necessarily bring out the type of topic insight and context that would make Jammed know-how reusable. We need more know-how behind the know-how. In this case, as facilitator, I pull out Michael Wilkinson's' generic information gathering moves:[6]

1. *Direct Probe*—"Why is that important?"
2. *Indirect Probe*—"And the reason you did that is. ..."
3. *Redirect*—"Good point. Can we put that in the parking lot?"
4. *Playback*—"Let me try to restate that. ..."
5. *Leading Question*—"Are there solutions in the area of ... ?"
6. *Prompt Question*—"What else might come into play?"
7. *Tag Question*—"That's important, isn't it?" (warms people up)
8. *Float*—"What about ... ? What are the benefits?"

It is important to help brokers take the lead during such moves. I model these, and I try to pull the brokers in by referring to brokers' previously voiced content goals. (For example, "Let me try to restate Joe's [originator's] comment in Jane's [broker's] terms, 'We need senior manager endorsement that has an impact,' not just 'senior manager endorsement,' right? That's an important distinction. Jane observed that her regional employees trust only local directives. Joe, how did local directives come into play in your senior managers' endorsements?")

Build a Container

A key role of the facilitator is to foster a climate of respect, curiosity, and safety so that the conversation engages all of the participants. Engagement comes from the very human and sincere interactions between the facilitator and the participants and among the participants. The facilitator is more than a microphone. She helps to hold the "container." The "container" is the sum of the interactions and histories of the participants, as we'll explore more in the Chapter 7 ("Heritage"). It is an experience-fed or time-tested rapport that we draw upon when we share with others. It can be strong and safe, or thin and leaky.

The facilitator initiates the container by setting up the intent of the Discover/Capture event, establishing the ground rules, and bringing the voices "into the room" (or virtual room) with initial participant introductions.

As the Discover/Capture event progresses, the facilitator continues to help hold the container-pressure, or the energy of the discussion. She does so by helping to probe deeper into the connections between events or processes or by drawing in diverse voices to extend or amplify concepts.

Larry King, the host of *Larry King Live*, was the master of the container. Writes TV Squad Blogger Joel Keller:

> *"Let's face it; to many, Larry is the doddering but curious grandfather people always liked talking to. And he used that perception to his advantage. He never, ever puts his guests on the spot as soon as they sit down. Often he opens with a question about their latest project or what they've been doing lately. He gently leads them to the point where he can ask [them] open-ended questions about real feelings they have, as opposed to canned PR-approved answers. To some, those questions were softballs. But to those who really knew his methods, those were his way to get people to relax."*

Keller goes on to mention Larry's 1988 interview with Frank Sinatra, where he got Frank to open up: "It looks like a Hoboken kid talking to a Brooklyn kid more than a legend talking to a show host."[7]

By managing the container, facilitators also make it possible for all participants to experience openness, diversity, and dialogue. These are three dimensions that characterize the Conversation disciplines. (I discuss these in detail in the next chapter.)

Be a Traffic Cop

Facilitators rarely pull off a Discover/Capture event without some form of dysfunction showing up. According to Master Facilitator Michael Wilkinson, "Dysfunctional behavior is any activity by a participant which is consciously or unconsciously a substitution for expressing displeasure with the session content or purpose, or outside factors."[8] Here are typical dysfunctional behaviors that the Knowledge Jam facilitator should be prepared to address:

- *Discourteous:* Participant arrives late. (*Tip:* Use ground rules. Consider sharing ground rules ahead of the event in the event reminder.)

■ *Impatient:* Participant is weary when the conversation is extremely detailed. (*Tip:* Take a pulse to see whether people are paying attention. Frequently ask the group whether the knowledge detail is necessary now or should be captured offline. Use a parking lot.)

■ *Distracted:* Doing email. (*Tip:* Engage people, call on non-speakers gently, or, when a speaker appears to be out of sync with the discussion thread, remind him or her and others where you have come from.)

■ *Silent:* Holding back knowledge or opposing the process. (*Tip:* Know the participants beforehand and/or establish sufficient trust that you can draw them out: "Sally, you had recently done something like that. Can you explain how you handled it?")

■ *Passive-aggressive:* Some participants may "vote" with absence. "If it's not my meeting, my participation is optional." (*Tip:* Make it worth their while. Give participants a clear sense of their responsibility and of knowledge gained/shared to support their goals. Use Table 3.1 Better still, plan ahead. Prior to the Discover/Capture event, make sure participants' incentives are aligned. Gain agreement on what decisions will be made in the Discover/Capture event by those present.)

■ *Resigned:* Feeling discouraged when the new ideas threaten the status quo. Not feeling empowered to make changes happen. (*Tip:* Discover/Capture events are not planning events, but often plans emerge from the conversation. Encourage participants to put their "enterprise" hats on and not constrain the creative thinking with fears of budgets, local resistance, etc. Secure sponsor commitment before the event, so that you can point out the sponsor's goodwill to support those participants who feel resigned or disempowered.)

■ *Argumentative:* Sometimes a participant may contradict the speaker. (*Tip:* Surface the arguments with equal treatment. Remind the group that differences are data, not just discord. Each speaker has an inherently positive role [ambassador for knowers or seekers], even when he sounds angry. More often than not, this is because he feels that his authority is limited. Don't let the argument be between the facilitator and doubter. Instead, use the group to inquire into how to address the argument. ("Should we take a moment to talk about X?") And use the group if the group should take any action or postpone the topic. ("Is there a need to do more than capture these divergent ideas?")

- *Cynical:* Participant says, "Knowledge Jam will blow over, like all fads." *(Tip:* Call upon the statements about anticipated outcomes by the sponsors and the brokers during the Select step. Remind them that, even if this Jam isn't their first priority, Jam skills are adaptive, even beyond this event. As appropriate, quote veteran Jammers' anecdotes or metrics.)

- *Doubting:* "You can't capture *that* knowledge," or "It's too complicated to explain," or "It becomes obsolete too soon." *(Tip:* Call on Knowledge Jam examples at other companies or in other groups. Get the group to agree on time limits for the Broker step. Schedule post-Discover/Capture gatherings among participants to dig down into details that may not be appropriate for the short-duration Jam.)

As Wilkinson points out, the best way to address dysfunction is *prevention.* Here are preventative facilitation moves I've adapted from Wilkinson:

- At the outset of the event, thoroughly review the objectives, ground rules, and roles of broker, originator, and facilitator. (Better still: Have them state those roles themselves.)

- Ensure that everyone speaks at beginning (round-robin, check-in, etc.), so that they feel present in the meeting, and so that they hear their own voices contributing to the sound-space of the Jam.

- Continue to position the Jam as being "about the wisdom of all participants" by facilitating conversations among brokers and knowledge originators and limiting those between the facilitator and the originators.

- Sustain flow and logic in the conversation. Allude to connections ("She said earlier, and I just heard also ...").

- Recap frequently.

- Acknowledge all voices, and note who hasn't spoken. Welcome the quieter participants' observations by relating to the topics discussed to their pre-event interview or their organization's pre-event interviews. (In a nutshell: *Know the participants.*)

- In longer Jams, schedule breaks and do a pulse-check with the group (Ask: "Should we move on to another topic?" "Should we change directions?" "Can we put that idea into the parking lot?" "Should we reschedule?") Always take a break before you feel you need it. A Jam is more akin to insight sprints than navel-gazing marathons.

- Vary your style and content (for example, interject summary points to "mix it up" with a monotone originator. Invite a variety of people to ask questions. Add some humor.).

- Accommodate introverted or reflective speakers by enforcing pauses. ("That's an intriguing comment. Let's pause for a second to let it sink in.")

- Accommodate remote speakers who may have trouble jumping in by having a chat feed monitored by the champion or another participant.

Wilkinson points out that if you can't prevent the dysfunction, approach the individual privately or, while in the session, *generally*. ("There isn't much coming from the phone line now.") Empathize with the *symptom*. ("We may be losing energy here, as we've been going at it for a while.") Address the *root cause*. ("I sense that this is a topic that hurts" or "It feels one-sided, doesn't it? Let's try to capture both sides of this story.")

Send Off and Extend Sense-Making

Facilitators draw out ideas and initiate sense-making during the session, such as by igniting, eliciting, and gaining agreement on vocabulary. To help participants appreciate that sense-making really happened, at the close of the Discover/Capture event, facilitators can remind participants what all have accomplished, and, in so doing, they help to propel the participants into the Brokering step. Generally, when I close a session, I cover five things:

1. *Review Knowledge Jam Process:* Review the activities (during the Discover/Capture event, before, after), and address how they mapped to the Knowledge Jam purpose;

2. *Review Content:* Summarize the content that has been captured, acknowledging contributors;

3. *Review Parking Lot or Actions:* Review action items, parking lot, decisions, and next steps;

4. *Offer Thanks:* Thank all the participants;

5. *Reflect:* Evaluate the process, results, and meeting outcomes relative to the objectives. In the short event, where time is precious, I sometimes will look for a show of hands or a vote from the group, "Did we accomplish what we planned?" or "Did you learn something new?" If done well, the reflection may also continue after the event, among the core team, or in an email exchange with the participants.

In general, it is helpful for all participants to start the Brokering process by seeing key themes or cross-currents in an executive summary, such as an MS PowerPoint presentation. Within a few days of the Discover/Capture event, facilitators clean up the Discover/Capture document, eliminating typos and smoothing out phrases, and drawing out decisions, actions, observations made by the group, and highlighting patterns in insights now visible when one stands back and looks at the whole.

4. FACILITATING THE BROKER STEP

During the Broker step, facilitators are both process managers and networkers. They assist the brokers' translation—publishing, extending, integrating, and promoting the knowledge. At times, facilitators themselves transfer elicited knowledge to specific knowledge-seekers.

Facilitators' responsibilities during the Broker step include:

1. *Target:* Working with the brokers, the facilitator helps revise the list of individuals or groups throughout the organization who could benefit from the knowledge surfaced during the Discover/ Capture event. This list of individuals may morph from Plan step to Broker step. For example, entering a Discover/Capture event, some of my Intel brokers thought that they were going to learn about suitability of current hardware for scaling huge databases. They did not expect originators to teach them about power use, know-how relevant to developers of power-saving products, not just to hardware capacity generalists.

2. *Publish, Extend, and Integrate:* When I first started doing Knowledge Jams, I used to describe the work of brokers as

"extending, integrating, and publishing." Now, with enterprise social software platforms and external social media, frequently, knowledge continues to evolve thanks to further input from participants, seekers, and the larger family of originators. The facilitator can help the broker release the knowledge in the right vehicle. As a result, related project teams or innovators can engage and continue to develop or inquire into the Jammed ideas. Brokering, as I describe in Chapter 5 ("Translation"), entails bringing the insight into new forms, such as procedures, product improvements, or competitive analyses. Once social media or other collaboration vehicles are part of the sharing, publishing in a formal sense may even be unnecessary.

3. *Project-Manage:* The brokers' role may be familiar to the organization (for example, authoring training materials) or new (creating and posting an idea for improving an old process). The facilitator may help the brokers to make sure that this work stays on schedule, in scope, and on spec. Facilitators may help with change management, a central theme for the brokers. Facilitators can also act as go-betweens to the sponsor, reporting back to sponsors on the concrete activities undertaken by brokers and identifying ways that sponsors can help.

4. *Network:* Facilitators help brokers promote elicited knowledge in the crowded market for ideas. In establishing Knowledge Jam programs, facilitators frequently also serve as a "node" for knowledge-seekers and knowledge originators in a formal way—a clearinghouse. Naturally, "Facilitator as Broker" becomes a more difficult combination as the dispersion of knowledge seekers and brokers increases. Then, Knowledge Jam portfolio management may entail managing scouts or "listening posts."

5. FACILITATING THE REUSE STEP

Facilitators' ultimate goal is reuse—no matter how knowledge reaches the seekers. Facilitators start by walking the talk.

1. *Model:* Facilitators model reuse even as they capture knowledge during the Discover/Capture event. For example, they may reference other Jams, borrow vocabulary, or echo good phrasing from originators.

2. *Measure:* Facilitators work with the brokers to record and report back to the Knowledge Jam sponsors actual reuse activity. Some reporting can be done online (for example, search hits and download counts), but the most effective is self-reported anecdotes, surveys, or interviews.

3. *Report:* Facilitators hold meetings with originators, brokers, and sponsors regarding impact and "stickiness" of the knowledge. In one of my client organizations, transferred Knowledge Jam knowledge was tracked, including the Jam source, the seeker, the themes, and transfer dates. Where possible, the facilitator-broker team also gathered testimonials from knowledge seekers. For more on Knowledge Jam measurement, see Chapter 9 ("Building").

Knowledge facilitators are on-point for all five Knowledge Jam steps, actively channeling the organization's energy and insight. Yet, their "centrality" diminishes progressively from Select through Reuse, as originators' and then brokers,' roles grow. Some colleagues have asked me to profile the facilitator so that they may begin building a "bench" of facilitators ready to be called on. I will profile the facilitator's skills in Chapter 9. Building facilitation capacity is valuable well beyond the Knowledge Jam and may fit nicely with the organization's leadership training. Primary facilitation skills—joining, eliciting, holding productive conversations, driving toward results—are much in demand for today's emerging leaders.

CHAPTER

DISCIPLINE 2: CONVERSATION

"Discipline 2: Conversation," shows how the "posture of openness," the "pursuit of diversity," and the "practices of dialogue" make collaborative knowledge elicitation possible. Bringing a diverse, widened perspective to respectful interactions results in more generative conversation. That, in turn, helps us to generate more useful know-how. Conversation also fuels a lasting rapport between originators and brokers from which we all can benefit as we take on the task of putting know-how work.

"At its heart, education is a social activity, not a solitary one. It's about the development of habits of mind, not the transmission of information. To be done well, it has to be experienced, by student and teacher, as a human interaction. Consider a modern thought experiment. Before the printing press, it was clear that to transmit knowledge from one generation to the next people had to come together. Outside the reading room of the New York Public Library are four huge murals depicting great moments in the development of writing—along with Moses, Gutenberg, and Mergenthaler hangs a depiction of the medieval scribes.... This activity, the gathering of learned people to conserve and transmit knowledge, gave birth to the university. But after Gutenberg one might have expected the end of this odd practice. Instead, institutions of higher education flourished."

ADAM FALK, PRESIDENT, WILLIAMS COLLEGE[1]

In 1988 I participated in the new employee training at Monitor Group, then a firm of about two hundred people. One hundred of us were there for this "intake" training—all new employees. The firm's leaders were standing at the front of the room describing our immense revenue growth targets, which hinged on all consultants' (new and veterans) delivering a well-defined set of core services with a great deal of skill. One of us newbies, an astute freshly minted Harvard Business School grad, said, "How do you expect to grow the revenues and maintain quality when half of the company is in this very room?" Monitor knew this could be an issue and had set out on an intensive program of training us. Central to our curriculum were effective communication practices. Management even invited Harvard Professor Chris Argyris to talk to the group. Monitor leaders' logic appeared to be this: If we teach people to be more productive in the way they interact with each other, they'll be more effective at solving clients' problems. For a management consultant of the Eighties, this was a game-changer.

As a naïve young analyst, it seemed to me that we were all about getting information. I could do that by myself if I tried hard enough, right? I was a geek. I didn't know how to dress like a consultant, dine like a consultant, swear like a consultant—let alone "crack the case" by extracting facts from the clients, their customers, or competitors. (Back then, there was no World Wide Web. Just the phone and a few journal-search tools.)

What I learned during that exhausting week was that intentional interaction is the medicine for both ailments—the loner and the geek. It was my first introduction to the ideas of "skillful conversation." I guess you could say that I was so bad at it that I decided to make it my life's work.

Consider the quote at the beginning of this chapter. Effective knowledge-exchange is social. It isn't transaction or "transmission," but a change in participants' repertoire or frame of reference. This is what Adam Falk calls "the development of habit of mind." Conversation allows us to not only expose our thinking, but to develop our habits of mind—to extend and refine our thinking in the presence of others who bring their own experiences and motivations. If *Facilitation* is the pilot, *Conversation* is the combustion engine. While the Knowledge Jam facilitator sets the direction and influences the tone, or "container"— that climate of common curiosity that we learned about in the last chapter—ultimately, it is the *participants* who make conversation into know-how.

In my experience, effective conversation has three main dimensions:

1. Posture of openness
2. Pursuit of diversity
3. Practices of dialogue

Openness sharpens our ability to see the bigger picture, *diversity* expands our problem-solving resources, and *dialogue* takes in these two ingredients and channels them into meaning and lasting relationships. Openness, diversity, and dialogue in Knowledge Jam conversations let knowledge surface that wouldn't have in an interview, appreciative listening exercise, or post-mortem. And those dimensions help to make the relationships between broker and originator develop and endure.

POSTURE OF OPENNESS

Openness, as an underlying posture in Knowledge Jam, is not simply quiet composure or self-control. It's how we jump in and participate with a good conscience. Openness has three ingredients: first is a practice of skillful inquiry; next is a selfless, almost spiritual, outreach; and third is a widened perspective, a willingness to see the larger system of parts.

Skillful inquiry, an open heart, and big-picture thinking are rarely sufficient individually. I describe them separately, in the same way my tennis coach broke down the serve into minute parts for me—to help me appreciate the contribution of each muscle in time. But to serve an ace, these elements have to come together in a holistic way.

Skillful Inquiry (Model II Behavior Trumps Model I)

The first ingredient to openness is an interaction discipline that harkens back to those orientation days at Monitor Group, when Chris Argyris shattered our sense of certainty. At the orientation event, and then in subsequent seminars, Argyris challenged our notions of "good" and "bad" conversation.[2] First, he described a set of behaviors which he called "Model I." Model I behavior is characterized by taking positions, being certain, and using abstract (as opposed to tangible or data-rich) language. Model I speakers also tend to advocate what they think they know (as opposed to inquiring about what they could know). With Model I behavior, well-meaning speakers tend to shut down discussion through their defensive posture. By making statements with definitiveness and holding ridged positions of "I am right/you are wrong," often a Model I type speaker's certainty could make a group overlook facts and talents right in their midst. While Model I was prevalent in our colleges and graduate schools, it had reduced our ability to understand and be understood, to collaborate, and to bring about change.

Argyris then went on to describe what he called Model II behavior. Model II behavior is about:

■ Being transparent and sharing the data one uses to reason and decide

■ Not jumping to conclusions (not taking positions)

■ Letting in the possibility of not always being right, of being wrong, and maybe even more human for it

■ Allowing ourselves to be challenged and to respond to challenge with curiosity, not defensiveness

Using Model II interactions, we invite others to share, to stay open to insight, and to co-evolve ideas with us.

Imagine trying to surface knowledge if even one participant in the Knowledge Jam were using Model I behavior. If that person were an *originator*, he would resist being asked to unpack his reasoning. The originator would defend his narrative with a tone or self-righteousness that discourages investigation. Or he might even clam up, for fear of losing his high position as "expert." Then imagine if she were a *broker*. By her posture of certainty, that person would neglect to probe deeper into the facts being shared in the Jam. She would seek out only ideas that would confirm what she already "knew." Unwittingly, both or them would return to their respective organization simply with strengthened convictions and only limited new insight. (Smart colleagues at the home organization might mistrust them and, potentially, mistrust the Knowledge Jam process.)

Model II, by contrast, takes the focus away from protecting one's positions or one's "correct" status and opens the possibility of unspoken (even forgotten) concepts showing up, combining, and forming something new. Members of an *originating* team could calmly narrate an embarrassing failure and even learn new facts from each other that they had missed in the fog of a project. A *broker* could feel safe enough to carry surprise and curiosity back to the seeking organization, and perhaps even inspire the seeking organization to shift direction entirely.

Model II behavior is effectively parking one's ego so that some shared insight may emerge. Following is an example of two originators (consultants) describing what happened when they used Model II:

Excerpt from Jam Using Model II

Conversation	Observation
Originator 1: One person was a squeaky wheel, but I realized he was competent and I shifted how I acted toward him. He didn't like [government agency] people at the top. He felt that they were bureaucratic and not particularly effective, especially at working across agencies. He associated us with them. He threatened us. But we chose not to fight him, but to include him without judging him and hear what he had to say. After a few meetings, he warmed to us. We found out that he had already done this type of analysis [infrastructure consolidation, complexity reduction]. He had done some system improvements, for example, improving bandwidth, but he felt "stuck." He complained that the organization didn't make changes effectively across agencies.	Consultants took a Model II orientation. We see a Model I skill set of Mr. "Squeaky Wheel."
Originator 1 (continuing): When we wrote the report, we highlighted this: "One can only get benefits (and scale economies) like this when this effort is cross-agency. ..." We not only quieted his objections, but I think we also improved the overall collaboration with the client.	Results of Model II interactions with the client.
Originator 2: Yes, I felt that our report would be vulnerable to scrutiny, given the limited time for data collection, and the assumptions we had to make. We expected them to attack, but they didn't. ... Our fear of their resistance ended up unfounded!	Model II shift appears to have extended beyond the "squeaky wheel."

The consulting team in the story was taking a Model II stance with their ornery client. They were listening, not defending. The first consultant noted that he learned important insights about the organization that might have gone unsaid if the client had felt threatened by Model I interactions. The second consultant noted that using Model II meant that the client organization was more ready to engage. As a result, the clients were ready to take in more ideas and, as change agents, the consultants were more constructive and helpful in their report than they might have been.

Preparing Your Heart to Listen

A second form of openness is less about learning a new skill and more about learning a new attitude. What I call the "prepared-heart" form of openness is having the readiness to be surprised and changed in an interaction with someone else. Carl Gaertner writes about this in his chapter in Olivia Parr-Rud's *Business Intelligence Success Factors.*[3] He describes this as the act of "preparing your heart to listen." Among religious thinkers it is also called "sacred listening." It suggests a form of mindfulness that we grant to other human beings *because* of that humanness—indeed, their validity as an agent of their own truth.

Gaertner describes this dimension of openness as coming about in two steps: first listening to our conscience, and then, while listening to another, being ready to set aside (at least temporarily) a conviction or worldview to which we are attached. It involves hearing what could challenge our idea or identities and responding with equanimity. We stand open to the possibility that we, ourselves, may change in the course of the conversation.

Imagine that you are a broker in a Knowledge Jam and an originator is describing their program management philosophy. You are child of Sixties-generation parents, and you believe fervently that, while self-directed teams may be slower, they are more motivated and, in the end, they provide more enduring solutions. Your originator proudly reveals he's just set up his daughter in an arranged marriage, and that he feels that the concept of parental wisdom ought to carry over to program management. How does your heart-preparedness help you deal with this in a productive way? You still your convictions for a moment. You think of elements of parent-ness (and child-ness) that do and do not apply to program management. You set the stage for an interaction with your originator that is not just transactional, but transformational, maybe even for you.

The difference between the heart-preparedness and Model II is that heart-preparedness comes back to our identity. In offering an open heart, we become a sort of medium for the tacit knowledge of others in the Knowledge Jam—not just a polite mechanism for getting them to talk. At a profound level, heart-preparedness is taking a risk. I feel vulnerable when I expose myself to the very real possibility of changing myself.

Words attributed to Pericles' are comforting when I consider this: "What you leave behind is not what is engraved in stone monuments, but what is woven into the lives of others." We are weaving and being woven into. With the practices of dialogue below, we'll explore how the heart-preparedness mindset can play out in our topic and language choices.

Systems Thinking

When we are open to hearing opposing or surprising perspectives—even from surprising sources—we are better able to construct the big picture, and we are better able to stress-test conclusions we might be drawing. Argyris would claim that we are authentically open *only* when we insist on hearing those opposing or surprising perspectives.

For most Knowledge Jam groups, drawing, not just writing, theories and facts can go a long way toward improving comprehension, retention, and curiosity. I've found that a highly effective tool to force this is systems thinking, a central capability that the organizational learning community invented. Systems thinking is the practice of identifying resource scarcities (or abundance) in our business, community or environment, and then inquiring into the interrelationships and forces causing those resources to rise or fall. A "resource" in this case can be a concrete thing (water, revenues) or an abstract thing (reputation, consumer confidence).

Consider the forces and scarcities in this example. Population growth stresses water supplies in the dryer western part of the United States. It also puts political pressure on governments to invest in both conservation technologies and regulations. Those investments, in turn, increase real estate desirability. As a result, we see an increase in net migration *into* those states, and that further stresses water supplies! More stress, more political pressure, more conservation, but more stress as a result!

When you draw a system on a piece of paper or a whiteboard, the behavior of that system (growth, collapse, oscillation) can be easier to understand. What systems thinking—and its simpler cousin, concept mapping—do is to widen our view of a problem. They encourage us to ask, say, in a Discover/Capture conversation, "What might be the unintended consequence of that HR decision?" or "What might have been the influencers of that line of business' growth?" With systems thinking, we'd consider both influencers that increased sales and influencers that potentially constrained or cannibalized growth. I'll dive into systems thinking and concept mapping concepts in Chapter 7 ("Heritage"), where we explore the origins of Knowledge Jam. Suffice to say here that systems thinking provides a widened view by standing back and being objective about the unintended consequences of our actions and the non-intuitive influencers of us.

To wrap up, openness takes the shapes of Model II behavior ("skillful language"), sacred listening ("prepared heart"), and systems thinking ("a widened view"). All three together form the "posture of openness" for the Knowledge Jam conversation. None by itself does the trick. You could go about mechanically practicing the Model II behaviors and be "competent" in Chris Argyris' non-defensiveness framework, but the space you offer others is not necessarily safe and compassionate ("prepared-heart"). On the other hand, you could be compassionate, but not very good at Model II language, and fail to help an originating team to dig into their collective experience and remember relevant details. Similarly, you could nicely direct the conversation through Model II language and a prepared-heart, and, without a widened view, you might still represent only those parts of the system that are familiar and be blinded to non-intuitive, but potentially life-saving forces at play.

PURSUIT OF DIVERSITY

One thing that puzzled me in my earliest Knowledge Jams was how originators and brokers who all sat in one function tended to settle into rather routine ideas. It went something like this: Someone would remind the others about standard process, such as the testing cycle, all would grunt in agreement, and the conversation didn't go much beyond that. Consider the dialogue among software application engineers in the excerpt on the next page.

This doesn't sound like a very productive Jam, at least from the broker's perspective. He is probably thinking that it may be expensive to reverse the application architecture decision in testing. But here the originators were of the one mind. If they had someone around recounting a different project experience (broker or originator), where the

---

Jam Excerpt with Conversation Among Software Application Engineers

Broker: We're going to use your software application architecture in our division. But the requirements phase of your project seemed to be compressed. Were there requirements that challenged you to change your application architecture up-front, say the existence of a user who had a high transaction volume?

Originator 1: We tended to push off issues like that into the testing process.

Originator 2: Yes, that's always covered in the stress-testing phase of the testing process, so we don't need to worry about that.

---

architecture "broke" because of the load on the system, they might have had an entirely different conversation.

Jams with highly similar participants didn't seem incisive enough, and I felt, as facilitator, that I was somehow letting people down when no one challenged assumptions. Out of desperation, I found myself marketing the upcoming Jams to brokers and originators outside of the originators' function, product area, or market. I sold the "outsiders" on the idea that the lessons learned would be portable. I was convinced of that. But what I didn't realize fully was that this portability was more than the good analogies and translations I produced for the outsiders as their facilitator. Instead, the portability resulted from challenges and explanations that surfaced directly as a result of having diverse people in the Jam. The "outsiders" provided contrasting opinions in a way that made it possible to not only adapt the knowledge to their newer environments, but it also made it possible to *adapt the knowledge better to the questions of the first brokers.*

Consider inviting marketing to the engineering Knowledge Jam shown in the example earlier. Having the "outsider" present actually improves the likelihood that the deeper questions are asked and that everyone benefits from a more complete picture of the originators' story. Now reconsider this conversation again with the marketing manager joining in. A Jam excerpt is shown on the next page.

Jam Excerpt Between Software Application Engineers and Marketing

Broker: We're going to use your software application architecture in our division. But the requirements phase of your project seemed to be compressed. Were there requirements that challenged you to change your application architecture up-front, say the existence of a user who had a high transaction volume?

Originator 1: We tended push off issues like that into the testing process.

Originator 2: Yes, that's always covered in the stress-testing phase of the testing process, so we don't need to worry about that.

Broker 2 (Marketing): That's good that your testing is so thorough. As a marketing person, I tend to spend more time on requirements, and I pull in all sorts of users. But I do that for another reason: I see what they need, and I involve them. Then, if we have to go back to the drawing board as a result of failing a stress test (which I would hope we could avoid by making sure we built to their volume specification), at least they'd be "with us" when we go to testing. They'd know we made a calculated risk with their spec in mind.

Here, the second broker comes at the issues of requirements and testing from a different angle. She is considering a relationship with a application user, not just a time-bound requirements process.

My impulse to "invite colorful friends for a great dinner party," and the occasional fortunate results, were not an attempt to remake the "Emperor's New Clothes." In *The Difference*, Scott Page explains how he spent several years at the California Institute of Technology in Pasadena, California, studying decision making and problem solving in diverse groups. He concludes:

"Diversity trumps homogeneity: Collections of people with diverse perspectives and heuristics outperform collections of people who rely on homogeneous perspectives and heuristics."[4]

Page even showed that the *predictive* capacity of diverse groups was greater than that of homogeneous groups. In effect, expanding the variety of perspectives and heuristics that are shared raises the level of insight. So my impulse to open the doors of the Knowledge Jam was consistent with good research. I was witnessing Page's diversity factor in the Knowledge Jam.

Page takes pains to clarify the definition of "diversity." He refers to cognitive differences, not identity or culture differences. Specifically, he includes perspectives (ways of representing situations and problems), interpretations (ways of categorizing or partitioning perspectives), heuristics (ways of generating solutions to problems), and predictive models (ways of inferring cause and effect).[5] Page does not claim direct benefits from *identity* diversity (religion, language, or dress). However, he elaborates, "If well managed, identity diversity can create benefits, provided it correlates with cognitive differences, and provided that the task is one in which diversity matters."[6]

The pursuit of cognitive diversity has proven to be well worth the effort for Knowledge Jam. Variety in perspective, heuristics, and predictive models translates into branches of conversation and then layers of meaning. More practically, if well-managed, cognitive diversity among Jam participants can result in novel ways of inferring cause and effect or context. Bringing out more context broadens the range of applications for the found know-how in the brokers' world.

Consider an example of cognitive diversity in the Institute for Healthcare Improvement Knowledge Jam, shown on the next page. The group was critiquing a draft definition of how multidisciplinary hospital quality teams "gel" as they come together to implement improvement practices. The topic was: "What would you add to or take away from this description of what team 'gelling' is?"

In the excerpt on the next page the nurses, doctors, and IHI staff contributed a spectrum of ideas to the definition of team "gelling." For example, communicating, having mutual respect, recognizing each team member's work and life burdens, building relationships, and accomplishing quality improvement goals together all came into the "gelling" definition. By joining forces, the definition (and, later in the Knowledge Jam, the recommendations) were far more thorough, decisive, and useful.

Excerpt Showing Cognitive Diversity

Originator 1 (Nurse, New Hampshire Hospital): Open communication is a big piece of it. There needs to be a process to work through disagreement. By "open communication" I mean safety in the group to say what you think.

Communicating openly

Originator 2 (Nurse, Connecticut Hospital): Taking the appropriate steps (intervention) to obtain the results. Having agreement about what those interventions will be.

Working for multidisciplinary agreement on interventions

Broker 1 (IHI Staff, Statistician): A team may gel before it actually has results.

Note: A team can "gel" before it has results.

Originator 1: A willingness to hold each other accountable for each piece of the project. That includes committing to having that hard discussion about desired results and assuring that you are getting those results out of the process.

Holding each other accountable

Broker 2 (IHI Faculty, Psychologist): For me what we are describing is a "functional team." There needs to be a relationship factor, beyond just our functional needs.

Having relationships at human-, not just task-level

78

Facilitator: Please can you elaborate?

Broker 2: You need to know people as humans, and not just be task-oriented. That means developing a relationship that has to do with our personal space—for example, what we are working on. It means acknowledging that life gets in the way. To me, that makes it a more sustainable team.

Originator 3 (Nurse, Louisiana Hospital): A mutual respect within your team. — Respecting each individual's role in the program

Facilitator: How is this different from the personal getting-to-know-you?

Originator 3: If I am working in a multi-dimensional team, there is more than just "respect." What I mean is "knowing what each other is doing." For example, [implementing a change] means step A to J for nurses, and for physicians that means Y. So when we meet collaboratively we are taking the time to see what the implications are for each area. — Knowing more about each others' task and what it takes to get the job done.

Originator 2 (commenting at the end of the Discover/Capture event): We all have the same goals, but it is interesting that the way we meet them may differ. It has to do with culture, structure, management styles of the organization. Maybe it's the styles of people who have quality improvement roles, who bring their uniqueness to the table).

PRACTICES OF DIALOGUE

A posture of openness and a diversity of inputs are both essential for propelling the conversation. Together with these, a solid agenda and thoughtful facilitation can help keep the flow of ideas on track. However, our basic interactions may still become stuck in familiar "cerebral" processes and debates. What unleashes uncommon insights and makes the Knowledge Jam conversation remarkable is *dialogue*.

Back in the Nineties, with his research on "dialogue practices" organizational learning practitioner William Isaacs asserted that the conversation concepts that we talked about so far—non-defensiveness, deep listening, the widened view, diversity—were a set of goals that could only be met by a fundamental shift in group actions. Out of this need he and MIT co-researcher, Otto Scharmer, developed the "Practices of Dialogue": listening, respect, suspension, and voice.

Brought into the Knowledge Jam conversation (with its backdrop of openness and diversity), these practices form a quality of talk that propels shared meaning and new relationships forward. The practices bring out and make sense of what we know in a disciplined way. Knowledge and context both come to the surface with more people engaging. In Chapter 7 ("Heritage") we'll learn more about the origins of the dialogue practices. Here we'll talk about each dialogue practice and how it plays out in the Knowledge Jam.

Dialogue Practice 1: Listening

In dialogue, *listening* is turning to the speaker in a way that is both selfless and open and directed to the goal of surfacing knowledge. Listening without interruption, and with skillful inquiry (similar to the questions in Chapter 3 ["Facilitation"]) improves the depth of detail and the richness of context. Often what emerges is a perspective beyond one's immediate assumptions. As a result, application, or *translation*, of knowledge through any kind of decomposition and re-assembly is more possible than had brokers simply read a white paper or diary. Brokers and their seeker organization have more rich content and context with which to work.

The facilitator encourages listening in two ways. First, she models openness by holding a posture of attention to the speaker. Second, she stays loyal to the speaker's words, not paraphrasing or making connections between ideas until she has captured the speaker's content and asked permission to edit. For example, a facilitator might say, "Sarah, I need to paraphrase here to catch all that you just said. Is that ok?" (Note that this is different from active listening, a technique that tends to lead the speaker. An active listener-facilitator tends to push harder or sooner for conclusions and interjects other themes and facts.)[7]

Dialogue Practice 2: Respect

In dialogue, *respect* means taking the originator or broker at face value and being open to understanding the origins of his choices and actions. It is not simply according them respect as the culture would have it (because of rank, fame, wealth, or age), but rather giving them space to contemplate how they and their team navigated a set of choices. In Knowledge Jam, it means looking at the pattern of causes—such as budget shortfalls, talent gaps, or team dysfunction—and seeing a decision or action not as a "failure," but as the product of those conditions.

Consider the excerpt below from a Knowledge Jam in which originators are chronicling the evolution of a mid-sized company:

Excerpt with Broker Using the "Respect" Dialogue Practice

Originator: That quarter we missed the target Earnings Before Interest, Taxes, Depreciation, and Amortization [EBITDA] that we had promised investors, and, as a result, our investors threatened to pull out. It was a harrowing scene, and we were worried we'd have to sell off parts of the company at just the wrong time. Fortunately, we won back their favor, and they stayed with us.

Broker: That must have been painful. Can you describe what was going on in the company and economy when your EBITDA dropped? What, in your view, made those investors open to staying with you?

Here, a respectful broker is getting out a rich story of the conditions that caused the drop in profit. A disrespectful broker might have focused entirely on the investors' threat (or managers' personal foibles that led to the profit drop) and might have ignored the complex set of factors which put the originator in the painful spot. As a result, they could have put the originator on the defensive during the Jam, and not surfaced particularly useful know-how.

Facilitators also practice respect by probing into the "why" of the decisions or narratives of the knowledge originators and brokers. They help the group to seek to understand and not to judge. The "learning history," a graphical rendition of the organization's chronology, can be a tremendously powerful illustration of respect.

Just an additional note: When we are fully present for others in a respectful way, not judging or inserting, we are more likely to remember the insights we hear. We aren't filtering. We're just using language in a way that opens a door. And we are more likely to remember who was there when we reached those insights.

Dialogue Practice 3: Voice

Voice in dialogue, is our sense of agency or authority. In Knowledge Jam, the originators' voice is an expression of their sense of ownership for their own truth and their urgency to get that truth out. Originators' voice-practice is the reflection of both experience and emotion. Sometimes, insight and emotion come out at the same time, and the emotion is as much data as are the facts. This is where its helpful to keep the posture of openness and to practice respect and listening. ("When you described the EBITDA shortfall, you seemed more pained than when you described the investors as you know them today. Why was that?")

For brokers, practicing voice is expressing a desire to collect and use insights in their specific functions or divisions and to put those insights to work in the most effective way possible. Practicing voice increases the brokers' stewardship for knowledge, once found. Change management practitioners agree that we are more likely to make use of a new idea or change effort if we had a hand ("voice") in creating it. Similarly, when our quest for knowledge is triggered by our specific needs (our "voiced" need, task, or puzzle), we are more likely to use ideas that fill those gaps.

The facilitator encourages *voice* by giving participants a sense of ownership of their own story (and according them attention and respect as they do so). Facilitators type speaker initials in front of the comments on the Discover/Capture template, even when the agreement is that people will not be directly quoted in any "public" Jam outputs. When facilitators and other participants welcome voice, originators can speak with conviction (not just to please people). Brokers can then ask more nuanced questions about the prospective applications for knowledge, and, as a result, they feel more like knowledge stewards than knowledge transmitters.

As facilitator, I encourage voice directly. I bring people in from the edges of the conversation and remind them about their "skin in the game." For example, I allude to a knowledge-gap that a broker described during Plan steps, such as how they can sell a technology similar to that of which the originators speak. Or I use simple analogies that are familiar to the originators. ("Meeting EBITDA targets in that market was probably like hanging wallpaper with one hand.")

When I first learned of the concept of voice, I found it quite startling that the dialogue process, that so focuses on selfless listening, would also have something that seems as *selfish* as voice. But with Knowledge Jam, it fits. Encouraging voice is providing a welcome mat for all participants' purpose—and even pride. Purpose and pride are often needed when originators are reluctant or even embarrassed about what they've learned from experience. And purpose and pride are needed when brokers sense that the originators' shared know-how is threatening to the seeker organization's status quo.

Dialogue Practice 4: Suspension

Suspension is about holding back our mental models or frameworks when we listen to another person. It's not just simply pausing to "reload," as William Isaacs likes to say, but going further and letting alternative constructs emerge from the conversation. We refine our thinking and assemble new insights only through suspension. A prerequisite to sense-making in Knowledge Jam is being able to hold in check our impulse to judge. This suspension practice heightens our ability to see new ideas and look for the cues for making them translate into new applications.

Systems thinking is a useful tool for encouraging suspension. For example, I could believe that all the extra money my generation spends on organic food is wasted. But, in suspending, I'm willing to hear Martha Stewart tell me that all vegetables are not created equal from an organic perspective. ("Spray fertilizers don't wash off my lettuce

Excerpt of Dialogue Practices in Jam for a Virtual Team

Originator 1 (Project Manager): It also helps having a person working on the ground with us [in Australia] to do a skills transfer. I believe the biggest problem we have in Australia is time-zone difference.

Voice

Broker (Training Executive, in the U.S.): You had not worked on a project with this scope before?

Listening

Originator 1: It was new to us. The actual scope, statement of work, etc.—that was new to us, but we knew the basic technology. There's "competency" education and there's "technical" education. We didn't spend time on that during the project. This is your territory, and I would like to know how you think about it.

Suspension

Originator 2 (Business Analyst): We feel it is very important to have the knowledge base to rely on, like [names of people in the U.S.] whom we consulted.

Voice

Broker: I would have expected there to be an expert there [with you on the ground] permanently. I try to do that as a matter of course.

Voice

Originator 3 (Business Analyst): (A bit defensively) We've gotten up to speed very quickly. We've gone 0 to 60 miles per hour in very little time. I don't think the customer thinks that we are winging it, but it would have been scary had they found out how fast we've learned.

Voice

Broker: You're working at a pace and confidence level below where you could be. I see unnecessary stress and discomfort for your local team. One of the reasons we have attrition is because of this type of stress. You are heroes; you are the technical people in the project organizations who are solving problems. I want you guys to go out on a project and be challenged and not be frustrated and worn down. We've improved on the competency-building front, but this is still an issue I will address.

Respect/Voice

Originator 1: We agree. Burnout is a risk. Please can you tell us what you are thinking of doing?

Listening

easily," she reports.) Buying more organic can expand the market, production, and ultimately scale- and price-parity with traditionally cultivated food. Here's a credible feedback loop. And, despite my Scotch heritage, I might want to spend a little more on organic Romaine today in hopes of an affordable low-pesticide lettuce tomorrow.

Translating to Knowledge Jam, suspension makes it safer to share (and practice voice) as a knowledge originator and safer to probe as a knowledge broker. The facilitator encourages suspension among participants while drawing out new patterns. Where suspension is going on, facilitators can recap and integrate several comments, and participants who have loosened their grip on their version of things are more likely to help each other with connecting ideas.

The excerpt on page 84 illustrates for a virtual project team how practices of voice, respect, listening, and suspension in a Jam allowed the broker, a training executive, to not be defensive, and to commit to action.

In this example, the Australian project team was tremendously overworked, and opinionated about how training was an issue (expressing voice). But they became open (suspending) and asked to learn about training, even despite their workload. The project team showed eagerness to hear how the training exec might address the problem (listening). Note that the training exec did not blame the project team for struggling along without going through formal training channels (respect).

The list below succinctly brings together the dialogue practices with the Knowledge Jam roles. Going left to right, it shows how the practices represent specific Knowledge Jam conversation interactions, which, in turn, yield concrete Knowledge Jam outcomes.

Deep Dive: Dialogue Practices

Dialogue Practices	*Interact*	*Act ("Translate")!*
1. Listening	Depth/Context	Application
2. Respect	Presence	Retention
3. Voice	Ownership	Stewardship
4. Suspension	Sense-Making	Interpretation

Dialogue Practice Opposites

The dialogue practices take some experience to recognize and to get right. An instructional technique I use as facilitator is one I learned when

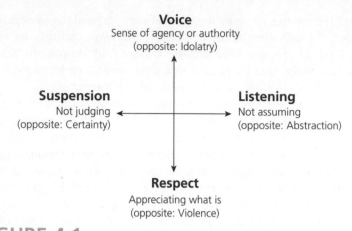

FIGURE 4.1. *Practices of Dialogue and Their Opposites*

I worked with William Isaacs. Participants remember dialogue practices more vividly when they imagine what it feels like when those practices are *absent.* Here are dialogue practice opposites:

- *Listening's* opposite is *abstraction*: Moving quickly to summary or framing the concepts without letting the speaker finish.

- *Respect's* opposite is *violence*: Disregarding someone's sense of agency or authority by dismissing the story or not drawing out the context around it.

- *Suspension's* opposite is *certainty*: Holding fast to one's preexisting mental models as if they were universal doctrine, not personally felt or individually formed.

- *Voice's* opposite is *idolatry*: Not using one's own voice, but speaking from someone else's (or the organization's) viewpoint and acting more out of fear or convention than out of conviction.

I like the way the axes represent energy. For the Knowledge Jam this seems to convey that all participants are capable of both movement and stillness. The brokers are not just recorders; they are asserting a new context for applying the insights they receive from the originators. And it goes without saying that the originators are asserting what they know and how they came to that knowing. But both the originators and brokers may also need to let the wider system emerge in the conversation. By all participants' suspending (in effect, by holding back their sense of certainty) new causes and effects can emerge, and the thinking of the whole group can rise to a new level. People who have participated in dialogue share a certain victory over the bland and the conventional. And they often take that sense of common achievement into their relationships beyond the Jam.

A truly productive conversation combines a posture of *openness*, the readiness include others or to jump in and add *diversity*, and the intention and courage to engage *dialogically*. Conversation like this has both a higher capacity for sense-making and a higher capacity for knowledge-relevance. More useful content flows. And more diverse perspectives and heuristics shape it, keeping an eye toward how it's going to be useful in future applications. Through dialogue, we're open to emergent—even serendipitous—translations for know-how. It seems, then, that when the dimensions of openness, diversity, and dialogue come together, Knowledge Jam doesn't feel like collecting words into a report. It's constructing collective intelligence. In the next chapter we'll see how translation carries that intelligence forward.

CHAPTER

DISCIPLINE 3: TRANSLATION

"Discipline 3: Translation" provides a how-to for Brokering, that is, knowing and representing the knowledge-customer or "seeker," remixing content for reuse, promoting and modeling reuse, and capitalizing on the relationships triggered in the Knowledge Jam to help refine ideas. Here I also describe how social media best broadcast and integrate know-how, improve originator-seeker networking, and extend knowledge velocity and durability.

> "I got some very, very good training with the Guadalcanal men that had just come off of Guadalcanal. And I always considered that an advanced course, because they got a lot of training before I ... ended up with the 1st Marine Division. Being with those veterans that had been there and done that— that was really something.
> "And I give them credit even till today for me still being alive and being here, because they would sit around and tell stories, what happened and how it happened, when it happened. And I listened and I asked questions because I knew that there was—that we will be going into something just as bad or maybe worse. And so I wanted all the details that I could find. ... I was so very fortunate of being with them for—I was with them for about nine months before we hit New Britain."
>
> NEIL CONAN INTERVIEW WITH R.V. BURGIN, AN EIGHTY-SEVEN-YEAR-OLD VETERAN OF WORLD WAR II, NATIONAL PUBLIC RADIO'S "TALK OF THE NATION," MARCH 11, 2010[1]

In Chapter 1, we looked at Larry Prusak and Al Jacobson's 2006 research on Knowledge Transaction cycle time, where they showed that elicitation and adaptation together represented 38 percent and 46 percent of the cycle time, respectively, for a total of 84 percent of the entire cycle time. (That amounts to about eighty-seven hours in my Indian offshore team example from that same chapter.) Prusak and Jacobson pointed out that these time investments dwarf the other steps in the transaction, what they called "search" and "negotiation with the originator(s)." Their hypothesis, consistent with the Knowledge Jam construct, was that people have a hard time making sense of knowledge they receive, for example, in a Word document, because so frequently it is context-poor. That is, it assumes that the knowledge recipient "just knows" how the originators' constraints at the time influenced their problem solving. It also assumes that the reader can "just figure out" how to tease out those constraints when trying to apply the knowledge today.

That's rarely the case. In a 2001 article Rob Cross, Andrew Parker, Larry Prusak, and Steven Borgatti showed that knowledge-seekers were more likely to reuse knowledge that was delivered by individuals, as opposed to knowledge-bases. Here, the numbers are equally dramatic: People prefer the personalized delivery over documents by a ratio of seven to one.[2] Their conclusion, which foreshadowed Prusak and Jacobson's later research, was that seekers like interacting with an originator because we can riff with them. In that interplay, we gather the context behind the facts and even receive advice on our own planned uses for the ideas we glean. Drawing out ideas from our conversation with the originator, rather than from a database, we are adding a bit of ourselves. We're representing our own (or our stakeholders') interests, and getting the nuance where we need it.

The intent behind having brokers in the Knowledge Jam was just that: To have the seeker (or broker, their ambassador) in the selection and planning of the Knowledge Jam, then having them in the Discover/ Capture conversation, helping to direct the inquiry, and later, remixing and promoting content for the other seekers. I call this work of the brokers "translation."

Translation is more than transforming. Transforming connotes a *re-shaping*: to change, possibly past all recognition. With the Latin root, latus, meaning "carried," translation suggests lifting something (adding energy) and moving it across toward something or someone. We may change the hue and add punctuation, but the shape stays largely intact.

On the other hand, translation is also different from *interpreting*. Interpreting suggests doing something on one's own (interpreting the music of jazz composer Claude Bolling, as I play it in my own tempo and style). Whereas interpretation connotes adding energy into *my* product, translation, by contrast, entails using that energy to meet another's specific need.

Decidedly, brokers, as "translators" are sense-making and moving know-how from point to point at the behest of the seeker.

This chapter focuses on the translation process—a process that starts long before the Discover/Capture event. Here I ask, "How do people come to be brokers (or translators)?" "How do they speak out for the needs of the divisions, teams, organizations, or governments they represent?" "What helps them to follow through on the commitments they make to their home organizations and to the Knowledge Jam process?" "How do they put the knowledge into circulation (targeting it, packaging it, marketing it, and contextualizing it)?"

Collaboration tools, particularly social media used within an organization (what Andy McAfee calls "enterprise social software platforms (ESSPs)) are changing the translation process these days. These can be effective vehicles to connect brokers with originators and sponsors, and brokers with the seekers they represent across geographies and time zones. Even invisible seekers. We'll dive into the role of collaboration tools in the translation process below.

BROKERS' MOTIVATORS

During the Select step of the Knowledge Jam process, Facilitators work with management to consider a portfolio of subjects. What drives the selection of the knowledge to be "jammed" is the possibility of leveraging know-how in the pursuit of new product design, more efficient processes, or deeper skills. (For example, we might ask, "Is transferring sales know-how between regions or with our resellers more important than transferring know-how about machinery from retiring engineers to newer engineers?")

As I will discuss in Chapter 9 ("Building"), often it is the seekers in those target organizations who make the case for the Knowledge Jam. For example, a new engineering team designing a fermentation process for a new biofuel might seek to learn techniques from another engineering team that used fermentation to produce a biopharmaceutical.[3]

Sometimes it is management who know their teams' knowledge has value (and that it is perishable), but they haven't quite figured out which seeker organization should receive it. For example, they might be motivated to capture old-timers' wisdom before those employees retire. (This is a threat to many corporations as the Baby Boomers age. My friend Robert Hoffman, at the Center for Human and Machine Cognition, calls this the "Grey Tsunami.")[4]

Regardless of whether the seeker organization can be identified and counted, or whether it is just in the division's "best interest," a central Knowledge Jam principle is seeker *stewardship*. That's the broker. With Knowledge Jam, I generally say, "No brokers, no Jam."

Whether they are representing known seekers or "standing in" for potential seekers, brokers embody four primary motivators: need, involvement, reflection, and other-centeredness.[5]

1. *Need:* Our active search for knowledge is triggered by specific needs (a problem, task, or puzzle that we or our organization or our network is experiencing). When we *need*, our senses are heightened. We are most likely to remember ideas that satisfy those needs.

2. *Involvement:* We are more likely to make use of new ideas if we had a hand in creating them. We're even more ready to adopt them if we've sounded out those new insights with others.

NGOs have demonstrated *involvement* as a broker-motivator in projects with African farmers. Farmers failed to adopt fertilizers and other crop technologies until they themselves engaged in the crop experiments. But with their *involvement*, the very crop-rotation approaches and fertilizers on which they couldn't previously be persuaded moved into the mainstream. More, their adoption rates grew when their involvement was augmented with some collective sense-making. Consider this excerpt from researchers in Malawi, Zimbabwe, Kenya, and Catholic Relief Services, Baltimore:

"The researcher-led and farmer-managed approach is the most cost-effective because it optimizes joint learning among farmers, researchers, and extension agents; facilitates development of skills for farmers to implement the new technologies; and strengthens traditional African collective learning methods. Analysis of farmers' perceptions of good and bad practices used at various stages in the research-development-diffusion-innovation process reveals that investments are most likely to generate impact if targeted at building farmers' capacity to experiment with new technologies and improve collective learning systems."[6]

Involvement for Knowledge Jam brokers plays a similar role to involvement in the field of change management: employees who discover and plan their destiny are more motivated to advocate for it and less likely to resist or obstruct new ideas.

3. *Reflection:* It is not just experience that teaches us, it is reflection on that experience that brings us practical lessons. By reflecting and sense-making, we begin to adopt new patterns of understanding. As we saw in the Southern Africa example, we do sense-making best when we are in a familiar group. With their home work groups brokers make sense of know-how that they bring back from the Jam. In *collective* sense-making, conversations can deepen a shift in mindset. We have the luxury of bouncing ideas off of someone who knows us and understands our context.

4. *Other-Centeredness:* The broker has constituents in mind as he participates. By imagining another use for the knowledge—in another vehicle, in another voice, with another audience—the broker is like a personal shopper. Brokers know their clients' coloring, body type, fabric preferences, and budget. They participate in the Knowledge Jam, imagining it as a new outfit on their work group's frame. They'll strive to integrate the textures and lines vital to the new style, while keeping the garish and uncomfortable out of the wardrobe.

In effect, by participating in the Knowledge Jam steps, the broker is both "in the game" (helping to elicit know-how, using sense-making to see if the new ideas really work in his new projects), and he has "skin in the game" (being responsible for adapting knowledge for his constituents).

So brokers carry a special burden. Like the seekers in a peer assist or knowledge-elicitation interviewers, they are involved, sometimes alongside other functions' brokers, in the discover/capture process. Akin to the peer assist, they have a sense of ownership of the knowledge they've gathered.[7] But here's where the Jam is different from both peer assist and interviews: Knowledge Jam brokers are ambassadors for their home teams and partners in change.

BROKERING BASICS

Likening a broker to a personal shopper is not intended to make light of the broker role. Sometimes life and death (at a minimum, *livelihood*) ride on the brokers' effectiveness at rapidly translating insights for their seeker organization. In this section I summarize the broker's responsibilities throughout the Knowledge Jam process.

Broker Responsibility 1: Knowing and Representing the Knowledge Customer or "Seeker"

Life and death were, in fact, at stake in a Knowledge Jam at Institute for Healthcare Improvement (IHI), discussed in Chapter 4 ("Conversation"). As introduced in that chapter, the Jam was for one of their national, virtual communities of labor and delivery (perinatal) quality improvement teams. During the two-year community engagement, IHI observed a sizeable range in time-to-proficiency for member teams of physicians, nurses, technicians, and administrators. IHI practice designers were eager to understand what made some member hospitals' quality teams come together or "gel" as productive change agents within weeks. Meanwhile, many other hospital quality teams lost months in false starts, reorganizations, and distractions.

The IHI community designers and faculty considered the real possibility that lives could be spared in other hospital departments or disease areas if quality teams could "gel" as quickly as those high-performing teams.

As *brokers*, the IHI planners and program designers arrived at Knowledge Jam with a sense of how typical teams "form" when chartered to reduce medical errors. And they could readily list several specific obstacles that most teams faced (for example, conflicting incentives, aptitude, or competition between levels or disciplines). These brokers were motivated and prepared to translate what they learned.[8]

Brokers like these are spanners, bridging across people and across ideas. They understand future contexts for the Knowledge Jam insights. As IHI brokers participated in the Select and Plan steps of the Knowledge Jam, they focused the conversation on sorting out those obstacles. In the Discover/Capture event they probed as educated and respectful peers. In brokering, they were equipped to translate today's insights to tomorrow's contexts.

A few years before I conducted a Knowledge Jam with a group of project manager originators where the subject was a cost-overrun on a

Excerpt from Knowledge Jam with Project Managers

Broker [Marketing Manager]: What could we do differently with the statement of work?

Originator [Project Manager]: The number one issue with the statement of work [SOW] that I'd change is the "timely access to stakeholders for review." This was the biggest "gotcha." Not having access put us over our hour and time limits. In the SOW this should not be open-ended. We could have had recourse to bill more for the added hours. But we didn't want to "pick at that," just as we were signing another $700K deal. If we had put it more squarely into the SOW, we might have been able to ask for more money for overage, without disrupting the follow-on project negotiation.

Broker [Marketing Manager]: In retrospect, we should have gone over the Ts and Cs with the client beforehand and given them a better appreciation for the potential overruns."

project. A marketing manager participated in the Knowledge Jam, representing other project managers who would one day be proposing similar work to other clients. Marketing was brokering on behalf of future project teams who could be blind-sighted by similar cost overruns. An excerpt from that Jam is shown above.

The marketing manager went on to translate what she learned into changes to the statement of work methodology. For example, she recommended talking with the client about assumptions and contingencies and spelling those out with the help of boilerplate contract language. This would make it less awkward to bring up the client's role in cost overruns in the heat of the moment.

Surrogate brokers sometimes need to stand in for a seeker who hasn't been named. This is frequently the case when we are capturing the insight of a retiree and we have a sense that we'll one day need to use that insight in future work, even though we hardly have the time to find the right seeker organization before the retiree hits the golf course.

Surrogate brokers may also be needed to Jam with a team that is disbanding or reforming to start a new project. All too often teams disband without a coherent sense of how they have made collective decisions, and their reluctance do this sense-making is amplified by the time pressures they are under. You have to strike while the iron (or the brains) are hot.

Another common example of when a surrogate broker is needed is when the seeker has little political power. For example, junior or offshore employees often don't have a seat at the table with powerful subject-matter experts. Sadly, those employees' effectiveness is greatly diminished by their blind spots and the organization's knowledge mismatches and knowledge jails.

In some situations, the facilitator may have to double as a broker. This is a tall order, because it requires subject-matter expertise and can limit the facilitator's neutrality and perceptiveness during the process. Whenever surrogate brokers join a Jam (or facilitators double up as brokers), it is helpful for those brokers to compile a punch list of the variety of concerns and scenarios their seekers might experience.

As I explained in Chapter 3 ("Facilitation"), Knowledge Jams may have two or three brokers, each one representing a different organization. When that occurs, brokers need to be ever more precise with their questions, as they are sharing the "space" with other brokers. This gentle competition is helpful, provided that there's some agreement about how the time will be allocated to topics. In my experience, when brokers represent multiple seeker organizations, they almost always begin to see value in ideas that they might not have anticipated.

Broker Responsibility 2: Re-Mixing Content

Translation's *latus* root, "lifting across," means adding some energy, so someone *else* can get something done without expending lots of energy. The brokers think about this throughout the Knowledge Jam process. The payoff is highest if they put in the right effort to discover and to network during the Discover/Capture event.

During the Discover/Capture step, the conversation among the brokers and originators begins the re-mixing of ideas. Consider this instructional example: An intranet search tool entrepreneur, Frederic Deriot of Darwin Ecosystems, was a knowledge originator in a Jam with a number of MIT Sloan students. The students were in broker roles, representing marketing, engineering, venture capital, and operations.

The marketing brokers needed to create an "elevator pitch" for Darwin's collateral. The marketing team asked how the search tool stacked up against Google.

Deriot explained how Darwin's statistical algorithm didn't respond to hit volume or re-linking frequency (the standard Google search algorithm). Rather, it reflected the frequency of directly related terms (and indirectly related terms) that appeared in live news or social media sites. He went on to explain that, in the Darwin Awareness Engine, these terms are rendered in an "attractor cloud" (displayed like a "tag cloud," but generated statistically by the simple presence of related terms in the material). In just a few short minutes, marketing brokers had coined the elevator pitch, "We retrieve the *relevant*, not the *popular.*" As marketers, they combined the Darwin Awareness Engine's strengths with their knack for coming up with the "bumper sticker," tools of the marketing trade. In this act of respectful translation, they didn't transform, they "re-mixed." (Not bad, considering the propensity of brilliant marketing students to be spin doctors!)

In re-mixing, brokers amend, amplify, annotate, or otherwise improve the reusability of Jammed know-how for their target seeker organization. In general, brokers also transfer knowledge into vehicles that make it accessible and reusable. Table 5.1 is a sample of such re-mixings.

Brokered, re-mixed knowledge frequently applies outside the initial seeking division or function. For example, in a financial services company the customer feedback gleaned from a marketing team was folded into new customer service practices. In a more timely example, lessons learned and practices from corporate restructuring during the global recession could become a best-selling (and enduring) transition kit to help specialized change management teams around the globe. At one Cambridge, Massachusetts–based software developer, their home-grown tools for application configuration management were so popular outside the organization that they spun them off into a new product line and a new revenue stream.

In this last example, an effective *process* for one division ends up as a *product* that another division sells. Or vice-versa, as we'll see in the "home team" excerpt from a Jam on page 99.

In the excerpt, the product team broker found the highly graphical model used by the originators for outside clients to be applicable to the home team's own infrastructure projects. This kind of serendipitous

TABLE 5.1. Illustrative Brokers' Remixes of Knowledge Jam Knowledge

Type of Knowledge	Seeker Profile	Brokered Form	Knowledge-Delivery (Brokering) Vehicle
Process, for example, how we ramped up a fabrication plant	Another region or division planning to build a fabrication plant	A process flow with process step annotation	Plant engineering tools' process flow
Product, such as how we defined a product map	Another product team building a similar product	Definitions of features, feature prioritization, template	Product strategy presentations
Market, such as how our target customer segment responded to an offer	Customer service organization evaluating staffing levels	Customer service representative (CSR) screens incorporating segment-related business intelligence	CSR stations, sales portal
Program, such as how we taught our special-needs kids math	Another school district educating special needs	Annotated curriculum, lesson plans	Online district-wide sample curriculums, teacher training resources
Organization, how we managed internal stakeholders during a restructuring	Change management teams for a restructuring in another division	Stakeholder matrix, organization plan, message samples	Online transition kits

Excerpt from Jam Helping the Home Team

Broker 1 (Product Team): Your final client report has a very cool "business case" for a future investment. Check out the four-quadrant graphic!

Originator 1 (Technical Consultant): We use that all the time. It shows: "Impact on Business" along one dimension and then "Probability to Realize Impact" on another dimension.

Originator 2 (Technical Consultant): There are actually two versions. First you see potential investments inside the quadrants. Next you see "threats" inside the quadrants. It has color-coding of value (in the first), and risk severity (in the second). The graphic helps with collaborative decision making. How could you use it?

Broker 1: We could use this for our own investments. I see us using this as we have hardware and other similar capital investments.

remixing of ideas into applications beyond the ones brokers originally planned, is not uncommon in Knowledge Jams.

Broker Responsibility 3: Transmitting Content

I define collaboration tools as any vehicles that help bring groups of people together across space and time to share content. Today, the options are almost unlimited—they range from a conference call to instant messages to Twitter. Recall that asynchronous collaboration tools figure prominently in the far-right column "knowledge delivery (Brokering) vehicle" in Table 5.1.

Social media are collaboration tools that land content onto "platforms" as opposed to narrow (and often ephemeral or hidden) "channels." (A wiki or Facebook is a *platform*. Email is a *channel*.) Social media are ideal for convening seekers around drafts, for re-engaging the originators, for storing captured know-how, and for extending it into useful forms that knowledge seekers may use in their day-to-day routines.

As we'll learn more in later chapters, ESSPs are social media within the corporate firewall. They have a particularly important role as they are locked down to the organization, and thus enable confidential company ideas to develop in safety. ESSPs enable many different forms of interaction and knowledge-dissemination. For example:

■ *Wikis* (PBworks or Wikipedia) can be used to build out narratives based on an initial structure established by the facilitator, brokers, or the planning team.

■ *Social bookmarks* (Delicious) can push Jammed knowledge out to the forefront as originators or brokers feature those pages and documents they most use.

■ *Microblogs* (Yammer, Lotus Connections, and Socialtext) can enable brokers to inform seekers about knowledge found and can be used to vet or extend ideas prior to any formal packaging. They can also help the whole Jam team broadcast to the organization about how new know-how contributes to success.

■ *Topical alerts* (like RSS feeds) can be used to track Brokering progress, say in a document being co-authored by brokers and originators in a wiki, to help the seekers know when someone has Jammed about ideas, or simply to let the facilitator and sponsor know when members of the Jamming community have contributed in some way to the Jammed content while it is being remixed for distribution.

■ *Discussion forums* (such as those in Microsoft SharePoint) can be used to engage brokers and originators to expand on topics that are first surfaced in a Knowledge Jam. Discussion forums operate a lot like microblogs, but may limit participants to only Jammers while content gets fleshed out.

MIT Principal Research Scientist Andrew McAfee describes the remarkable versatility of Enterprise 2.0 to expand the quantity and spread of good ideas:

> *"Enterprise 2.0 increases the number of good ideas that an organization develops and delivers to its constituencies. Some of these—for example, a better process for taking and filling customer orders—can be incorporated into an ERP system and so disseminated throughout a company. Others can be directly integrated into products. Still*

others can spark a productive conversation or meeting, or put hours back into the week of a busy knowledge worker. The ESSPs themselves are largely indifferent to these different types of ideas; the new collaborative tools of Web 2.0 and Enterprise 2.0 simply provide forums in which people come together with few preconditions or constraints and get remarkably powerful content and ideas."[9]

In my experience, Jammed ideas spread more quickly—have a *higher velocity*—when we use social media. Velocity comes from social media's access, interaction, reach, and as transport vehicle.

- *Access.* First, *social media accelerate the process of identifying both originators and applications for knowledge.* In the sea of online interactions, participants tend to self-identify. A good search engine pointed at social media chatter can rapidly shed light on networks of experts or expressed knowledge gaps, and can speed up both Knowledge Jam Plan and Broker steps.

- *Interaction.* Second, velocity rises because *brokers, originators, and seekers can participate efficiently in an extended conversation,* filling in details that may not have come up in the Discover/Capture event, or which didn't make the Planning agenda "cut." No one needs to set up another meeting, provided that the right parties are in the social media and the ingredients of conversation—openness, diversity, and dialogue—can flourish. As we learned above, involvement of this type is likely to increase the seeker's comfort with using the knowledge and reduce adoption hurdles.

- *Reach:* Third, velocity rises because *social media tools provide remarkable reach–broadcasting to secondary and remote or previously unknown seekers.* At the extreme, we can tweet to our Twitter followers (and, with re-tweeting, to our followers' followers) just-in-time during a Discover/Capture event and get the Brokering process rolling even before the conversation ends. (A word of caution: it can be helpful to prepare originators and their managers for the possibility of sudden rock stardom!)

- *Transport:* A fourth source of velocity is the flexibility of *using social media not just as a conduit or broadcast to announce, but as a knowledge delivery vehicle.* Where social media tools house the final knowledge indefinitely, seekers need go no further for updates. U.S. Army Training and Doctrine Command saw with the

Army field manuals wiki, which now house regularly updated field Army tactics, techniques, and procedures.[10] Contrast that to static formats like hard-copy field manuals, hard-coded workflow or online support screens that require lengthy batch processes to be re-coded, re-tested, and installed.

For some organizations, an asynchronous (especially platform-based) collaboration helps accommodate multiple time zones and ways of working. An online asynchronous interchange, say between a Boston-based team and a Bangalore-based team, has two advantages. Not only does it enable participants to respond to ideas on their own schedules (in this case, India being nine and one-half hours ahead), but it also levels the playing field. Slowing down the pace of conversation can help the non-English speaker keep up. Sometimes slowing down also helps hesitant brokers and seekers to ask follow-up questions that might feel embarrassing to them or offensive to the knowledge originators. Conversation will work provided that participants work in the dimensions of openness, diversity, and dialogue.

Broker Responsibility 4: Being a Change Agent

Change agents are those who articulate a shared vision, and also enable others to act around that vision. Brokers are the consummate change agents. Change agents who inspire action are those who are first and foremost trusted as a conduit for ideas. Brokers credibility in the eyes of their seekers improve the odds that Jammed knowledge will actually be put to work by the seekers they represent. (In contrast, a broker with a "salesman" reputation may have little success in bringing "home" know-how, particularly when that know-how conflicts with commonly held beliefs.)

Broker credibility can come from reputation or affiliation. A broker is more credible to me if she has served my organization before or she is legitimately connected to a reputable source or program. We emphasized the importance of sponsorship for generating credibility in Chapter 3 ("Facilitation"). Sponsors not only get people into the Jam, but they also can "have the back" of the broker.

A second characteristic of a broker-change agent is *collaboration*. Brokers' collaboration starts early with their participation in the Knowledge Jam planning, where they collaborate with other partici-pants to ensure that the Knowledge Jam topics will suit the seeker organization that they represent. Likewise, they collaborate in the Discover/Capture event conversations by engaging in a way that is expansive for multiple seekers, not just those they represent. Back at "home" among the seekers they represented during the Planning and Discover/Capture steps, brokers find constructive ways to collaborate with different types of seekers. A hand-off, even by the most trusted broker, may not result in a change in seeker behavior. Just as we saw that *involvement* by the brokers in the Discover/Capture event improved the brokers' commitment to the process, brokers will find that involvement by the seekers is critical to getting seekers to invest in the change. Finally, broker change agents take Knowledge Jam's Conversation discipline with them. Brokers need to know when to tread lightly and to not threaten the egos of the seekers, especially when Jammed know-how conflicts with the way seekers have been doing things up to now. Brokers must guard against being perceived by their seekers as colonizers. Brokers are wise to take a page out of the conversation chapter:

- They practice *openness,* that is, expressing ideas grounded in data, inquiring into others' reasoning, engaging people in the big picture, and staying away from blaming comments. This serves brokers well, especially when they are conveying "how *not* to do something."

- They pursue *diversity*. They stress test the translation for the know-how from the Jam by going beyond the most familiar audiences. A broker from HR might bring in IT to see how know-how might be applied.

- Brokers even need *dialogue practices, listening*, for example, when seekers muster the courage to explain pride and regrets; *voice* when they have to convey conviction; *suspension* when they have to imagine working within the current (admittedly broken) system; and *respect* for the history that has led to the behavior patterns that need to shift.

Broker Responsibility 5: Promoting Translated Knowledge and Modeling Reuse

Brokering knowledge doesn't *end* with a wiki posting or broadcast email with elaborate attachments. Even in the lucky situations where

Jammed know-how is in a new procedure, brokers can't yet hang up the change agent hat. They *promote*.

Promoting means assembling Jammed ideas with some creativity and carrying that creativity into messages. Brokers can borrow a page out of *Made to Stick* by Chip and Dan Heath.[11] The authors show that effective promotions need to be:

- Simple

- Unexpected

- Concrete

- Credible

- Emotional

- Conveyed in stories

Translation of Jammed knowledge needs to be all of these things. So does the communication about that translation. For example, if know-how about how to construct a bridge to withstand 100-mile-per-hour winds is hidden in the body of a lengthy whitepaper, and the whitepaper is dry and routine, maybe this time the broker should try a sending around a flash video of the Tacoma Narrows or arrange a field trip.

Brokers' best promotion is when they actually use new know-how themselves. For example, a teacher may feel strongly that a teaching approach she learned at a teaching conference makes sense for her local district. Sharing lesson plans and recounting the lectures from educators at the conference may not do the trick. The teacher-broker may need to show how a pilot among her students yields some credible changes in student performance. Often know-how takes hold only when the new ideas show some value *at home*.

Following is an excerpt from an interview with a broker who charged into translation with just enough passion to attract several other organizations into the Jam.

This exuberant broker took full responsibility for taking knowledge forward to product teams and regions. *Note well:* What wasn't clear initially to the broker was that translation isn't just about publishing. It's also about engaging the seekers. As it turned out, a pilot made this journey a lot less lonely.

Excerpt from Brokering Plan for Technology Design

Broker: The Knowledge Jam would enable us to provide scenarios, with documented engineering protocols and annotation regarding benefits and constraints of the associated designs under each scenario. The learning curve would be reduced. We would not take the client down a path that is a waste of time. I propose the following: (1) let's Jam scenarios from [client] and package them like other design "kits"; (2) next, let's review them with our product team and other regions; then, finally, (3) let's publish them in a scenario folder on our product space on the portal.

Broker Responsibility 6: Handling Knowledge Perishability

A final note on *durability*. That's an antonym for knowledge perishability. Very often what drives the need to do a Knowledge Jam is the sense that the recent insights (of a team, subject-matter expert, soon-to-be-retiree) are ephemeral, and that we need to put them to work in another part of the organization *now*. In this case, there is a greater pressure on the broker to make sure that knowledge reaches the seekers quickly. Brokers need to alert the seekers to the role they will be playing in the Jam so that seekers are prepared. After the Discover/Capture event, brokers can use alerts, blogging, tagging, broadcast (email, microblogging). They also can label the knowledge (or the opportunity to use it) "perishable" by making the connection to the seekers' context explicitly. (In our bridge example, the broker could say, "This is the bridge design the Blue Bird Team used in St. Louis. Cardinal Team, this is timely for you before you start design selection in Indianapolis.")

At Intel we did a Knowledge Jam with a team that had developed a remarkably valuable protocol for one of our highest revenue consulting services. As it turned out, the consulting methods team revised the consulting "solution delivery-kits" only on an annual basis. Brokers knew that we had a small window to promote the new protocol, so we called a "knowledge transfer conference call" with originators, brokers, and the kit update team and moved the Jam to the front of the queue.

Because Brokering is the last mile of the Knowledge Jam process, and sometimes time elapses between Discover/Capture and Brokering (and Reuse) steps, it can be elusive. I assert that translation is a process that the seeking organization and their brokers should initiate even before a Knowledge Jam plan is hatched. Translation calls on brokers to represent seekers well, to help the most useful know-how and context to surface, to be change agents, and to be deft social media users. If the Facilitation discipline is piloting the car, and Conversation is the engine, then Translation is the sturdy chassis, transporting insights across sometimes treacherous terrain.

CHAPTER

BESPECKLED, MARRIED, AND EMANCIPATED

"Bespeckled, Married, and Emancipated" revisits the "blind spots," "mismatches," and "jail"—thorny problems from Chapter 1—and recaps how the Knowledge Jam's boundary-spanning (Facilitation discipline), participative knowledge-elicitation (Conversation discipline), and stewardship (Translation discipline) are a viable combination for overcoming those hazards.

"All Mankind
Not just purposeful mankind
But mankind unrelated to what is important to just us
Without a fuss and thus
Live totally within
Emancipated dialogue"

FROM EMANCIPATED DIALOGUE, BY BLACKRABBIT9X.[1]

In Chapter 1 I talked about three obstacles to tacit knowledge transfer: blind spots, mismatches, and knowledge jail. These are truly thorny problems, and some of our best efforts fail to discover and capture relevant knowledge, frame it appropriately, and raise it above the fray. Knowledge Jam offers an alternative:

1. Boundary-spanning to overcome knowledge blind spots (*Facilitation*)

2. Surfacing the reusable knowledge, and reducing knowledge mismatches (*Conversation*)

3. Putting knowledge to work, that is, releasing captive knowledge from knowledge jail (*Translation*)

In this chapter, I show how the Knowledge Jam cycle and disciplines address the thorny problems directly. Facilitation, Conversation, and Translation provide business alignment and direction, relevance, and continuity, and these are best understood after absorbing the preceding chapters. (Later, in Chapter 8 ["Comparing"], I'll also consider how these characteristics differentiate Knowledge Jam and complement other approaches to knowledge transfer and innovation.)

BOUNDARY-SPANNING

Blind spots come from our being unaware of relevant knowledge (until it's too late) or being unaware of the need for connecting specific insights across people, groups, or organizations. Blind spots are failures in *boundary-spanning*. Blind spots that we saw in Chapter 1 ("Rationale") were knowledge flight and separated puzzle pieces. The Knowledge Jam *Facilitation* discipline helps with boundary-spanning:

- *Facilitators' number 1 mission is to identify and advocate for knowledge that can be Jammed.* During the Select step, facilitators play an important alignment role. They try to know what's where (and what's missing), while at the same appreciating the economics of surfacing and reusing knowledge. In effect, whereas brokers are like personal shoppers for their represented seeker organizations, facilitators (and their listening posts) are like the enterprise's personal shoppers, pointing out potential knowledge subjects.

■ *Facilitators bring people together who might not otherwise connect.* Facilitators assemble many lenses for looking at problems and set the tenor of the interaction and conversation. For example, they could do this by scanning the landscape for knowledge originators' stories about inventing a product and propose Jams that draw in teams who are researching both similar and different products.

■ *Facilitators bring together ideas that might not otherwise have been juxtaposed.* That means corralling different parts of an issue into one place and time (or virtual place). This entails assembling not just different organizations, but genuinely different facets of an issue. We learned in Chapter 4 ("Conversation") that diversity can improve collective decision making and predictive capabilities. As we saw in the Application Testing example in that chapter, introducing a variety of perspectives and heuristics improves the ability of the group to see and connect separated puzzle pieces that can reframe our thinking on about a problem.

■ *Facilitators' "container" of common curiosity is conducive to idea exploration and risk taking.* When the container is strong, participants take off their blinders and talk openly and reflectively about patterns of events or decisions. When they do this, all the participants can participate in making logical connections between facts and theories, even those that are embarrassing. In that sense-making facilitators help participants to bring ideas into light that wouldn't have come up in one-on-one interviews, repository submissions, or team-to-team transfers.

SURFACING USABLE INSIGHT

Three mismatches I described in Chapter 1 were mixed incentives, lack of context, and mis-alignment of content. Coming together for the Knowledge Jam provides an opportunity for the group to get out usable know-how. That is, know-how that is more appropriately matched to the seeker organization's need and that has sufficient context around it so that it's easy to translate. Group reflection pulls and shapes know-how in a way that could not happen if a single team member journaled, or even multiple members co-authored a report. The *Conversation* discipline in Knowledge Jam helps bring out usable insight:

■ *The Knowledge Jam dialogue makes the undiscussable discussable.* For example, a researcher-broker can safely explain how he is thinking about a question and gain input from originators. (A well-respected academic researcher once admitted to not discussing his project with his colleagues in the same department: "I fear that if I tell them, someone will run with the idea before I have a patent.") Rather than avoiding a topic (or diverting the discussion after superficialities), a conversation with the dimensions of openness (including ground rules), diversity, and dialogue can be safe.

■ *Conversation brings context, separating the unique from the universal.* In sense-making in a group, we can draw out the context of the originators' know-how. As a result, when brokers translate, they are better able to present seekers with both insight and choices. Much solo work is context-poor: it simply doesn't have a lot of narrative about the narrative—even terms can have different meaning in different contexts. I repeatedly saw the need for context in my financial services days. Analyses by corporate planners were very difficult to translate from one division client to the next, and even within the corporate planning function. Elaborate Excel reports didn't typically show decision paths, nor forks in the road that caused the analyst to change assumptions or to swap methodologies. Report readers were on their own to discern whether an Excel report could be applied to another product or division. Reuse was even more hazardous when the analyst took for granted economic or sociological conditions (high inflation or politically sensitized report audiences). In a conversation, a broker might reduce these reuse risks by asking questions about the context.

■ *Brokers bring new perspective to the originating team.* As we saw in the straw and paper-plate tower building role play in Chapter 3 ("Facilitation"), thc Jam can be enlightening even for the originators. Originating team members leave the Planning and Discover/ Capture events with new awareness—insights into how their success or failure occurred, as well as insights into where they could improve on the next project. It's also worth pointing out that peer recognition for an originating team is a motivating force for continuing high performance.

■ *Brokers are driven by need and involvement.* When the broker genuinely needs (or needs on behalf of the seeker organization that he represents), he arrives at the Jam events with the intensity of purpose and curiosity that result in focused questions. Brokers' involvement in the discussion can feed that intensity, as they become more determined to draw a line from the originators' historical context to their seeker organization. I saw this with fundraiser brokers from an educational non-profit who attended a Knowledge Jam with a recently retired Harvard University fund raising executive as originator. As the conversation progressed, the brokers' intensity showed in their body language and in their questions— clearly they saw this as an opportunity to learn the type of fund-raising techniques and relationship-management strategies that they could put to work.

PUTTING KNOWLEDGE TO WORK

In Chapter 1 we encountered the following issues with knowledge jail— info glut, language barriers, and prose erosion. The antidote for jail is setting up the right conditions for making it easy to move knowledge to those who need it and how they need it. That is, *translation.* Here are some ways that the Translation discipline gets knowledge out of jail:

- *Translation surmounts "language" barriers.* Brokers (and the seekers they support) mold the knowledge, listening for what was going on as the originators recount how they made decisions, and mentally mapping that into their context. ("That drilling team was dodging hurricanes. We're going to fend off icebergs. We need to keep temperature in mind.") When the broker packages Jammed knowledge in a usable knowledge product, such as a requirements document, a product spec, or a training curriculum, she is translating from old context to new context, from the language of the originators to the language of the seekers.

- *Form matches the need: prose erosion (or excess) ceases to be a liability.* Receiving know-how in a familiar vehicle or format (like the marketing management system, the customer relationships management [CRM] station, or the microchip design blueprints), a knowledge seeker has a shorter learning curve and he can go quickly into using the knowledge. Conversely, when lessons-learned documents are prepared for "everyone" or with too many or too few explanations, they tend to be useful to few.

- *Brokers use their networks to push Knowledge Jam outputs to the forefront.* In promoting Jammed knowledge, brokers need to not only re-mix the knowledge in seeker-appropriate forms. They also will use their networks and collaboration tools to single out the knowledge product from the info glut. During and after the Jam, brokers expand those networks to include the originators. Now the path to connection is strewn with less clutter. As a result brokers

TABLE 6.1. **How the Three Differentiators of Knowledge Jam Achieve Business Benefits**

Facilitation	Conversation	Translation
Boundary-Spanning (Shedding Light on "Blind Spots"— Reducing Knowledge-Flight and Drawing in Puzzle Pieces)	Surfacing Useful Insight (Informing "Mismatches"— Aligning Incentives, Surfacing Context, Improving Placement)	Putting Knowledge to Work (Springing from "Jail"—Overcoming Info Glut, Language Barriers, and Prose Erosion)
Facilitator and the selection process bring a laser-sharp focus on business-relevant knowledge.	Sense-making in conversation helps us to see systems and feedback structures so we better grasp how to apply knowledge.	Brokers are ambassadors—self-interested and motivated to see knowledge surfaced for effective reuse.
Facilitator bridges between originator and broker organizations.	Jamming, participants take responsibility for connecting between different knowledge applications.	Brokers helped "wrap context around" the knowledge surfaced during the Jam, reducing reuse effort.
Facilitator models respect and common curiosity, making it easier to draw connections.	Knowledge Jam aligns incentives, and ignites a network among originators and seekers; shifting from push to pull	Brokers use their social media and team relationships to elevate Jammed content above the noise.

(and the seekers they represent) find it easy to re-engage Jam participants at a later date, when they come up against challenges not covered in the Discover/Capture event, or find solutions to puzzles participants encountered there.

Table 6.1 summarizes how the obstacles we encountered in Chapter 1 are addressed by the Knowledge Jam disciplines.

Knowledge Jam, with its three disciplines of Facilitation, Conversation, and Translation, addresses knowledge blind spots, mismatches, and jail. Knowledge Jam gets that hidden know-how out into the daylight and into our products and practices *intentionally.*

Knowledge Jam should be part of a broad knowledge reuse program whereby various knowledge-sharing processes and tools are fine-tuned to knowledge types, originators' profiles, or seekers' needs. (This is the subject of Chapter 8.) Knowledge Jam can also be part of a larger change initiative, where the disciplines of Facilitation, Conversation, and Translation as *culture* (intention, openness, and stewardship) improve planning and technology adoption. (More on this in Chapter 10.)

But first, taking a page out of our own book, let's apply the dialogue practice of "respect" and consider Knowledge Jam's heritage. That will help us to more fully appreciate the research and practice from which it evolved. I hope that this journey back in time also stirs in you this hope that Knowledge Jam disciplines become components of your culture, enabling and accelerating innovation and change.

CHAPTER

KNOWLEDGE JAM HERITAGE: PREQUEL TO THE THREE DISCIPLINES

"Knowledge Jam Heritage: Prequel to the Three Disciplines" shows how the disciplines of Knowledge Jam (Facilitation, Conversation, and Translation) derive, respectively, from three business practices developed over the last twenty years: intelligence acquisition, organizational learning, and collaboration technology. Rooted in those business practices, Knowledge Jam may also be in for an exciting ride, as those practices are not standing still. They evolve as work becomes more wired, more globalized, and more interdependent. Knowledge Jam as a practice will also evolve, but it won't forget its origins.

"As a rule, there are in everyone all sorts of good ideas, ready like tinder. But much of this tinder catches fire, or catches it successfully, only when it meets with some flame or spark from the outside, that is, from some other person. Often, too, our own light goes out, and it is rekindled by some experience we go through with a fellow man. Thus we have each of us cause to think with deep gratitude of those who have lighted the flames within us."

ALBERT SCHWEITZER, *THE DIGNITY OF THE INDIVIDUAL*[1]

Though I fancy myself an innovator, I am, by my nature, a bit of a scavenger. Most people involved with knowledge are unabashedly borrowers and adapters, drawing from others as we build and inhabit our relatively new science.[2] Perhaps because we are not bound by centuries of tradition, we have the luxury of drawing from other business practices and thinkers without the risk of seriously offending. Like the brokers I described in Chapter 5 ("Translation"), we have a knack for pulling together unconventional practices in an innovative way.

This chapter is about Knowledge Jam's eclecticism. It is also shamelessly autobiographical. I talk about some of my (and Knowledge Jam's) origins—intelligence acquisition, organizational learning, and collaboration technology. These fields of research have inspired and informed the three disciplines of Knowledge Jam—Facilitation, Conversation, and Translation, respectively. I believe that remembering our practice heritage is critical to our integrity and authenticity as individual practitioners, just as Albert Schweitzer expresses his gratitude for others who have "lighted the flames within us."

Star Wars Episode 1 "Phantom Menace" came almost eighteen years after we first met Star Wars' Luke Skywalker and Han Solo. So it is with this "prequel" to the KM disciplines: may this help you appreciate the pioneering, and sometimes colorful, characters that brought us here.

INTELLIGENCE ACQUISITION

Intelligence acquisition is the prequel to Knowledge Jam's Facilitation discipline. Intelligence acquisition, at its simplest, is the process of gathering and synthesizing information, generally to inform decisions and improve processes. Its cousin, business intelligence, goes further and applies quantitative tools like cluster or regression analysis to mine for data patterns and inform a set of conclusions. Both "intelligence" practices involve data collection—either direct (interviews, surveys), or passive (observation, click streams, revealed preferences).

Intelligence acquisition began with the heyday of strategy consulting firms Bain, BCG, McKinsey, and Monitor in the Eighties and had its geeky adolescence as customer relationship management (CRM) and data mining tools came out in the late Nineties. Consultants came by the planeload to the world's top companies, NGOs, and government agencies to gather and process data about organizations, markets, and constituencies. They used business school–tested frameworks to draw pictures and make conclusions about all types of phenomena.

As a young consultant, one of my first case teams generated an activity-based cost model for a large steel mill. Our team spent many long hours in interviews with client executives to better understand how decisions were made and resources allocated. At a first pass, we defined all activities within the major processes, such as iron smelting and steel chemistry. Then for each of the several hundred activities, we asked dozens of employees what triggered its start and what influenced its intensity. (For example, a customer order triggered a scheduled run of the cold roller, and the rolling specification was driven by the steel finish tolerances.) Many hours of listening to operators describe their decisions enabled us to draw up a system map. That map, in turn, we fed into a computer model that showed which customers and which products improved or diminished average profitability. (We ran this on an Intel 286 with a multi-hour batch cycle, so getting the input correct was critical.)

What made that intelligence acquisition more than the computational work of today's business intelligence systems was the fact that 95 percent of the information derived from a human perspective. An explanation. A judgment call. An ah-hah for both interviewer *and* interviewee. What seemed to begin as data collection became more of a discovery jointly (and proudly) formed out of the collective experience. Importantly, the focus, flow, and the feel of the shared experience mattered. I call these three elements of intelligence acquisition intentional insight, container building, and shared values. Let's look at these in more depth.

Intentional Insight

Intelligence acquisition begins with establishing a rationale and a plan to expand what we know about a subject. It combines the ego-ful activity of establishing a framework (a set of starting questions) with the ego-less act of listening (hearing what's being said and what's not being said). Thus, it is far more than typical knowledge capture, like journalism or "harvesting." (We'll size these up in Chapter 8 ["Comparing"].)

Consider the interviews with the steel mill operators. We had to help the interviewee understand how we were thinking about triggers and drivers, but didn't want limit them to our framing of the problem. We hoped to frame it so that they could summon up their years of insight and talk about what they felt, in their gut, really made cold-rolled steel so expensive to produce.

Here, intelligence acquisition is a balance of the planned and the emergent. Paradoxically, by meticulously setting the stage to see patterns across our interviews and by striving to position an idea into framework, almost always we helped the interviewees discover the new, the unexpected, and the serendipitous. Bells went off. They could describe a common situation and discern what was repeatable and what was exceptional.

This type of learning had many names at the time, but today I call this "intentional insight." In contrast to chaos theory, which proposes that statistically identifiable patterns emerge out of the random, complexity theory states that the path you take to get into a situation matters as much as the starting and ending points.[3] Intentional insight is in the latter camp. It proclaims that "framing" matters. When people introduce multiple frames, our eclecticism (and even our arguments about the frames) better equip us to understand how our experience measures up, to discern what insights are meaningful or missing, and to generate new models for action.

In that pre-Google era, I would pour through reams of LexisNexis printouts, trade news articles, 10Ks, and annual reports. My consulting colleagues and I, at times overwhelmed with the volume, would use our catalogue of business frameworks, such as value chain, Porter's five forces, and buyer purchase criteria. A little victory came each time we found the exception to our frames and could imagine a new frame altogether.

Once I was doing intelligence acquisition for a paper converter who wanted to understand the market for various adhesive innovations. We noticed that each customer responded to innovations with delays, as predicted, but those same delays weren't the same length across different downstream business models, say large office suppliers versus distributors. That forced us to rethink the role of the channel. What made us effective was that we had bounded the problem to a degree (by looking at patterns in purchases at the time of innovations), but we were open to some serendipity. In effect, we kept our view wide enough for "intentional insight."

Container-Building

Intelligence acquisition processes that involve interviews were far more challenging for a twenty-something than reading and synthesizing. My university studies in the Eighties had taken me to the library, not to the phone, cocktail party, or conference room. I was cordial and informed, but very mechanical. My interview outcomes were never as juicy or memorable as those of my more self-assured or garrulous peers. I remember listening to phone research by my colleagues. There were riotous outbursts of laughter. They were joking and "present" in a way that I wasn't, and it was working for them.

I learned that I had to set the stage for knowledge transfer. It didn't just happen.

My manager brought this to light with some good-hearted imitation. He hunched over his interview guide and started barking questions. I was mortified. He explained the importance of setting a tone with my words and posture, inviting the "whole person" into the conversation, and being a whole person myself. "Meaning," he explained, "is not born out of a transaction, but out of a kind of co-creation. *You* have to set the conditions for this."

I later learned a term for setting those conditions from another sage boss, William Isaacs—"building a container." I discussed container-building as a key facilitator role in Chapter 3 ("Facilitation"). The container is the metaphoric space in which we interact. It is the sum of the ideas, experiences, personalities, and appreciations that we've brought into our shared spaces (be that in a place or over phone lines). Isaacs explains that the well-built container between or among people effectively provides a barrier around the energy of the interaction, thereby making it safe to explore:

"As [containers] become more stable and conscious, they can hold more pressure. It seems to take a certain amount of pressure for human beings to think together. As people come together and bring their differences out, the pressure builds. Then the question arises, Is there a container to hold this pressure? If not, people will tend to try to avoid issues, blame one another, resists what is happening. It is possible to create containers that can hold the fire of creation. When this is the case, those within the container do not have the feeling that they will be 'burned' or that things are 'too hot.' They may feel stretched, but included and safe."[4]

Only upon co-existing within a container—some common ground, be it a shared experience, the weather, politics, or laughable Red Sox scores—can deep and insightful knowledge-exchange begin to occur.

As an interviewer those years back, I had to make this happen. I had to offer up an element of humor or personal interest or shared life and make my interviewees feel comfortable sharing a bit of themselves. We had to invest in the container of common curiosity before we could be effective at bringing out know-how.

Another paradox: In making ourselves just a bit vulnerable, we were, in fact, collectively more powerful over the complex topic. Successful intelligence acquisition calls for interactions that contribute to the container. Now, this comes naturally for me. It doesn't feel like work, but it works.

Shared Value

Another lesson from intelligence acquisition is the importance of aligning (and voicing) a shared set of objectives or shared value. This is perhaps the simplest dimension of intelligence acquisition to describe, but the most difficult to bring about. Shared value involves aligning:

1. The business drivers of the intelligence acquisition initiative with the intelligence acquisition approach and

2. The intelligence acquisition approach, with some concrete value that the knowledge originator holds.

Shared value is different from "shared values," which are often the short-hand definition for the word "culture."

Later in my career I did quite of bit of knowledge management strategy and planning. I implemented KM processes and technology. In one project a number of older-time engineers were avoiding our program. Some did this outspokenly, some subtly by using time-scarcity as a defense. We quickly abandoned the initial goal of amassing volumes of documents from these knowledge originators. We found that shared value (and, hence, participation) would require improving those origina-tors' current work overload problem. We shifted our focus from knowledge-collection to launching a number of communities of practice where those same originators felt they were getting something in return (a network, new insights, exposure, a tidy repository). Shared value became a binding force for the community of practitioners.

With the Knowledge Jam, the *intentional insight, container-building,* and *shared value* of intelligence acquisition become the key ingredients of the Facilitation discipline. A facilitator embodies the concept of intention—he plans and coordinates the Knowledge Jam, first vetting of subjects with sponsors, then generating the agenda (framework), then facilitating knowledge-transfer in the Discover/ Capture event. Finally, he helps to align ongoing Brokering efforts to the business objectives to ensure ongoing *shared value*. Here, the facilitator helps topics change direction in mutually insightful ways. Facilitators are always on the lookout to create shared value for participants. Most importantly, facilitators help to build the *container* by setting a tone of common curiosity. By putting a piece of themselves into the mix, facilitators model and encourage respectful, informed inquiry and discourage defensive, criticizing or protective attitudes.

ORGANIZATIONAL LEARNING

Organizational learning, a field of practice focused on how groups and companies learn, is the prequel to the Conversation discipline. Organizational learning philosophy—the potential for collective improvement even in adversity and diversity—as well as it tools and practices have been taken up and rebranded by many other fields. Below I use the traditional organizational learning language, but you may know some of this from such practices as "virtual teaming," "positive deviance," or "wisdom of crowds." We'll look at the field and how it fed the Conversation discipline.

The Organizational Learning Field

Peter Senge introduced organizational learning to business executives and non-profit leaders while he was at the Massachusetts Institute of Technology (MIT) Sloan School of Management in 1991. Organizational learning was seen as a way of improving the resilience of our organizations, ecologies, and economies. The Center for Organizational Learning became a gathering for organizational behaviorists, engineers, and education experts, led by Senge and frequently joined by MIT and Harvard researchers Daniel Kim, Ed Schein, Chris Argyris, Donald Schön, and progressive companies like Harley-Davidson and Visa International.[5] Their aim was to combine the principles of "systems thinking" at the level of the "organization" (school, company, nation), and to help unveil the way we *learn how* we *learn* ("double-loop learning"[6]). They posited that entire organizations could be learning units, but that it took courageous individuals in collaboration to bring this about:

"In 1991, the Center for Organizational Learning was founded at MIT by Peter Senge with a mission of fostering collaboration among a group of corporations committed to fundamental organizational change and advancing the state of the art in building learning organizations; its initial focus was on developing new learning capabilities in the areas of systems thinking, collaborative inquiry into tacit mental models, and nurturing personal and shared vision."[7]

Talking about mental models (worldviews) and shared vision was actually quite radical at the time, when corporate HR departments spent resources motivating and training the individual. Rarely did they bring up the worldviews of those individuals (fearful, invincible, wounded, beleaguered), let alone the potentially paralyzing worldviews of groups of individuals.

Organizational learning contributed to Knowledge Jam's Conversation discipline three central capabilities:

1. *Systems thinking.* Systems thinking is a tool for building a shared understanding of how a number of interacting parts work together.

2. *Cognitive diversity.* Cognitive diversity capitalizes on the organizational learning principle that learning is *social*. It claims that we learn more by coming together and by naming and bridging our worldviews or mental models.

3. *Dialogue.* Dialogue is the practice of generating shared meaning through a shared unimpeded flow of ideas.

Together, these three contribute to Knowledge Jam by widening the perspective, welcoming idea breadth, and by giving us a very real set of tools for talking about ambiguous, but valuable, tacit knowledge. I'll describe each in turn.

Systems Thinking

Systems thinking is the first ancestor of Conversation discipline. We visited systems thinking briefly in Chapter 4 ("Conversation"), and here we'll dive a bit deeper. Often considered the starting point for all organizational learning, systems thinking is rooted in system dynamics. System dynamics describes and quantitatively models a group of interdependent things, such as beer stocks and diaper purchases, to discover the non-linear (and, often, non-intuitive) interactions between them.

System dynamics was based on the theory of electrical control systems. It is highly mathematical and relies on non-linear programming. My dad, Alexander (Jack) Pugh, worked on system dynamics in the Sixties with Jay Forrester, founder of the System Dynamics Department at MIT. Dad would bring home system dynamics drawings and describe the quirky, sometimes oscillatory behavior that resulted when you quantified some feedback loops and interactions. For example, extreme pile-ups of inventory in response to an overly optimistic sales force, depletion of a fish stock due to fishermen acting autonomously, or huge cost overruns for mega projects, like aircraft carrier and rocket construction.

By the time I was ten, I was drawing feedback loops on my school notebooks and had one eight-syllable word in my fourth-grade vocabulary: "unintended consequences."

Scroll forward. In 1990, Peter Senge, then a graduate of Jay Forrester's System Dynamics Program at MIT, wrote *The Fifth Discipline,*[8] a brilliant translation of system dynamics for a general business audience. Peter named this "systems thinking." Systems thinking focuses on drawing feedback arrows and interdependencies and illustrating why some of our most sincere efforts backfire, with unintended consequences. Systems thinking is more easy to grasp than system dynamics for most people, as it leaves out the quantitative models and numeric plots of stocks, flows, and behavior. Growing up with system dynamics, I took to systems thinking like a fish to water: I felt at home in that tremendously descriptive (but flawed) world.

As a tool for visualizing know-how in the Knowledge Jam conversation, systems thinking is in good company. Many knowledge-elicitors use the technique of concept mapping,[9] which has many similarities to systems thinking. Concept maps represent relationships among concepts, and concept mappers use verbs to define those relationships. ("Cats → [eat] Canaries.") Systems thinking also represents relationships among concepts. What systems thinking additionally provides is a focus on second-order outcomes and a measure of time. It does this through the distinction between "stocks" and "flows," and through the notion of a resource growing, shrinking, or even oscillating over time due to feedback loops.

For example, the "stock" of canaries goes down as the "stock" of carnivorous cats goes up. This relationship (or "flow") could be linear or exponential. The term "flow" is used to describe a driving relationship (or influence, or impact). "Eat" is a flow that has the property of

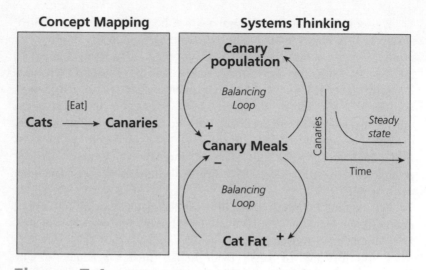

Figure 7.1. *Comparing Concept Mapping to Systems Thinking: Cats and Canaries*

impacting canaries (and making cats fat, of course). A feedback loop might be "Fat cats are less nimble and can therefore catch fewer canaries." This is what we call a balancing loop, because it serves to reduce something (pouncing cats) and, on net, the counter-effect of dwindling canaries.[10]

Figure 7.1 shows the flow relationship between cats and canaries for concept mapping and for systems thinking. In the systems thinking panel, on the right, it shows the second-order effect (balancing effect) of cats growing fat.

Read the systems thinking graphic on the right by saying, "If X goes up, it has a negative (–) or positive (+) effect on Y." The negative and positive signs go over the arrow heads. Here, for example, "If Canary Meals goes up, the Canary Population goes down," and "If Cat Fat goes up, Canary Meals goes down."

In systems thinking, we force ourselves to be open to the unexpected. A causal relationship that can be particularly insightful, albeit sometimes disturbing, is one that is contrary to our basic intuition. For example, many of us have seen (or attempted to build) an incentive system that creates exactly the opposite result of what we intended. In early KM programs, managers rewarded or required employees to contribute to the knowledge base. Managers' goal was sincere: they wanted to improve the volume of submitted documents, giving the program some credibility, and therefore increase the likelihood that knowledge would be reused. Diligent employees submitted materials in the spirit of reuse. Or so they thought.

Unfortunately, managers overlooked one other feedback loop: quality. A reputation for good quality resulted in trust in the knowledge base and higher reuse (a "reinforcing loop"). A reputation for lower quality resulted in mistrust, and some backing off (a "balancing loop"). Where there was no explicit quality-certification, and employees got their incentives for just submitting documents, the resulting repository was suspect. Few believed that it housed anything of value. Seekers would have to winnow through documents and call the originators before they felt confident about reusing documents they found. Here, the goal was increased reuse (and the accompanying lowered operating costs through reuse), and the unintended consequence was clutter and the *higher* operating costs associated with training and attracting knowledge-seekers, beleaguered knowledge originators, and even a plateau in submissions.[11] (See Figure 7.2.)

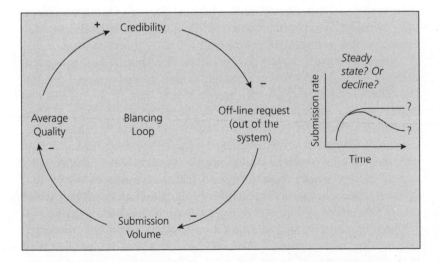

Figure 7.2. *Systems Thinking Illustration for Content Submissions Where Incentives Focused on Volume, Not Quality*

Read Figure 7.2 by saying, "If X goes up, it has a negative (–) or positive (+) effect on Y." Here, for example, "If credibility goes up, it has a negative effect on off-line requests. People use the system instead of going around it." Conversely, "If credibility goes down, it has a positive effect on off-line requests. People use the system less."

Systems thinking would become a critical skill for drawing out tacit knowledge as part of the Conversation discipline. In the Discover/ Capture step Knowledge Jam participants find that visualizing such causes and effects (for example, how policy, investments, attitudes, or other factors interact) causes us to slow down and look for unexpected insights. Such insights make know-how more reusable.

Practical Diversity

The second ancestor of the Conversation discipline is diversity research. As with our African farmer example in Chapter 5 ("Translation"), pioneers within the Organizational Learning Center (OLC)[12] argued that learning is social. We learn best when we have a shared teachable moment, or when our co-workers or fellow citizens serve as sounding boards for exploring learning experiences.

The notion that learning is social brings up an interesting dilemma: How do you get collective learning when the people don't all agree on fundamentals? This answer isn't obvious. Doesn't difference (read: disagreement) thwart our sharing of ideas and our listening to each other, and thereby limit our learning?

Organizational learning practitioners like Daniel Kim set out to determine whether diversity of thought within groups could help learning. The starting point for this research was mental models. Mental models are our individual world-views about how things happen. They are our individual stories about the causes and effects within our companies, communities, and families. For example, one manager may argue strongly for a change to sales incentives because her mental model is that the underlying sales problems are always due to motivation; while another manager may argue for product feature changes because his mental model is that underlying sales problems are always caused by uncompetitive products. These two managers will talk past each other and grow increasing frustrated unless it becomes clear that they have different mental models of what underlies the poor sales figures and can talk about each.

Organizational learning practitioners hypothesized that unvoiced (unwritten, tacit) mental models could be obstacles, preventing us from agreeing on actions and thereby preventing us from effectively adapting to competition, scarcity, or opportunity. Their research showed that when we make our mental models explicit (for example, in pictures, system thinking diagrams, stories), those mental models are discussable. Outside of our heads, pictures and narratives give us a bit of distance from our thorny problems, and we increase the possibility of bridging our differences. At the same time, when we look at the clash points in our mental models, we expose a part of the problem that none of us could have fully seen on our own before. In the sales argument above, seeing the clash point of "motivation versus uncompetitive products" could enable each camp to see that sales force motivation and weak product features could both be related to a company-wide misconception of customer needs.

Combined mental models yield greater incisiveness to tackle today's problems. Mental model variety also makes us more adaptable to the potential variety of tomorrow's problems.

This idea echoes arguments many scientists make today for biological diversity. It shields us from mutating bugs. Organizational learning in other fields also found compelling examples of when collective learning and problem solving improved when contrasting world-views were intentionally included—crossing department, division, function, and even organization. We introduced this notion in Chapter 4 and Scott Page showed mathematically in *The Difference* that diverse mental models can improve both performance and predictions.

Organizational learning practitioners pondered: If breadth and adaptability are good things to have, then why not *fabricate* mental model diversity?

Dr. David Kantor, a family and organizational psychologist, took this on by exploring dimensions of diversity he called "structural dynamics." Examples include language choices individuals make (speaking with power, emotion, meaning), group interaction patterns (assertion, completion, opposition, reflection), and decision-making heuristics (democratic, linear, or emergent reasoning). He showed that some types of diversity can get a group stuck (for example, your talking about the deadlines, my talking about our team's morale). Kantor describes these dimensions of diversity in his "Introduction to Structural Dynamics" in the *Fifth Discipline Fieldbook*.[13] He explains a number of flavors of difference that he had observed in working with family and organizational systems. (See the sidebar on the next page.)

Kantor is an optimist and a pragmatist. Even as he describes people's habitual (and sometimes dysfunctional) ways of acting in a group, he notes that one's awareness of the group pattern (and what's missing) are enough to equip them to act in another way and inject new energy into the dynamic. For example, if everyone is coming up with suggestions, and no one is apparently moving to act, just adding "follower" energy ("OK, let's go deep on Option A") can shift the *group's* energy from overwhelming paralysis toward action.

SIDEBAR: STRUCTURAL DYNAMICS: STRATEGICALLY STIMULATING DIVERSITY
Here are a few diversity concepts David Kantor introduces from his research with families and corporate or non-profit organizations:[14]

1. Action Positions
We habitually make one of four moves while interacting in a group. These are what Kantor calls "action positions" (also called the "Four Player Model"):

- *Move* (advance, advocate, propose),

- *Follow* (agree, complete),

- *Oppose* (contest, correct, provide alternatives), and

- *Bystand* (observe, reflect).

Any of these moves can be annoying to other group members. Their good intention gets lost in the initial impressions they may make. *Movers* come across as bossy. *Followers* come across as spineless. *Opposers* come across as obstructionist. *Bystanders* come across as absent or distant. Where the diversity message is relevant is that groups that lack one or more of these roles, or that stay in an interaction pattern, can become "stuck." In effect, lacking diversity can reduce the flow of ideas.

- In Knowledge Jam, too much "moving" (say, declaring an objective) with no "following" (acknowledging and recording) becomes "all hat and no cattle," with no closure.

In other words, you can use your understanding of structural dynamics to *forge the diversity that the group lacks. Cognitive* diversity, as we called it earlier, to distinguish it from *identity* diversity (cultural), became a critical dimension of Knowledge Jam's Conversation discipline. Kantor called on us to vary language, energy, and decision-making paradigms—effectively adding to cognitive diversity. With some practice, you can help a group "come unstuck" and, in so doing, be more creative, cover more ground, and take any innovation forward.

- Too much back-and-forth between moving and opposing ("The spec was too tight." "No it wasn't. We were just sloppy!") becomes a "point-counterpoint," again, with no closure. (How about, "Have we calibrated our measuring instrument?")

- Too much following becomes "courteous compliance," with no insight or innovation (think: Looney Tunes® chipmunks).

- Too much bystanding becomes a "hall of mirrors," with repeated reflection on the process, but no substantive move to action ("We could change conference rooms." "We could change the sequence." "Have you noticed how many times Jane spoke?")

Kantor would point out that, once you know your favored action position and can see what the group lacks, you can fill it in. You up the diversity quotient directly.

2. Languages

Kantor talks about languages not as a syntax and alphabet, but as content. The language of *power* is language about accomplishment, competition, action, and comparison. When I talk about missing deadlines or publishing deliverables, I am speaking in the language of power.

The language of *affect* is about feeling, relationships, and emotional impacts. When I talk about the negative impact to families of a layoff, I am speaking in the language of affect.

The language of *meaning* is about concepts and patterns. When I talk about how my organization seems to "always put new executives on the firing line each time we hire one from the outside," I'm talking about a pattern, using the language of meaning.

(Continued)

Kantor points out that languages can get out of balance just as much as action positions can. For example, an excess of power can cause team members to retreat. The energy can be softened with some affect. ("Yes, the project was on time, but at what cost to the team's health?") or an excess of affect can be grounded with meaning. ("I see this pattern, and it's destructive. We get paralyzed when layoffs are announced.") Again, you are upping the diversity, and, in so doing, moving the conversation out of a stuck pattern and into the realm of more ideas.

A Knowledge Jam was conducted with a team of Intel Solution Services consultants who were the first to establish Wi-fi for a commuter train in August of 2006. In the excerpt from a Knowledge Jam below, notice the shift from cost (language of power) to pride/identity (language of affect).

Excerpt Showing How Shifting Language from Power to Affect Can Help

Originator 1: [Client] was very happy with our work. We delivered the results, we demonstrated the [efficacy of the technology] to the right level, and we had a good relationship with the [partner organizations]. We kept quiet on the issues of our cost-overruns, in the interest of selling the next phase. What did that cost us?

Originator 2: Preparing for the media event was driving a lot of this [cost overrun]. We are also generating case studies. But clients find the slide presentations, with pictures, very appealing. The architecture pictures helped [client] execs understand how much was involved. And they are proud! They got a great appreciation of the magnitude of the project. (They originally thought, "Oh, you will put up a bunch of antennas on the train and then you're done." Now they think we're geniuses.) Rail operators appreciate pictures, as they saw themselves in them, too.

As a facilitator, broker, or originator the goal is to see whether the lack of a certain language (power, affect, or meaning) is keeping the discussion stuck. If it is, inject the missing language. In this example we see a shift from monetary issues (power) to clients being enthralled with pictures (affect).

3. Paradigms

Kantor points out that we naturally fall into preferred ways of interacting when we speak, decide, or build coalitions. He calls these ways of interacting "paradigms." An *open paradigm* is democratic and fluid in including a variety of ideas. Second, a *closed paradigm* is more linear or structured in its approach, allowing fewer unspecified inputs, and generally more hierarchical. Third, a *random paradigm* is one that incorporates new ideas as needed by the decision-maker holding the paradigm, but their approach doesn't appear to follow a given structure or standard consensus approach. Random-paradigm people can be immensely creative, as they are able to bring in ideas (and improvise on the fly) and add those directly to existing structures.

Conflict arises in a Knowledge Jam when different speakers assume their paradigm is universal. A person in an open paradigm may speak quickly and with frequent requests for validation and input from others. Meanwhile, a person in a closed paradigm may hold back and look for validation from superiors or the facilitator. Or they may speak dogmatically and not provide any validation at all. A person in a random paradigm might become frustrated with a closed paradigm speaker, as the person doesn't seem to be welcoming the idea of serendipity. As with languages and action positions, Kantor would suggest that participants can gently shift their paradigms to expand the ideas coming out.

For example, I could prod a closed-paradigm speaker with a question like, "Have you ever had to try it another way?" "When younger employees come on board looking to learn, they may need to do Step 3 first. What have you done when someone needs you to go out of order?" or I could take a random-paradigm speaker and remind her that closed and open paradigm people can't track with them. Those with closed and open paradigms expect a structure. You might remark, "When we don't conclude something, but move on, I have trouble concentrating. May I propose that we use the 'parking lot'?"

4. Heroic Modes

The last of the diversity components Kantor expresses is the "heroic" modes. Derived from Jungian psychology, the heroic modes are the narratives we tend to act out when we are in groups and that can become ugly when we are threatened.

(Continued)

- The *fixer* heroic mode solves problems and organizes people and solutions quickly. But their shadow is an *abuser* (meaning they push their ideas on others too assertively or too soon, without regard for the others' need to engage or "fix" themselves).

- The *protector* heroic mode looks after the feelings of the people and the needs of the group. Their shadow is the *accuser* (meaning, they see the "protected" and the "oppressing" as two very distinct camps).

- The *survivor* heroic mode marches forward on the original plan and heads toward the agreed-on goal, regardless of the swirl of activities that conspires to destruct the process. The survivor's shadow is the *abandoner* (meaning that they abandon emotionally or literally, sometimes unexpectedly, after a long period of stoic endurance).

Though Kantor stresses that our native heroic modes are deeply rooted in our gender, individual, and family narratives, we all have the ability to see and act out patterns of fixer, protector, or survivor and to intervene in constructive ways. For example, in a trusting relationship with a fixer, I could invite the person to consider using some of the "fixing" energy to listen for signs of people's fatigue. Or with a survivor, I could

Dialogue

The third ancestor of the Conversation discipline was the "Dialogue Project." This was an OLC group led by William Isaacs and Otto Scharmer. Dialogue had a unique role in the Knowledge Jam heritage. I first learned about this while studying with Isaacs as an MIT Sloan student. I later worked for Isaacs and experienced this at his company, a spinoff of the OLC, called "Dialogos."

Like their friend David Kantor, Isaacs and Scharmer sought to describe the real-time interpersonal practices that enable a conversation to be not just *transactional*, but "generative of new meaning." Isaacs, who drew in concepts from particle physicist David Bohm, sought to teach people about dialogue by juxtaposing "discussion" (which can be transactional, combative, or close-ended) with "dialogue," which, by contrast, was more translational, integrative, and open-ended. In the language of physics, a *wave* rather than a *particle*. Isaacs used to introduce dialogue through its etymology. *Dia* is Greek for "flow" or invite the person to consider whether the task is really a "life sentence" or whether some creative additions might make it more collective and more fun. Finally, with a protector who may be tending toward his accuser shadow, I could encourage a greater sense of voice or agency. ("Consider how your project could meaningfully influence management's views.")

When taken together, the way you self-assess along the structural dynamic components (action positions, languages, paradigms, and heroic modes) makes up what David Kantor calls your "boundary profile." Knowing your boundary profile (or an organization's boundary profile, at a summary level) can be very enlightening, as it enables you to plot out ways to improve diversity in all types of conversations in which you participate.

Knowledge Jams will benefit from diverse perspectives and heuristics when we make timely shifts in different boundary profile dimensions—blends of action positions, languages, paradigms, and heroic modes. New patterns emerge where the stale routines were thought to live. Values become distinct and discussable. Interdependence becomes clear. This lesson goes beyond the Knowledge Jam. Across most organizational interactions, we can improve many dimensions of diversity (and thereby performance) instantaneously and improve the breadth and quality of insight.

"through," and *logos* is Greek for "word" or "meaning." Dialogue was quite simply "meaning flowing through."[15]

In Chapter 4 I explored the practices of dialogue—listening, respect, voice and suspension. At Dialogos, Isaacs represented the practices along the axes shown in Figure 7.3. Further, he named the axes to correspond to the organizational learning ideas of advocacy and inquiry.[16]

The "axis of advocacy" is one of assertion, advancement, or forward energy, and can be focusing on the self. Voice and respect stand opposite each other on this axis, as each represents a sort of movement toward the speaker.

The "axis of inquiry" is one of opening and receiving. Suspension and listening stand opposite each other, as a gift of stillness or of "letting in," as a listener takes in someone else's ideas.

In Chapter 4 we learned all about the practices. We didn't talk about what led Isaacs to them. At Dialogos, Isaacs taught our clients about the principles behind the practices of dialogue. I'll paraphrase them and map them to our Conversation discipline:

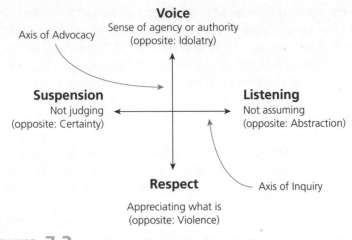

Figure 7.3. *Dialogue Practices (Reprise)*

Copyright © Dialogos Inc. Reproduced with Permission.

- *Mutuality:* Dialogue is not just democratic, but collective, in the greatest sense of the word. In dialogue, each participant is responsible for keeping the ball rolling, the ideas flowing, and group contributing. Knowledge Jam conversations involve surfacing the context or conditions around the facts ("Why did you decide to do that *then*?") When context is drawn out with the many-to-many interactions in dialogue participants better understand how ideas can be reusable across places and time. Moreover, context drawn out in a dialogic way gives the brokers ownership—a personalized take on the knowledge. ("We have a different value system, but we can do this, too. We can pull off this change in *our* branch if branch managers, rather than *function* managers, support it.")

- *Container:* A prerequisite for dialogue is a container (as we introduced with the Facilitation discipline). A container is an essential backdrop as one engages in dialogue—a vehicle for holding the tension (and possibility) as participants listen and speak.

- *Double-Loop Learning:* Dialogue calls upon us to see how we learn (or impede our own or others' learning) and to do something about it. As I participate, I am responsible for examining my prejudices or blind spots. That responsibility applies as much to whom I decide to recognize as a "source" as much as to what I consider to be "truth."

- *Identity:* The most radical element of dialogue is that I come with the very real expectation that I could be changed. I can expect to have new ideas woven into mine in a manner that fundamentally changes me and my identity. Recall that this concept of identity also shows up in the openness dimension, as heart-preparedness.

- *Emergence:* I join a dialogue with the expectation of being carried by the conversation, as opposed to forcing my agenda or requiring participants in the dialogue to follow a line of reasoning that I have planned out a priori. But I'm not a purist: Knowledge Jam has a knowledge-elicitation objective (rather than being unstructured and fully emergent, as is often the goal of "pure" dialogue). So Knowledge Jam's being facilitated (rather than leaderless, as dialogue purists would have it), means that Knowledge Jam conversations channel the dialogue practices toward a shared knowledge product that is tangible: a populated Discover/Capture template, a set of knowledge nuggets, and enduring relationships between participants.

In a Knowledge Jam conversation, participants use the dialogue *practices* of voice, listening, respect, and suspension to draw out meaning in a collaborative and intentional way. But even further, Isaacs' dialogue *principles*, as we just saw, influence all three dimensions of the Conversation discipline—the posture of openness, pursuit of diversity, and practices of dialogue.

COLLABORATION TECHNOLOGY

Collaboration technology is the ancestor of the Translation discipline. Collaboration tools—from email and shared folders to instant messages, wikis, and blogs—are an inseparable part of today's knowledge work and our organizational lives.

It wasn't always that way. In 1989[17] Lotus Corporation (now part of IBM) released Lotus Notes and proudly called it "groupware." It combined databases and virtual working places for distributed teams to store, share, classify, and converse around documents. With Release 2.0

in 1991, Lotus Notes scaled to ten thousand users with a client-server architecture that enabled global teams to collaborate.

I remember working for an ad agency that year. We were pitching the Lotus account. The partner on the account spoke in hushed tones, "This is really going to be big. This is going to revolutionize how we do work." I remember being puzzled. How can a database do *that*? Well, it did.

Adaptation

With technology advancements, collaboration tools soon blended the easy graphical user interface of the web, with the structure and order of folders, document versioning, and personalization. Additionally, notifications or "alerts" made it possible for a user to know who was working on what and where the process stood, even without going back to the groupware space. With mounting management attention to collaborative virtual work, teams began realizing big increases in productivity and job satisfaction. Online collaborations reduced the need to co-locate and fly across the country for meetings. And improved document sharing made it possible to share documents across groups and to reduce versioning errors.

Teams that had shared paper or emailed drafts through a convoluted (and precarious) chain now were able to collaborate on documents, plans, and spreadsheets with tremendous transparency. They had a "space" to call their own, with their own norms and trappings.

What came to interest me was not how documents and processes were controlled, but how this new collaboration experience enabled things to happen spontaneously. Work seemed to morph to accommodate a diversity of participants, customers, or other changing business circumstances.

I explored this in my master's thesis.[18] I listening mesmerized in 1995 when the first webmaster for a leading IT industry analyst organization admitted that even that progressive technology oracle's offerings were morphing with the new web interaction:[19]

> *"Before we rebuilt the web around the [new] concept, it was just me. I came up with new terms just because I wasn't familiar with some of the practices. For example, we had to respond to inquiries about getting reports. I had to communicate to the site visitors that TechFuture has a policy not to sell single reports. I didn't know exactly how to phrase it, so I invented the term 'membership.' I knew we*

had to put an answer out there, but I didn't have anyone looking over my shoulder. Then, when we brought in the consultant to talk to us, she pointed out to me that nowhere in the TechFuture literature is the term 'membership.' I had invented it."

My master's advisor, Wanda Orlikowski, professor of information technologies and organization studies at MIT's Sloan School, captured this nicely in a 1997 *Sloan Management Review* article case studying collaboration tools: "[T]echnological change is an iterative series of different changes, many unpredictable at the start, that evolve from practical experience with the new technologies."[20] As we adapt, we become.

Exposure

Collaboration tools became a way of life for us who were doing team-based project work every day. After several years of Lotus Notes, I had to learn (and implement) other collaboration tools like EMC Documentum's eRoom, Microsoft's SharePoint, and portals like those of OpenText and Oracle. This was long before their current brands and corporate ownership. Then "standing up a site," as we now put it, took months and hundreds of thousands of dollars. Today, I can go onto Google, PBworks, Ning, or CubeTree and start up at pilot collaboration space in twenty minutes with no money down.

By the early 21st century, as the distinction between the portal and the collaboration tools started to blur, these tools brought further advances in the publishing and promotion of shared ideas. We all were the webmasters. We all were inventing products on the fly, just as the pioneering webmaster did at the technology research firm. Whereas once we would draft editorials, project plans, and analyses in private groupware sites, tucked into folders, and behind sign-ons, now we also had a way to broadcast and obtain feedback on our ideas from co-workers and partners around the globe.

Today's social media sites take that "exposure" concept to a further level. Public sites like Facebook and The Huffington Post and enterprise tools like Jive ClearSpace, Lotus Connections, and SocialText shift the discourse from the channel to the platform. As MIT Senior Research Scientist Andrew McAfee, puts it:

"Now contributions are globally visible (everyone with access to the platform can see them) and persistent (they stick around, and so can

be consulted and searched for). Access can be restricted ... , but the
main goal of a platform technology is to make content widely and
permanently available to its members."[21]

Having Knowledge Jam content "globally visible" can be an immense advantage during the translation process in the Brokering and Reuse Knowledge Jam steps. Content velocity increases because content is exposed to knowledge seekers–visitors, searchers, or subscribers who exist outside of corporate teams, traditional publications, subscriber lists, and personal contact lists.

Co-Creation

By around 2002, a decade after Lotus Notes' auspicious beginnings, we were ripe for the "social" part of today's social media, such as wikis, microblogs, social networking, and web-bookmarking. These tools are unique in that they emphasize co-creation. By contrast to document-centric groupware tools and soapbox-like blogging tools, these thrive on the idea of incrementalism. That is, annotations, re-broadcasts, and new contexts extend the ideas of others. For example, with microblogging software Twitter, I can annotate and "re-tweet" to my whole follower group someone else's tweet that I like. And with collaborative-bookmarking like Delicious, I can open up my classifications ("tags") for your perusal so that you can discover my approach to finding and ordering the web.

Much research is ongoing today about the co-creation phenomenon of social media. Not only do these tools enable co-creation of content, but also the co-evolution of our identities and our products' identities. When I post something, I have come to expect that my co-creators will take it to a higher, more meaningful level. Co-creation will make my ideas better suited to my shifting audiences. Provided that my co-creators are representative of my ultimate target audiences (and I pray that they don't quote me out of context—the fate that befell innocent Shirley Sherrod when she was quoted by blogger Andrew Breitbart. President Obama *fired* her).[22] Stress testing an idea in social media improves its adaptability. But it may also change how I perceive myself in association with my (morphed) content. A blogger friend of mine, Gil Yehuda, expressed this sentiment:

> *"I blog to reach out and invite others in. This process creates engage-*
> *ment. I have to refine my thoughts before blogging, which is good*

for me. But more importantly, I get to learn more when people react. This improves me, while also allowing me to engage with others. As an extrovert, I take the risk of being out there—and sometimes being wrong. But getting the engagement is rewarding. It's also transformative."[23]

Collaboration tools, Web 2.0 (and its corporate cousin, Enterprise 2.0), inspired the *Translation* discipline of Knowledge Jam. Starting at the Select step, collaboration tools can be used to solicit subjects and to collaboratively track and expose a portfolio of Knowledge Jam targets. As the participants plan, they may share background information, artifacts, templates, and opinions in collaboration spaces, on both those spaces sponsored by the Knowledge Jam team as well as other spaces owned by the participants' product, division, or functional areas. Finally, brokers will use collaboration tools to translate and transmit the Knowledge Jam outcomes into forms that are useful to their teams. A sales rep may learn in the Knowledge Jam about an awkward delay (and silence) in certain customer service transactions. This idea could land in the sales team wiki in a section on "cross-selling opportunities."

Simply updating and announcing the revised sales protocol may not change the behavior of sales employees. As I have argued already, anyone presented with a resource to make a change—a change to a decision-making process, product profile, or process step—is more quick to make use of that resource if he feels he has been represented substantively (as the broker does during the Discover/Capture event), and if he can contribute something of himself to the ideas. A broker using Web 2.0 and E2.0 collaboration technology to engage other seekers will likely enjoy greater velocity in the translation of Knowledge Jam outputs into action.

Thanks to the journeymen and women before us, Knowledge Jam solves thorny problems with shared responsibility, diverse perspectives, and transparency (as Andrew McAfee would put it, out of the "repository" and onto the "platform"). From intelligence acquisition, organizational learning, and collaboration tools derive the core disciplines of the Knowledge Jam—*Facilitation, Conversation,* and *Translation.* In a nutshell, we glean the *intention* and *container-building* of the

Intelligence Acquisition	Organizational Learning	Collaboration Technology
▪ "Intentional Insight" ▪ "Container-Building" ▪ "Shared Value"	▪ Systems Thinking ▪ Practical Diversity ▪ Dialogue	▪ Adaptation ▪ Exposure ▪ Co-Creation
Facilitation	*Conversation*	*Translation*

Knowledge Jam Disciplines

Figure 7.4. *Knowledge Jam's Inheritance*

intelligence acquisition, the *participation* and *diversity* of organizational learning, and the *adaptability* and *exposure* of collaboration technology. (See Figure 7.4 for a roll-up of the Knowledge Jam inheritance ideas.)

Having these ties will serve us in the long run. Our business models, practices and markets are anything but static. They evolve as work becomes more wired, more global, and more interdependent. So, too, must the Knowledge Jam. By rooting itself in disciplines that flex with the times (flexing intelligence forms, flexing the boundaries of the organization, and flexing the technology of collaboration), then our foundation can adapt to the ideas, organizational models, and tools of our future.

CHAPTER

COMPARING KNOWLEDGE JAM TO OTHER KNOWLEDGE-CAPTURE METHODS

"Comparing Knowledge Jam to Other Knowledge-Capture Methods" proposes a model for looking at Knowledge Jam's properties alongside other knowledge capture/transfer methods. Many managers have asked, "What's new here?" To help you answer that question, I provide a side-by-side comparison so that you can consider when Knowledge Jam might replace or complement other methods that you are currently using to bring out and share know-how. Knowledge Jam is in good company, but it is the only practice that scores high on all three method components: structure and intention (Facilitation), sense-making (Conversation), and knowledge pull and integration (Translation).

> *"It was quickly evident that 'one size' does not fit all. I did not find reliable principles of transfer that could be generated across all organizational and all knowledge management practices. But in this diversity I began to discern what it was that made a method work in one place but not in another ... I found three criteria that determine how a transfer method will work in a specific situation: who the intended receiver is, in terms of similarity of task and context; the nature of the task in terms of how routine and frequent it is; and the type of knowledge that is being transferred."*
>
> NANCY DIXON, *COMMON KNOWLEDGE: HOW COMPANIES THRIVE BY SHARING WHAT THEY KNOW*[1]

The number of knowledge-transfer approaches is dizzying. In one Conference Board study, the authors identified fifteen transfer methods.[2] Doing your own survey of knowledge-transfer choices, you will find many salient options, and Knowledge Jam is certainly not the answer to all of your knowledge-transfer problems. Consider these scenarios:

■ If your team wants to improve its own capacity to organize and process insight, and reuse is primarily for that one team, *after action review* or *post-mortem* could be appropriate.

■ If you simply want to understand an expert's knowledge in its own context, and without an intent to re-apply it, *interviews* may be sufficient.

■ If you know what knowledge is out there, who your originators are, and you know the exact needs of your target seekers or learners, *instructional design* may do the trick.

■ If you need to collect a known knowledge type, such as application documentation, disciplined *repository submissions* may be sufficient.

■ If you are not concerned with the integrity of content nor its consistency and structure, but you are seeing knowledge-transfer as part of new culture evolution only, *appreciative inquiry* will get you on your way.

■ If you have a single known seeker team and matched known originator team, a *peer assist* may meet your needs.

■ If you want to focus on individuals' professional development or their learning from an expert for their individual benefit, *mentoring* is helpful.

If you didn't see yourself above, or you told yourself, "Sometimes, but only on a good day!," then you are not alone. As we saw in Chapter 1 ("Rationale"), organizations are plagued with blind spots, mismatches, and knowledge-jails, and many of the knowledge capture-transfer methods fail to get at the root of these problems.

A FACILITATION-CONVERSATION-TRANSLATION SCALE

We learned in Chapter 6 ("Bespeckled") that the Knowledge Jam disciplines of Facilitation, Conversation, and Translation bring boundary spanning, usable insight, and intentional knowledge application. Those three disciplines are not unique to Knowledge Jam, at least not individually. They are present in a host of knowledge-capture approaches, such as the *interviewer-as-facilitator* in appreciative inquiry, *conversation* in teams' post-mortems, and *inquisitive translation* by the novice team who interview originators in the peer assist.

Table 8.1 and Figure 8.1 characterize a number of knowledge capture and transfer methodologies according to the dimensions of Facilitation, Conversation, and Translation. In them we ask:

■ How much *Facilitation* is going on? That is, how much subject selection, planning, process management, container building, and knowledge recording are systematically directed by a facilitator?

■ How much *Conversation* is going on? That is, how much does the group, as opposed to the originators or the interviewers (or web crawlers), engage in dialogue in a way that draws out ideas and context and shapes the discovery and application of insights?

■ How much *Translation* is going on? That is, how much are the seekers or their representatives drawing out knowledge to meet seekers' needs? How much are they re-mixing it and shaping it for a specific use? How much are they promoting it (even when resistance calls for applying good change management practices)?

Table 8.1 shows the diversity in the thirteen capture transfer methods as they use the three disciplines of Facilitation, Conversation, and Translation.

Figure 8.1 is a map of Table 8.1 using the same Venn diagram we introduced in the Introduction to this book. I encourage you to add other knowledge-transfer methods that you are considering (or inventing) to address your unique originating teams, knowledge types, target uses, and culture.

The methodologies that come closest to Knowledge Jam are peer assist, instructional design, and community of practice. Peer assist is a close cousin. Although peer assist differs in that it is generally a direct originator-seeker exchange where the topic is driven by one seeker team, the peer assist is often facilitated and a lively conversation ensues on the seeker's topic of choice. (Innovation jam also shares a great deal with its namesake, though less driven toward relationships and not as laser-beam focused. It is worth noting that Knowledge Harvesting[3] shares the intense planning and facilitation of Knowledge Jam, though it typically lacks the collaborative, group-driven elicitation and the formalized broker role.)

TABLE 8.1. Facilitation-Conversation-Translation Comparison of Various Knowledge Capture Transfer Approaches

Knowledge Capture Transfer Approach	Good For	Facilitation	Conversation	Translation	Comments
1. Knowledge Jam	Five-step process for eliciting and putting know-how to work using a facilitated conversation and engaging representatives of the seeker team or brokers, in the elicitation and transfer. Primary knowledge-elicitation is a real-time discover/capture event (may be in-person or virtual).	H	H	H	Intentional planning, facilitation, business alignment. Conversation or dialogue used systematically to surface know-how (Conversation spawns new relationships, and thus continues after Jam). Extensive participation of brokers who steward the remixing, reformatting, and promotion of knowledge to seekers. Draws from many frameworks such as intelligence acquisition, organizational learning, collaboration, and cognitive task analysis.

Knowledge Capture Transfer Approach	Good For	Facilitation	Conversation	Translation	Comments
2. Individual Journaling or Procedure Writing	Self-awareness, individual development	L	L	L	Lacks the inquiry from an outsider (broker or facilitator) who brings his or her own context. May result in format that works for the originator, but not for the future seeker of the knowledge.
3. After-Action Review or Post-Mortem (Systematically discuss a team or individual's history on a project or program)	Team building, shared lessons learned for a specific group. Done selectively, in alignment with trajectory for this team in question, can improve team's processes.	L	M	L	AAR requires leadership or sponsorship to ensure that knowledge goes into practice, rather than just file folder or file drawer. Content surfaced is limited. AAR does not generally use dialogue practices unless they are part of the organizational culture or brought in by a facilitator.

(Continued)

(Table 8.1 continued)

Knowledge Capture Transfer Approach	Good For	Facilitation	Conversation	Translation	Comments
4. Knowledge Harvesting™ (Interview-based elicitation of tacit knowledge)	Deep dive on content that individual expert or team would not have seen or considered capturing on his or her own	H	L	L	Knowledge Harvesting uses a highly structured facilitation approach, addressing systemic, procedural, conditional, and social knowledge. Content depth and format are limited by creativity of the Knowledge Harvesting planners. By contrast, with Knowledge Jam, topics are pulled by more inquiring brokers, who bring their own context. Additionally, Knowledge Jam broker puts knowledge into new formats suitable to seekers more quickly. (See Appendix A.)

Knowledge Capture Transfer Approach	Good For	Facilitation	Conversation	Translation	Comments
5. Mentoring (Pairing a novice or apprentice with an expert for the purpose of knowledge-transfer.) *Note:* Different from mentoring arrangements focused purely on career planning.	Transferring one skill set to one individual in a way that is limited to the needs of that individual. Building self-esteem in the novice. Navigating knowledge requirements for given industry or company.	L	M	L	Like Knowledge Jam, learner seeks out of "need" and is involved in the learning. Mentoring can be efficient from the seeker's perspective, but not the organization's perspective. With mentoring, most learners do not package what they learned, and the beneficiary of the mentoring investment is limited. With Knowledge _am more topics are pulled by more diverse, inquiring brokers.

(Continued)

(Table 8.1 continued)

Knowledge Capture Transfer Approach	Good For	Facilitation	Conversation	Translation	Comments
6. Journalistic Interview (Interviewer asking questions of an expert. Includes exit Interview with retiring or other leaver.)	Understanding what makes individuals effective, how they decide, how they "know."	M	L	L	Knowledge Jam (like Knowledge Harvesting™) is more facilitated, interactive, structured, and reflective. (Knowledge Jam is oriented toward understanding "systems" collectively, joining different lenses on a problem). Journalistic interview is generally oriented toward surface facts and history than toward getting an understanding of the underlying "system" of know-how. Knowledge Jam is also more oriented toward applying the knowledge, rather than stopping with a piece of writing or publication.

Knowledge Capture Transfer Approach	Good For	Facilitation	Conversation	Translation	Comments
7. Appreciative Inquiry (Organizational transformation through inquiry and action, focusing on what works, rather than dwelling on failures)	Improving overall affect and encouraging inquiry over advocacy	M	L	L	Appreciative nquiry is a guided probe into motivations and outcomes. Knowledge Jam is focused on a given knowledge loss or knowledge application issue, rather than behavioral or attitudinal change. (Although this type of content may be present.) Knowledge Jam does not steer away from negative realizations and provides a structure for unpacking failures and driving insights about those failures into the brokers' processes.

(Continued)

(Table 8.1 continued)

Knowledge Capture Transfer Approach	Good For	Facilitation	Conversation	Translation	Comments
8. Peer Assist (New project team does a talk-back with veteran project team with the new project team's plan at the center. Often facilitated.)	Starting a new project with very similar dimensions to previous project or program	M	M	M	Both peer assist and Knowledge Jam involve a group in the elicitation of knowledge. However, peer assist is mostly bilateral. It is scoped narrowly for just one future project audience. Knowledge Jam may have several seeker groups represented and benefits from the diversity. Peer assist engages future project teams in the elicitation process, although it does not explicitly call for conversation (openness, diversity, dialogue).

Knowledge Capture Transfer Approach	Good For	Facilitation	Conversation	Translation	Comments
9. Innovation Jam (Event where employees can contribute over a twenty-four-hour time period online to a number of topics using a discussion or microblogging type tool, as with IBM's "Innovation Jam." Generally moderated. Topics are defined ahead of time)	Getting insights from far-flung employees who are not likely to contribute to corporate innovations	L	M	L	Innovation jam may require surprisingly significant facilitation (online moderation) to ensure that the conversation is productive and continues, but many innovation jam program managers don't budget for this. Innovation jam conversation may not be deep enough to flesh out topics until after the event. Threads often come throughout the day, from different contributors, without deep inquiry into meaning between broker (or facilitator) and originator. Requires considerable investment in marketing, employee time, and technology across the organization. (See sidebar, "The Price Is Right," in Chapter 9.)

(Continued)

(Table 8.1 continued)

Knowledge Capture Transfer Approach	Good For	Facilitation	Conversation	Translation	Comments
10. Instructional Design (Elicits knowledge and compiles existing knowledge into training programs)	Knowledge is known and agreed-on. Target learners are known and agreed on. Instructional design puts information into an intentionally translated format, e.g., training.	M	L	M	Similar to journalistic interview, inquiry is limited by the facilitator's skills and scope. Knowledge Jam seeks deeper meaning during the elicitation—not just know what, but know how and know why. This comes from the participation of the brokers who spontaneously ask for clarification and contextualization with their seeker organization in mind.

Knowledge Capture Transfer Approach	Good For	Facilitation	Conversation	Translation	Comments
11. **Community of Practice** (Collective that comes together around a common practice or objective, crossing organizational boundaries, and driven to build out a body of knowledge and to network)	Group seeks to network, build a general body of knowledge, and interact in ways that are not afforded by organizational hierarchy, organizational boundaries, or functional distinctions.	M	M	M	Many CoPs may use a Knowledge Jam approach, where planning, facilitation, and translation are intentional. Most CoPs, like Knowledge Jam, benefit from the real-time interactivity of interested practitioners. Although Knowledge Jam topics may be "emergent" like the CoP's, in the Knowledge Jam conversation, topics are selected with the sponsor, broker, and originator ahead of time. CoP conversation rarely has dialogue practices. Intentionally (lack of translation) is a frequent complaint about CoPs.

(Continued)

153

(Table 8.1 continued)

Knowledge Capture Transfer Approach	Good For	Facilitation	Conversation	Translation	Comments
12. Search/Alerts (Use of online crawling or structured hyper-linking technology to find content)	Large volumes of explicit knowledge can be compiled and crawled, and then the user can be alerted.	L	L	M	With Knowledge Jam tacit, not just explicit, knowledge (and its context) surface through a dialogue between brokers and originators. Search is less often collective, and more often individual. Knowledge Jam selection of strategic knowledge is generally collective. With search, intentionally often collective. With search, intentionally often lacks, though subscriptions are improving this. With search, translation occurs at a primitive level. The search and RSS or other alerting tools are "moving across" content according to the seeker's specification, but the adaptation is up to the individual.

Knowledge Capture Transfer Approach	Good For	Facilitation	Conversation	Translation	Comments
13. **Wiki** (Use of an easily accessed shared web interface for sharing ideas directly on page. Allows review and reversion of content and changes to content. Long-form microblogs have similar attributes, though without the ability to revise.)	Co-authoring asynchronously by a variety of participants across geographies and times. Version tracking. Low cost (often free in the "cloud").	L	M	M	Wikis enable a number of different people to engage, co-author, and synthesize know-how. Because wikis can be unstructured, meaning may be elusive unless a wiki gardener or curator emerges or is voted in by contributors. In addition, lack of translation (intentionality of reuse) is a frequent complaint about wiki. By contrast, Knowledge Jam is highly selective of subjects. Knowledge Jam's elicitation/translation roles are explicit. Unlike Knowledge Jam, wikis usually lack the immediacy of the human real-time interaction. (See the sidebar, "The Price Is Right," in Chapter 9 ["Building"].)

FIGURE 8.1. *Venn Diagram for Comparison of Capture/ Transfer Methods*

When we look at the Venn diagram in Figure 8.1, we see that Knowledge Jam stands apart. It is more focused and facilitated (from its intelligence acquisition heritage), more collectively emergent (using conversation, from its organizational learning heritage), and more directed toward the translation process or toward putting knowledge to work (from its collaboration heritage).

Knowledge Jam addresses blind spots, mismatches, and jail. It focuses on bringing ephemeral or inaccessible knowledge out into the daylight and into our products and practices. But it is not a standalone KM program. Knowledge Jam relies on having in place basic collaboration resources and a knowledge sharing mindset. Organizations may also employ a variety of other methods, for example, a digital asset management repository to ensure that a body of documents and digital media are searchable and reusable, or a reflection discipline, like after action review, to ensure that any team, no matter how small and obscure, gets "permission" to slow down and do some sense-making.

In the next chapter, I'll give you some perspective on what choosing a Knowledge Jam approach entails. There we'll discuss how to launch a Knowledge Jam effort with a solid business case.

CHAPTER

BUILDING A KNOWLEDGE JAM PRACTICE

"Building a Knowledge Jam Practice" shows how to define, sell, staff, launch, and evaluate a Knowledge Jam program. You'll also find frameworks to model your Knowledge Jam business case. I invite you to explore how to integrate Knowledge Jam into a larger KM or innovation strategy. And I propose Knowledge Jam facilitation—with its strategizing, planning, eliciting, and motivating—as a leadership developmental opportunity.

"We don't make money when our planes are on the ground."

SOUTHWEST AIRLINES

So it is with knowledge: the ROI for capturing knowledge is zero (or worse) if it isn't in motion. In an economy where market dominance is fleeting and corporations, governments, and non-profits seek more work with fewer labor dollars, managers can't afford to let the valuable insights of experts, teams, and partners go unused. Nor can they invest blindly in knowledge-capture and transfer without having the confidence that the outcome is that reusable, market- or organization-appropriate knowledge is getting out and being put to work.

As we saw in Chapter 1, knowledge right under our noses, within our workforces and networks, could:

- Streamline our processes, improve our cost structure, or improve our consistent compliance with regulation;

- Improve how we interact with customers and partners, thereby solidifying our reputation as a partner, and reducing our market or supply risks;

- Inform our product innovations and help us to (re)capture markets;

- Reduce our single points of failure (for example, spread scarce machine know-how, application know-how, or customer know-how); and

- Improve our employee job satisfaction.

Such benefits are elusive with knowledge capture and transfer approaches that don't directly address blind spots, mismatches, and jail, as we saw in Chapter 8 ("Comparing"). And, once we determine we can gain the benefits, the approach has to be practical. Managers need a program that has a reasonable footprint in terms of time, cost, and executive attention; that fits into the existing organizational processes; and that is easy to learn. In this chapter I describe how you start a Knowledge Jam program in a manner that achieves such affordability, fit, and adaptability.

Right-brain readers, please bear with me here; this is probably the driest chapter for you. Take comfort in the fact that establishing the Knowledge Jam practice on sturdy footing is your ticket to a rewarding (and rewarded) program. On the other hand, right-brainers can be tremendously effective. Language matters. All too often investments of this kind are de-prioritized because of a mismatch in language. You'll avoid this fate. As I introduce language from industry, consulting, and academia, I help you shape the themes of affordability, fit, and adaptability into a credible message.

BUILDING A BUSINESS CASE AND SELLING KNOWLEDGE JAM

A business case typically consists of benefits (qualitative and quantitative), a reasonable estimate of costs, competitive differentiators, and a clear articulation of risks and their mitigations. I'll describe each in turn.

Business Case Message 1: Identifying Qualitative and Quantitative Benefits

A Knowledge Jam program begins with the end in mind, just as a Knowledge Jam itself begins with the end in mind ("putting knowledge to work"). Your starting point should be a vivid picture of Knowledge Jam program in full swing with purposeful planning, people engaging together in productive and continuing Discover/Capture experiences, and many seeker organizations using know-how that came out of Knowledge Jams.

To build a business case for a Knowledge Jam program requires having both quantitative and qualitative messages. In *quantitative* messages you articulate the benefits like time savings, improved market share, efficiencies, and employee retention, attraction, or development. For example:

- New project teams complete prototypes in a fraction of the usual time as they leverage best practices from previous product development teams.

- Improved sales processes incorporating effective customer messaging result in longer-lasting, more profitable customer relationships.

- The proportion of new product initiatives that fail late in the product development cycle drops considerably, due to insightful up-front customer testing and environmental testing methods.

- New employees become attuned to how the business makes money in half the usual ramp time; they take appropriate actions, with appropriate attentiveness to valued customers, profitable products, and relevant market events.

In parallel, with these measurable benefit messages of knowledge put to work, *qualitative* messages place a value on benefits that can be agreed on, but which are difficult to measure. For example:

■ Innovation options are expanded due to diversity of perspectives and heuristics (such as cross-functional diversity, cross-product diversity, cross-geography diversity, and cross-tenure or generational diversity).

■ The organization becomes better at problem solving and adapting to market changes, as they have a routine for discerning news or competitive developments and sense-making.

■ The organization reduces its risk as information flows more quickly, operations are more portable (around the globe), and all this with a lower dependence on subject-matter experts.

■ Subject-matter experts and experienced teams are less likely to be "knowledge bottlenecks" (spending time answering questions) and can come to rely on learners and apprentices to get work done.

■ New leaders are more able to facilitate meaningful discussions, resulting in more functional teams, greater employee engagement, and more collaborative responses to opportunities.

Business Case Message 2: Calculating Benefits Collaboratively

Knowledge Jam benefits most often result from combining Jammed knowledge with behavior, technology, and process changes in the seeker organization. Jam program planners (champion, sponsors, or facilitators) could estimate quantitative benefits from knowledge consumption. The seeker organization, in turn, could estimate benefits from making some investment, part of which is inspired by Jammed innovations. In my experience it's very difficult to avoid double counting. During the project budgeting process, the Jam program planners and seeker organizations each make their case to management, and they may over-represent, or even under-represent, knowledge Jam's benefits. In such cases, making the benefits case for Knowledge Jam requires a *partnership* between Jam program planners and the seeker organization.

Here's the double-counting remedy. The Knowledge Jam program planner joins up with the seeker organization to measure the "lift" that comes from Knowledge Jam outputs. First, they jointly estimate all changes in performance (for example, improvements in revenue, market share, profitability, customer satisfaction, or new facilitation or translation skills). From this, they subtract direct Jam costs and all investments (Jam-derived *and* non-Jam) by the seeker organization. Ultimately, in looking at new *net* benefits both organizations can begin to discern the lift from the Jam.

Let's look at an example: A seeker organization is improving a core product that has a starting value stream. Adding Jammed production process know-how could improve margins by reducing scrap and its associated labor. It would be difficult to tease out margin improvements that are from the new Jam-derived production ideas from other typical materials quality adjustments. (Designers, toolers, and operators will incorporate both the typical materials changes and changes related to the Jam, and it may be too disruptive to cost out those changes separately.) A reasonable approach would be to net out macro-level costs from macro-level benefits and to compare new margins to those resulting from typical scrap improvements. Consider Table 9.1.

Whether you use return on investment (ROI), net present value, or the payback period method, the lift from the Knowledge Jam can be quite evident. It takes thoughtfulness of both parties to use the experience-based big picture approach, and it does require some comfort with estimation. But it is better than the politics of double counting or hair-splitting activity-based accounting.

Having some examples may help in this collaborative effort. In Table 9.2 I provide some measuring and messaging that could be used jointly by Knowledge Jam program planners and seeker organizations as you sell your Knowledge Jams.

This interdependency is a common characteristic of horizontal programs, such as information technology, knowledge management, and quality. Those managers who can express their benefits as a partnership with other organizations are more likely to be credible and effective than those who spend time trying to articulate the minute contributions of each separately. Not "declaring victory" until knowledge is put to work is one of Knowledge Jam's fundamental tenets. Taking a partnership approach to claim Knowledge Jam's value motivates both sponsor and seeker organizations to live by that tenet.

Just a word on finance. Finance is a necessary ally for any organization where Knowledge Jam efforts fall under an investment portfolio process. Quantification of value needs to have finance's stamp of approval. Finance may limit "benefits" to realizable headcount

TABLE 9.1. **Illustrative Macro-Level Benefits Improvements Due to Adding Jammed Know-How**

Macro Accounting Item	Results from Typical Scrap Improvement Cycle ($)	Results from Knowledge Jam–Informed Scrap Improvement Cycle ($)
Investment		
Knowledge Jam–related (participants' time through the KJ cycle, Jam-related collaboration technology improvements)	(0)	(20)
Seeker organization (design and tests of new formulations and new materials handing; adjustments to process and machinery for materials preparations, tolerances, temperatures; training)	(50)	(100)
Subtotal, Investment	**(50)**	**(120)**
First Year Contribution to Margin		
Materials and Scrap, net	100	300
Production Labor, net	50	100
Maintenance Labor and Equipment, net	50	100
Subtotal, Contribution to Margin	**200**	**500**
Total Year 1 Benefits	**$150**	**$380**

Production Facility Benefits (Costs), in Thousands.

TABLE 9.2. **Selling Benefits in Partnership with Seeker Organization**

Type	Example Benefit Category	Benefit Directly Attributable to Knowledge Jam When Know-How Is Translated and Reused (Broader Message)	Seeker Organization's Additional Benefit (More Direct Message)
Quantitative	Accelerated employee on-boarding (reduced time-to-proficiency)	"Employees may receive the right messages to avoid errors in judgment."	"We were rolling out training anyway. Now we embed the experts' insights for greater accuracy and credibility."
	Process and project efficiencies	"Specific steps can be avoided or added to reduce time, materials costs, admin costs."	"We invest in continuous improvement programs periodically, but now we capitalize on internal know-how systematically for these classes of improvement."
	More profitable customer relationships	"Specific messages conveyed to customer segments, or specific offers could have a more reliable impact."	"We refresh customer messages and capitalize on internal experiences for these classes of messages."

163

(Table 9.2 continued)

Type	Example Benefit Category	Benefit Directly Attributable to Knowledge Jam When Know-How Is Translated and Reused (Broader Message)	Seeker Organization's Additional Benefit (More Direct Message)
Qualitative	Leaders' influencing and enabling competency	"Leaders learn facilitation skills and work in a highly collaborative Jam environment to surface insights, promote dialogue, and shift mindsets."	"We fund leadership and employee effectiveness programs. Now we have experiential learning for skills with proven benefits of these types."
	Accelerated innovation cycles	"Sources of innovations are routinely surfaced in the Discover/ Capture event."	"We fund R&D programs that miss ideas from the field, shop floor, or project team. Now we have a systematic pipeline."
	Improved agility	"Brokers, facilitators, originators all practice skills required for creating and internalizing change."	"We have funded change management approaches, but now the organization is overcoming defensiveness and delays in feedback using the Knowledge Jam disciplines."
	Reduced risk	"With sense-making conversations, we have better insight into risks, which are now readily identified (and translated) for seekers."	"We have a risk management process, but the time to refresh our list of risks and their impacts is too long. We now have a 'listening post' for risk and time to identify and review risks has fallen by X."

reductions. (For example, I've heard said 2,000 hours are "only saved if a job was eliminated.") That might leave many a Jammer intimidated when they envision the bulk of the benefits coming from efficiencies, not revenue or materials gains. However, this accounting restriction should not deter your business case. Having been in the finance organization myself, I know that when finance sees the whole picture—of new product revenue, improved operations, experts' time savings, and improved originator-broker networks—they can be ardent supporter of Knowledge Jam. Even if they put such benefits into the "general" or "qualitative" column, your joint calculations and shared benefits story go a long way to building your credibility.

Business Case Message 3: Calculating Direct Costs

As we saw in the scrap illustration, Knowledge Jam has direct and indirect costs: the investment in the Knowledge Jam cycle (time spent by the facilitator, originators, brokers, sponsors, and champions) and investments in seeker organization technology, process, or behaviors that help them to take advantage of Knowledge Jam insights. I tend to calculate seeker costs on a Jam by Jam basis as a change in trending costs.

It is possible to generalize Knowledge Jam's direct costs, and it is certainly advantageous to have these ball-parked when you are selling a Knowledge Jam program. They are considerably lower than the alternatives we saw in Chapter 8 ("Comparing"). Here are some rules of thumb for quantifying the time investment by the facilitator, originators, brokers, sponsors, and champions. I'll also provide a specific example of each.

- *Facilitators (60 to 80 hours):* Facilitators are present throughout the whole process, identifying and inviting the other participants, brokering the selection of the Knowledge Jam subjects, organizing and facilitating the planning meetings, conducting interviews with originators and brokers, facilitating the Discover/Capture event, packaging the initial Knowledge Jam outcomes, and vetting the findings with brokers and the core team (representatives of originators, brokers, sponsor, champion).[1]

- Facilitators stay partially engaged through the Broker and Reuse steps, ensuring that the brokers have what they need to move the knowledge into its next format for target-seeker audiences. Importantly, facilitators help ensure that measures are in place for

TABLE 9.3. Knowledge Jam Facilitator Time Calculations (Scenario with Two Discover/Capture Sessions)

Knowledge Jam Step	Individual Offline Prep/ Writing/ Analysis/ Compiling	Meetings or Calls with Core Team or Sponsor	Events Facilitation (Including Set-Up/ Tear-Down)	Broker Follow-Up Calls	Preparatory interview Scheduling, Delivery, Write-Up	KJ Facilitator Activities	Typical Timing
1. Select	5	3				1. Become familiar with challenges, objectives, language; review map, whitepapers 2. Educate sponsor/core team (co-facilitators) 3. Identify subject and themes with sponsor/core team ("subject" is refined into "topics" for during the "planning event") 4. Help select KJ "planning event" and "discover/ capture event" participants	Weeks 1 and 2 (can accelerate; depends on core team/ sponsor availability)

Knowledge Jam Step	Individual Offline Prep/ Writing/ Analysis/ Compiling	Meetings or Calls with Core Team or Sponsor	Events Facilitation (Including Set-Up/ Tear-Down)	Broker Follow-Up Calls	Preparatory interview Scheduling, Delivery, Write-Up	KJ Facilitator Activities	Typical Timing
2. Plan	10	5	3		5	1. Draft email invites (save the date/overview/KJ value prop) for Discover/Capture event participants. 2. Draft Planning event email for "Planning event" participants (represent brokers and originators) 3. Prep logistics for "Planning event" call 4. Facilitate "Planning event" call 5. Summarize "Planning event" outcome (these are "discussion topics" for Discover/Capture event) 6. Prep ogistics for "Discover/Capture event" 7. Draft email reminder (plus agenda) for "Discover/Capture event" 8. Help participants understand their roles (selectively call/ meet, especially brokers)	Weeks 3 and 4 (can accelerate; depends on coordination efficiency)

(Continued)

(Table 9.3 continued)

Knowledge Jam Step	Individual Offline Prep/ Writing/ Analysis/ Compiling	Meetings or Calls with Core Team or Sponsor	Events Facilitation (Including Set-Up/ Tear-Down)	Broker Follow-Up Calls	Preparatory interview Scheduling, Delivery, Write-Up	KJ Facilitator Activities	Typical Timing
3. Discover/ Capture	11	3	8			1. Final (in person) pre-meeting with co-facilitators on choreography 2. Prep event room, flip charts, co-facilitators 3. Facilitate D/C event(s) (assume two 90-minute sessions) (co-facilitator from core team) One 90-minute session only eliminates four hours from facilitation and four hours from individual offline preparation.	Weeks 5 to 7 (can accelerate; depends on review cycle)

Knowledge Jam Step	Individual Offline Prep/ Writing/ Analysis/ Compiling	Meetings or Calls with Core Team or Sponsor	Events Facilitation (Including Set-Up/ Tear-Down)	Broker Follow-Up Calls	Preparatory interview Scheduling, Delivery, Write-Up	KJ Facilitator Activities	Typical Timing
						4. Compile KJ event notes and summarize	
						5. Review KJ notes and summary with core team	
						6. Draft email text to accompany draft KJ notes, summary	
						7. Compile feedback from participants; edit	
						8. Draft text to accompany fina KJ notes, summary, broker instructions	
						9. Provide strategic reccmmendations to Core Team, sponsor regarding KJ(s) program, actions proposed, knowledge map	

(Continued)

(Table 9.3 continued)

Knowledge Jam Step	Individual Offline Prep/ Writing/ Analysis/ Compiling	Meetings or Calls with Core Team or Sponsor	Events Facilitation (Including Set-Up/ Tear-Down)	Broker Follow-Up Calls	Preparatory interview Scheduling, Delivery, Write-Up	KJ Facilitator Activities	Typical Timing
4. Broker	3	10		5		1. Meet with core team/ sponsor agree to brokering / reuse expectations 2. Meet with sponsor regarding brokers' activities, time-frames 3. As agreed with sponsor, meet with brokers on a schedule (over six-month period) 4. Report back to sponsor on broker progress, opportunities (monthly, quarterly)	Months 3 to 9 Ensures that non-profit gets a return on the KJ

Knowledge Jam Step	Individual Offline Prep/ Writing/ Analysis/ Compiling	Meetings or Calls with Core Team or Sponsor	Events Facilitation (Including Set-Up/ Tear-Down)	Broker Follow-Up Calls	Preparatory interview Scheduling, Delivery, Write-Up	KJ Facilitator Activities	Typical Timing
5. Reuse	2	2		5		1. Review Reuse activity, as agreed to with core team/ sponsor 2. Report back to sponsor on reuse/impact of reuse	Months 3 to 9 Ensures that non-profit gets a return on the K
Total Estimated Hours	31	23	11	10	5	80	

Notes:

1. Discover/Capture event is in-person (with some dial-ins, using desktop share).
2. KJ facilitator has advanced facilitation skills as well as KJ training.
3. Core team is sponsor + facilitator + co-facilitator(s). Co-facilitator(s) from non-profit are mostly connector/bridger during event (only basic facilitation skills needed for this.) Brokers are from non-profit.
4. Basic logistics assistance from non-profit (room, projectors, dial-ins, desktop-sharing apps, email list prep, etc., as agreed with core team).
5. Facilitator sets up all 1:1 interviews.
6. Mapping and environmental scan is performed by non-profit.
7. Non-profit sends out emails to participants for save the date and Planning event.
8. After events, facilitator sends draft outcomes (of Planning event, Discover/Capture event, Summary, KJ notes, etc.).
9. Brokers, not facilitator, are responsible for knowledge publishing, unless non-profit requests that the "summary" be converted into other distributable formats.
10. Facilitator checks-in with brokers (two to four non-profit team members) for half-hour monthly for six months (varies by type of brokering).
11. Primary reuse assessment falls within KM program or other assessment program related to the seeker organization activity.

assessing the impact of translated knowledge, and for communicating outcomes to the sponsor.

In Table 9.3 I add up typical Knowledge Jam time investments by the facilitator. This non-profit organization estimated facilitator time for a Jam with two Discover/Capture events. (As a rule of thumb, as much as twenty hours of interviews and participant education can be spread over multiple Discover/Capture events [with different topics]).

■ *Knowledge Originators (5 to 10 hours):* Originators have a lighter load than the facilitators and brokers. In general, the originators participate in an optional interview, the Planning event, the Discover/Capture event, and ad hoc discussions with the brokers and their teams after the Discover/Capture event. In my experience, this amounts to five hours (at the low end, where the originator has some written documentation to reference), to ten hours (at the high end, where the originator doesn't have any documentation, or where the originator invests considerable time after the Discover/Capture event to fill in details in conversation with the broker). A Knowledge Jam goal is to minimize originators' time—to honor them and to off-load their burden, not increase it. We also guard against needlessly having them compile information that may not be used in the translation process.

■ *Brokers (5 to 20 hours):* Brokers participate in an interview, the Planning event, the Discover/Capture event, some post-Discover/Capture event discussions with the facilitator, and translation activities directly with or for their seekers. Translation activities, as we saw in Chapter 5 ("Translation"), begin before the Planning event. They include strategizing on Discover/Capture event topics, sensemaking in the Planning and Discover/Capture events, re-mixing and packaging, and getting clarification with the originator after the Discover/Capture event. Direct interaction in facilitation activities during the Jam's first three steps amounts to about four hours.

Brokers' remaining time investment can vary considerably, depending on how they translate knowledge and how many (and how favorable) the constituencies they serve are. Time investment in interactions with their seeker organization—and in re-mixing, packaging, and promoting Jammed knowledge—will depend on the specific content, presentation requirements, social media efficiencies, and complexity of the know-how's translated form or vehicle.

This can be an elusive effort to measure, because some of the work of the broker would have happened *anyway*. For example, as we saw in Table 9.3 above, she might be a project manager who is defining phases in the project—now more intelligently, but with perhaps a little increase above her original schedule to accommodate knowledge review. Alternatively, she might translate Jammed know-how into a training or workflow module that could require working with software developers and testers. Generally, when the broker and her peers are making these significant investments, it is best to categorize them as seeker organization investments and use a framework similar to the one in Table 9.1.

- *Sponsors (2 to 10 hours):* At the outset of a Knowledge Jam program, sponsors invest several hours into understanding the benefits and costs of Knowledge Jam and contribute to the subject selection and measurement objectives. Sponsors participate periodically in the discussion with the facilitator and representative originators and brokers during the Plan and Discover/Capture steps. Additionally, sponsors may help with promotion. They call on various parts of the organization to be aware of, and participate in, the Knowledge Jam.

- *Champions (up to 10 hours):* Champions are key players when the facilitator is joining the group from outside the department, division, or company. In cases in which the facilitator is "native," a champion may not be needed. Champions help identify the players, organize the facility, set up the projection, phone, and web-conferencing equipment, and place timely communications, such as invitations for Plan and Discover/Capture events.

- *Systems:* Incremental systems investments for the Jam cycle are generally low if the organization already has a collaboration platform on which to publish templates, drafts, meeting reminders, and Jammed content. As we saw in Chapter 5 ("Translation"), tools such as wikis and discussion forums are invaluable for vetting subjects and topics (agendas), as well as for soliciting input from seekers and originators during the translation process. As many of these collaboration tools are now available within organizations or in the "cloud," they can be obtained for free or at a low cost.

Table 9.4 summarizes these time estimates. Note that the facilitator is 60 to 80 percent of the labor (70 to 80 percent if no champion). This

TABLE 9.4. Knowledge Jam Hours-Investment Ranges

Knowledge Jam Participant	Low	High
Facilitator	60	80
Originator(s), each	5	10
Broker(s), each	5	20
Sponsor	2	10
Champion	0	10
Total	72	130

Note: I've excluded the other seeker organization investments in technology and process.

SIDEBAR: THE PRICE IS RIGHT!   Consider this comparison between the cost of implementing Innovation Jam™ (a "wisdom of crowds" approach to knowledge capture and transfer) and Knowledge Jam. You'll likely spend twenty times more to do an Innovation Jam.

14 Nov 2006: *"IBM Chairman and Chief Executive Officer Samuel J. Palmisano today announced that the company will invest $100 million over the next two years. ... The largest online brainstorming session ever, Innovation Jam brought together more than 150,000 people from 104 countries. ... Over two 72-hour sessions, participants posted more than 46,000 ideas as they explored IBM's most advanced research technologies and considered their application to real-world problems and emerging business opportunities."*
2006 Press Release "IBM Invests $100 Million in Collaborative Innovation Ideas"[2]

"... In those 72 hours we got over 40,000 ideas. A hundred and almost fifty thousand people were online with us at some point

is quite different from other knowledge-transfer initiatives that place the burden on the knowledge originators. Also note that brokers may even out-work originators.

Business Case Message 4: Differentiating Knowledge Jam

As we saw in Chapter 8 ("Comparing"), Knowledge Jam is suited for situations in which putting knowledge to work is an urgent imperative and when know-how (and its context) are best surfaced in a conversation involving originators, brokers, and facilitators. Using the Facilitation-Conversation-Translation comparison in Table 8.1 will help you to differentiate Knowledge Jam from other knowledge-transfer approaches. Your business case could be more compelling when you explain why Knowledge Jam is more efficient, productive, and timely than other innovation or knowledge-transfer approaches, such as joint planning sessions, peer mentoring, or expert interviews. In the sidebar below, "The Price Is Right," is a back-of-the-envelope cost comparison of the Knowledge Jam to the Innovation Jam.

---

in those 72 hours. We only have 350,000 IBMers, so it's not a bad participation rate. ... We had to take those 40,000 ideas, and we had to reduce them, because I couldn't fund 40,000 ideas. They weren't all unique, so we had to go through a bit of a digital and analog refinement process for the next couple of months. Then we took the top 36. ... And then we put those 36 ideas back online for another 72 hours, *and we let people have at them to refine them, to nurture them, to massage them, to move them in a direction where they really stood out — or didn't stand out.* We then picked 10 from the 36, *to be candid with you. ... It's not always obvious that these things are going to stick in the marketplace. Some need even more incubation, they need more nurturing because they're great ideas, but they're so far out—like never in a million years would the world be ready for it right here and now."*

2007 Gartner Fellows Interview with IBM EVP Nicholas Donofrio. Used with Permission.[3]

(Continued)

	Knowledge Jam*	Innovation Jam**	
Participant/ Seeker time	$20K	$500K	Compared to crowd-sourcing, Knowledge Jam content is more *focused, timely* and *usable*
Facilitator/ moderator time	$10K	$100K	
Platform modifications	$5K	$100K	
	$35K	**$700K**	

K Jam is 1/20th the Investment

*Conservative (high) estimate; **Conservative (low) estimate;

FIGURE 9.1. *Comparing the Costs of Knowledge Jam to the IBM Innovation Jam™*

In a recent discussion with a large bank communications director, I learned that the Innovation Jam brings the benefits of finding and engaging people at the periphery of the organization. That, in and of itself, may have been worth his investment.

Business Case Message 5: Mitigating Risks

The last, but not least, message of the business case is risk. Risk is the "haircut" you give to your optimistic net-benefits case by considering what could go wrong. Risks for a Knowledge Jam are failure to get out the useful knowledge, failure to see that the knowledge be put to work within a reasonable time frame or failure to keep the program together, either due to distraction or resource poaching. A mitigation, or "counterweight," for risks could be something increasing the likelihood of obtaining the benefits, such as the know-how application being politically attractive, aligning nicely with strategic goals, or having a reasonable footprint in terms of time and materials. Many of these risks and their mitigations have been directly addressed in the preceding chapters. Table 9.5 is a quick summary of primary risks and the mitigations we've touched on throughout the book.

Relative to Innovation Jam, Knowledge Jam does spark such valuable networks, but it is more intentional, focused, and directed toward known problems. TRIZ experts would favor Knowledge Jam, arguing that it is more cost-effective to innovate *intentionally* versus with a shot-gun approach:

> "[TRIZ pioneer] Altshuller believed that inventive problems stem from contradictions [one of the basic TRIZ concepts] between two or more elements, such as, 'If we want more acceleration, we need a larger engine; but that will increase the cost of the car,' that is, more of something desirable also brings more of something less desirable, or less of something else also desirable."
>
> Wikipedia

In effect, when you look at the magnitude of the investment, Knowledge Jam is the TRIZ of Jams!

CULTIVATING KNOWLEDGE JAM FACILITATORS

Many of my clients and colleagues have asked where to find Knowledge Jam facilitators. I look for people with strong business savvy, good networking skills, good "asking" skills, and a genuine sense of interest in others. In casting about for facilitators, consider these critical responsibilities:

- Scans the environment for knowledge subjects that could help the business perform

- Prioritizes Knowledge Jam subjects and Knowledge Jam topics

- Coordinates, plans, and facilitates Plan and Discover/Capture events

- Identifies and includes the appropriate participants

TABLE 9.5. Risks and Mitigations in a Knowledge Jam Business Case

Risk	Mitigation
Failure to get out *useful* knowledge and context	Carefully manage portfolio of prospective Jam subjects, and get sponsors, originators, and brokers to agree to selection of subjects.
	Sequence Jams (and originators' participation) according to their receptivity to the concept of knowledge-sharing. Cultivate future originators purposefully.
	Work with leadership to ensure that originators and brokers are engaged and rewarded for participation, topic generation, and warm transfers.
	Manage the "container" and strive for the conversation elements of posture of openness, Pursuit of diversity, and practices of dialogue during the Plan and Discover/Capture events.
	Identify signs of dysfunction and address them early and collectively.
	Equip brokers to do deep dives with originating teams post-Discover/Capture event.
Failure to put the Jammed knowledge to work	Plan for success. Socialize the benefits of using insights in the seeker organization that brokers represent.
	Work with leadership to ensure that originators and brokers are engaged and rewarded for each effective translation of Jammed know-how.
	Identify and prepare for translation technology requirements before the Jam starts (such as collaboration tools, or seeker organization tools, such as workflow).
Failure to keep the program together	Find an enthusiastic sponsor and a persevering champion for each Jam.
	Position Knowledge Jam as a professional developmental program—facilitators doing a tour of duty to acquire leadership skills. (And prepare to cycle in new facilitators.)
	Continuously place the Knowledge Jam portfolio (and its potential benefits) in front of leadership, and keep Knowledge Jam practice and benefits on the corporate agenda.

- Educates participants on the Knowledge Jam and its components

- Facilitates/models a positive knowledge-sharing environment (holds container of "common curiosity")

- Participates in productive Jam conversations

- Draws out questions from participants

- Electronically captures notes for review by all stakeholders

- Summarizes effectively online and offline

- Reconfirms originators' and brokers' commitment to sharing and "brokering," and assists where needed

- Offers a "just in time" knowledge transfer during and after the Knowledge Jam cycle

- Models re-use in their own work by applying outcomes from other Jams

Not surprisingly, the people who are most competent as Knowledge Jam facilitators are also competent leaders. The parallels between the list above and leadership "profiles" or "action frameworks" abound. Consider Kouzes and Posner's leadership planks (paraphrased)[4]:

- Inspiring a common vision

- Helping others to take action

- Modeling the new behavior

- Challenging the way we've always done things

- Encouraging followers' passion

The Knowledge Jam facilitator does all of these. Most elusive is inspiring the common vision. Facilitators rally support and enthusiasm for the Knowledge Jam (and the seekers' benefits from the know-how expected), even as the conversation in which knowledge unfolds is emergent and quite unpredictable. Facilitators inspire a certain faith in the unknown—in hidden knowledge and in an emergent path. That calls on facilitators to bring an internal passion of their own.

Knowledge Jam can be a leadership development opportunity for facilitators and other participants. The Knowledge Jam hones important business skills: prioritization, boundary spanning, process facilitation, productive conversation, sense-making, measurement, and sponsor-management. Not surprisingly, great Knowledge Jam facilitators don't stay in place. Facilitators I've trained or hired were often "poached" by other programs or functions. They went on to play process facilitator, change manager, or program manager elsewhere in the organization or its larger network.

I recommend having the Knowledge Jam facilitator role be a rotation or "tour of duty." As facilitators, employees learn how to discern systemic relationships among ideas, to network, to lead sense-making, and to inspire creativity in others. It's helpful to plan a facilitator "bench" where employees rotate on and off after gaining skills through their facilitation experiences.

MEASURING AND PROMOTING SUCCESS

Positioning is critical, because selling the Knowledge Jam program can be a challenging, as we learned in the Building a Business Case section above. Knowledge Jam can be labeled as "intense," "invasive," and even "touchy-feely." While those might be tall compliments in some contexts, Knowledge Jam program planners need to get the image right for their stakeholders. For example, the benefits messages above (like "saves money," "improves reputation," "reduces single points of failure") need to roll off your tongue. Participants continually need to be reminded how they can contribute and benefit (the "What's-in-it-for-me?" factor we saw in Table 3.1 in Chapter 3 ["Facilitation"]).

Just as we discussed the promotion responsibility of the broker, for the Knowledge Jam program planner, measuring and communicating Jams' impacts help maintain attention on the program, attract originators or originating teams, and ensure seekers take advantage Jammed insights. Table 9.1 can help you prepare communications about benefits to be measured. To keep attention on Intel's Jams, we recorded testimonials from participants and seeker organizations similar to the ones in that table. We also compiled simple statistics:

■ Number of Jams

■ Number of participants in Jams

■ Number of (and which) organizations or geographies represented

■ Number of published "nuggets"

■ Number of receiving organizations

These we brought into the selection portfolio meetings with the sponsors so that they could gauge historical and prospective impact.

As we discussed in Chapter 3, collaboration resources are common today in most organizations, and a number are also free or cloud-based. At Intel Knowledge Jam fit within a larger knowledge-transfer program and took advantage of an existing collaboration platform. We had a web tool that alerted key stakeholders to Jam "impact summaries" with linked Discover/Capture notes and executive summaries. We also had a web-based "transfer log" to celebrate warm hand-offs to seekers by brokers and facilitators. We reached critical mass at about eighteen months, with approximately fifty published "Knowledge Nuggets" and at least twice that number of identified seekers, brokers, and originators.

In a nutshell, ingredients for building a Knowledge Jam program are agreement on business and knowledge-work problems (blind spots, mismatches, and jails), good planning, invested brokers and seekers, and high-energy facilitators. Knowledge Jam is not "ambulance chasing." Jamming needs to be built into the fabric of the organization. Over time a growing body of trusted, translated knowledge-exchanges, and trusted, experienced facilitators, originators, brokers and champions will legitimize the Knowledge Jam program. That momentum enhances employees' willingness to join in and reuse knowledge, and even their eagerness to volunteer subjects (or themselves) into Jams. Since momentum is key, I encourage you not to see this as three- or six-month project, but as a *roadmap*, where you can grow your own critical mass of Jammers and of Jammed know-how—visibly contributing new products, new efficiencies, and a new culture.

CHAPTER

KNOWLEDGE JAM FOR LEADING CHANGE AND LEVERAGING SOCIAL MEDIA

"Knowledge Jam for Leading Change and Leveraging Social Media" explores Knowledge Jam as a practice that can be used in making strategy—and "making it stick." Knowledge Jam brings about a culture of change—intention, openness, and stewardship—and brings that culture into today's tools of change, such as formalized strategic planning and transformational technology implementations. In this chapter, Knowledge Jam and social media switch roles: Social media efforts are not simply Knowledge Jam's enablers, but they can be enabled by it, resulting in better content quality, interaction quality, and velocity for ideas.

"I never 'worry' about action, but only inaction."

WINSTON CHURCHILL

183

Why do so many great strategies animate people at first, but fail in the implementation? Doing change management projects, I ask that question daily. Change failures might be due to strategic oversight, shocks to the market, competitors' hostile maneuvers, or new substitutes for the product. But most strategy researchers point back to the organization itself. They have shown that average strategies, solidly executed, almost always yield better outcomes than brilliant strategies when execution is poor.[1]

Why not have better-than-average strategies *and* solid execution at the same time? I'll be showing how Knowledge Jam can help with absorption of know-how into the strategic planning process and can help with the organization's change-absorption. Knowledge Jam fights a two-pronged war against change failures by improving up- and down-stream activities.

What strategy programs often lack is *credibility*, *fit*, and *engagement*. That is, they lack the data which convincingly point toward a direction, the suitability of that direction to the intended organization, and the genuine commitment to that direction from people whose lives are affected. These knowledge-absorption and change-absorption deficits are non-trivial—they routinely hamper mission critical changes, such as moves to more agile advertising processes or to automated sales technology.

Let's revisit the stories from the Introduction and Chapter 5. These are great examples of where inspired strategies, poorly elicited and translated, resulted in programs and plans that didn't stick:

> At a new production facility of a major computer hardware manufacturer, performance appeared relatively stable during the first month of operation. Yet, when veteran operators (who had been "on loan" to the new facility) departed, yields dropped and outages skyrocketed. Senior management couldn't comprehend why this could occur. Traditional knowledge-transfer methods, such as veterans' painstakingly recording procedures and one-on-one job shadowing, failed to sufficiently engage operators in their future roles and failed to draw out the range of things that could go wrong when all parts of the factory were up and running. (Missing: Facilitation!)
>
> In order to accelerate knowledge transfer between consultants, a leading strategy consulting firm decided to produce video recordings of veteran consultants. After hours of recording time, prepara-

tion, tagging, uploading, and promotion, the fifteen-minute videos were not looked at by new project teams, even when those new project teams were doing follow-on work at the same clients as the consultants in the videos. The follow-on teams didn't find that watching videos "fit" with their road-warrior schedules and provided little value over and above simply reading PowerPoints. They continued to interact directly with the veteran consultants to sound them out about how historical lessons learned would play out in the future projects. (Missing: Conversation!)

When NGOs tried to introduce fertilizer application procedures to African farmers, initially, the uptake was poor. The fertilizer process didn't fit in with the farmers' planting routine or the credit structures already in place for seed purchases. Unfortunately, fertilization didn't fit with the production methods or the local customs either. Until the community could be included in the process, farmers felt their new methods and values were in conflict. (Missing: Translation!)

Failed knowledge and change absorptions like these result in budget overruns, missed markets, flagging employee morale, even starvation. We often see one of two scenarios: When plans seem to be well-informed (with high credibility and fit), early change management efforts lack enough strength to sustain stakeholders' *engagement* throughout long and tortuous implementations. At other times, change managers are invited so late after the strategic planning that they cannot influence *credibility* and *fit* and struggle to be more than cheerleaders for what's been "handed off" to them.

USING KNOWLEDGE JAM FOR LEADING CHANGE

Fortunately, the deficits of credibility, fit, and engagement are the very strengths of Knowledge Jam:

- *Credibility* through well-targeted insight (via facilitation). Appropriate integration of know-how might have helped the new production facility operators in the first example.

- *Fit* through creative integration into future work (via conversation). A conversation with follow-on consultants might have helped the earnest videographers in the second example determine how to make videos more "navigable" or more interactive.

■ *Engagement* through collaborative sorting out and mapping of context (via translation). Translation, we found in Chapter 5, did eventually help the reluctant African farmers in the third example.

Knowledge Jam disciplines, brought into planning, may help avoid execution hazards. Over a planning cycle, successive Knowledge Jams can be applied in each phase of development—such as scoping, analyzing, designing, and implementing. By having a Jam "inside" (borrowing a phrase from Intel), managers choose knowledge inputs better, and strategy participants can innovate by drawing out the hidden insight in the organization.

Now the most radical change from traditional strategy cycles: As in Knowledge Jam, where knowledge ownership shifts to the brokers, in a Jam-like strategy process, it is "brokers" who take ownership, not the facilitator or consultants.

Using Knowledge Jam as part of a regular planning process may feel unconventional but it pays dividends:

■ Innovation processes are more effective when they are informed by hidden (and sometimes non-intuitive) insight from inside and outside the organization. For example, holding a Jam with a customer service team could yield new ideas around products. Call center associates may come up with features that R&D did not. Those product features may have greater fit with emerging customer segments.

■ A facilitated conversation welcoming a diversity of perspectives and heuristics (and encouraging people to challenge sacred cows) is likely to have better problem solving. This comes about when non-traditional groups like those call center associates are brought into the room.

■ Moreover, as these diverse teams use visualization tools like systems thinking loops or cause-and-effect diagrams to explore the root cause of a problem or to spin out potential options, they are more likely to consider interactions under a "bigger tent" of functions, facilities, or customer segments. This raises thoroughness and accuracy, and credibility over time.

■ Finally, as we saw in Chapter 5, implementation of innovative ideas meets with less friction when the actors are motivated to participate. Participants are more determined to act (engaged) after being part of the planning process.

Knowledge Jam at the Heart of the Strategy Process

Knowledge Jam flows from the Discover/Capture step to the Broker step and to the Reuse step. The brokers carry the knowledge out from the Discover/Capture event into their organizations and programs. Imagine a situation in which the brokering is not to an *individual know-how application*, but *the next phase in the planning process*. That is, "brokering" amounts to translating the collective insight further forward into the funnel of the planning cycle.

For example, if the planning cycle will be transitioning from "analyzing the problem" phase to "envisioning the future" phase, brokers (or managers in a brokering capacity) have two responsibilities. They are caretakers of the analysis phase content (which they carry to constituencies in the envision phase), and they are responsible for re-mixing what's known so far for who and what are at stake in the upcoming envisioning phase.

Brokering like this reduces cycle time in the planning process, as less time is invested in details that will not help in the downstream phases. It's as if the next phase is a familiar catcher squatting with a mitt. You throw him a baseball, not a Pacific salmon.

The sidebar "Jamming in the Boardroom—Shared Insight in Action" describes one method for putting Knowledge Jam into the planning process. Designed with several Knowledge Jammers, it holds promise of being a better way to select, invent, and mobilize change. And for a facilitator or consultant, facilitating a series of Knowledge Jams, rather than being an "expert," is a more effective and rewarding way to lead change.

Knowledge Jam as Culture

Embedding the Knowledge Jam into a change process puts into place the mechanics of Facilitation, Conversation, and Translation. In practice, fortunately, Knowledge Jam also spawns its own culture. If one defines culture as simply "shared values," then Knowledge Jam's culture could be summarized as:

- "Intention" stemming from thorough selection, intentional insight, and common curiosity (from the Facilitation discipline),

- "Openness" encapsulating conversation's open posture, diversity pursuit, and dialogue practices (from the Conversation discipline), and

- "Stewardship" embodied in the ambassadorship played by the brokers (from the Translation discipline).

In sum, Knowledge Jam as a business *process* may help with defining and mobilizing change. Knowledge Jam as a set of *values and behaviors*—an ecology for working with a group's know-how—provides a change-ready culture. By being based on intention, openness, and stewardship, a Knowledge Jam culture can transform strategy from an abstract plan to something we internalize. The Jamming in the Boardroom sidebar below provides an example of a structured way for putting Knowledge Jam inside strategic planning so that the culture shifts, too. For a manager, participating in a series of Knowledge Jams, rather than in a planning or budgeting cycle, is a more effective and rewarding way to lead people.

SIDEBAR: JAMMING IN THE BOARDROOM— SHARED INSIGHT IN ACTION

Using Knowledge Jam in strategic planning I call "Shared Insight in Action" (SIA). SIA seeks to generate insight and accelerate problem solving by using Knowledge Jam disciplines of Facilitation, Conversation, and Translation to add credibility, fit and engagement to problem solving, and to inject a *culture* of intention, openness, and stewardship into planning.

SIA Approach

SIA addresses business problems by accumulating progressive insight over successive planning stages. The planning stages can be traditional strategy development (frame the problem, envision a solution, plan to act, as shown below), or any other development frameworks, such as the six sigma's DMAIC (define, measure, analyze, improve, control), the waterfall software development lifecycle (SDLC) methodology (requirements, design, code, build, debug), or, SDLC's more iterative cousin "agile" development.

SIA has a Knowledge Jam at each planning step. Knowledge Jam surfaces insight intentionally and collaboratively, provides a sense of ownership, and promotes effective action:

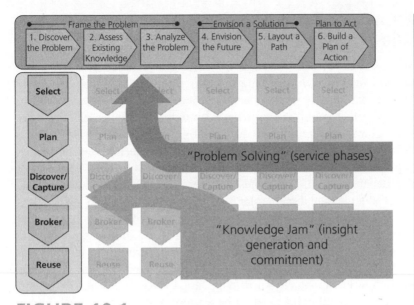

FIGURE 10.1. *Shared Insight in Action Approach*

The overall (horizontal) process is the stages of strategic planning. Vertical swipes are Jams. Collective knowledge grows and is shaped left to right. This very direct physical experience of the Jam within SIA gives participants a rhythm and a facilitated, manager-approved venue to model (and see others model) intention, openness, and stewardship.

Brokers can be product managers, analysts, program managers, or anyone who helps take know-how forward. Brokers think ahead to their future use of the knowledge (in the next stage of the process, such as "envision the future" after "analyze the problem").

SIA has a value distinct from many strategy planning processes: *client empowerment*. Because of their participation, brokers have sufficient documented knowledge to act on their own without further dependency on consultants. With SIA's regular collaboration and transparency, managers come to see themselves as allies up and down-stream through the process—change agents motivated by the shared opportunities and directed toward a common goal.

KNOWLEDGE JAM FOR BUSINESS TRANSFORMATION AND SOCIAL MEDIA

We just saw that Knowledge Jam disciplines—as a practice and a culture—can help *define* change. I also argue that they help to *absorb* change, particularly where change impacts knowledge workers. Change examples that could be improved with these disciplines include introducing new marketing methods, rolling out new enterprise resource planning (ERP) tools, or merging information technology or finance departments for two companies or divisions.

Because one of the biggest business transformations of our times is introducing social media, let's consider this example in depth.

In Chapter 5 ("Translation"), we saw that collaboration tools like enterprise social software platforms (ESSPs) had immense potential as supporting actors, helping the facilitators and brokers to identify participants and subjects, and then to disseminate, augment, and customize know-how elicited in the Knowledge Jam. Conversely, Knowledge Jam, as a practice and culture, could be a supporting actor for this big corporate change—social media–mediated interactions within and across organizations.

Social media business transformation is a good example because of the very real (and sometimes tragic) social media change absorption failures we are seeing in today's organizations. It turns out that intention, openness, and stewardship are three cultural dimensions that pundits claim many social media initiatives lack. Projects are haphazard, originators often hold back, and content accumulates and gets forgotten.

Meanwhile, Knowledge Jam's disciplines of Facilitation, Conversation, and Translation may raise the likelihood that the most sought-after experts and teams come to participate in Web 2.0 or Enterprise 2.0, and that the most relevant content flows to where it's needed.

Recap: Why Social Media Matter

We saw earlier that collaboration tools enable knowledge to be re-mixed, transmitted, and expanded with remarkable speed and reach. The democratic nature of social media tools—such as wikis, blogs, forums, shared digital media, and microblogs—make it possible to unite people with people, and people with content "frictionlessly."

As a broker, I can share insight on a forum with my colleagues in Melbourne, sixteen time zones away from Boston. Moreover, because of hyperlinking and alerting, if I or someone else tags my thread and exposes it to the corporate search (or, externally, to my community search), I might help someone whom I don't even know. Because collaborators don't need to know html, nor do they need to use a special desktop application, these typical mechanical obstacles to discovering know-how are lifted. The ideas I post may also accumulate and morph: When the discussion extends across different companies, functions, and countries, cognitive diversity tends to increase (thereby increasing perspectives and heuristics) and something smarter is likely to emerge.

For example, in one online forum in which I participate, we were riffing on the topic, "How do you get your online community members to contribute to a discussion forum?" Consider the perspectives expressed in the responses here:

- An executive, who led an online community at her company, proposed seeding the forum with starting comments, and thereby drawing out members. (Mental model: "Jump in. Lead by example.")

- An academic suggested that, for his organization, that type of leadership could be perceived as manipulative or just silly. Stand back and gently nudge contributors offline. (Mental model: "Let the online dialogue emerge.")

- A consultant countered that the focus should be on improving the quality of the question. Just start a whole new thread after taking a survey about which question most resonates. (Mental model: "Take time to get it right. Good questions beget good answers.")

So all of us in the online community could select among or combine these three, depending on our culture or relationship to members in each forum that we are trying to influence. This was a great example of where diverse (and unexpected) perspectives extended the problem solving.[2]

What's Wrong with Social Media Initiatives?

Andrew McAfee notes that E2.0 is naturally democratic, likening it to Chris Argyris' Model II, one of the dimensions of openness that we saw in Chapter 4. McAfee writes:

"Like Model II, Enterprise 2.0 is about abandoning the assumption that unilateral control is the best way to achieve desired outcomes,

and instead trusting in people's ability to interact productively without constant supervision from above."³

I agree with McAfee. The remarkably democratic nature of E2.0 is that it removes many of the encumbrances that might compel me to take positions, defend them, speak unilaterally, or consider topics undiscussable—all elements of the evil "Model I" style Argyris describes. With Model II, bringing the conditions of fairness and respect (which meet Scott Page's requirement of a "non-dysfunctional" interaction), we set the stage for both diversity and dialogue. We enjoy Page's better collective decision making and improved predictive capacity.

But McAfee ponders the idea that the simple *possibility* of Model II behavior in E2.0 doesn't always lead to Model II rich, unfettered participation. Nor does that possibility lead to knowledge relevancy. He goes so far as to invite his E2.0 leaders to take the challenge, that is, to invest in ways for their specific organizations to take up Model II and to "open themselves up to the conversation."⁴

Perhaps social media, like other game-changing technologies that call for behavior and attitude change, could benefit from the *whole* Knowledge Jam package. The tools of E2.0, by themselves, are the ham in the sandwich, but you need bread and condiments, too. Let's review what the bread and condiments do for that sandwich.

Conversation Is More Than Model II

McAfee reminds us that Chris Argyris himself stated that Model II is difficult to embrace, as our culture often pulls us back into defensive, self-protective, competitive behavior. McAfee is hopeful, but notes that all organizations don't suddenly become enlightened when they embrace social media.

In Chapter 4 ("Conversation") we discussed how Knowledge Jam's "posture of openness" blends the Model II behavior with a second, more psychological openness, what we call "heart preparedness." More, with Conversation, we use visualization tools (systems thinking, concept mapping) to enable a third form of openness, the "widened view." It takes a full "posture of openness"—*Model II language*, *heart preparedness* and *widened view*—for a truly productive conversation to unfold.

What that means for social media is that I, as participant, need to change.

- I need to go further than just finding pat Model II phrases that soften my declarative statements ("I think we should control our own budget. You see, I had a bad experience when I gave up control once.")

- I also can't just hold onto my positions so tightly ("I give IT autonomy, but let's check in every once in a while.")

- I also can't reject part of the widened view ("Let's invite all of the stakeholders to the discussion, but wait on IT, as they might hold us up.")

Instead, I have to surrender a bit. ("Maybe we should invite IT to talk about the whole program and find out what their pain points and objectives are for the year.")

Using the language of the Conversation discipline, when I am "willing to be changed or influenced by the conversation," the widened view feels less threatening. I can find the language to welcome diversity. Indeed, I can imagine how the container of our (now extended) group can survive a debate or two.

No Facilitation or Poor Facilitation

Social media yields remarkable creativity in the Conversation discipline alone. But is the Conversation discipline enough? Frustrated Web 2.0 and Enterprise 2.0 managers would say "no." There is no guarantee that the right people are out there on the wiki, blog, or microblog, sharing the high-impact knowledge. Nor is there any way to know whether that knowledge will be put to work. I would suggest (at the risk of being called a social media heretic), that social media lack sufficient "facilitative" or "coordinative" elements.

Many knowledge management and IT organization leaders have decried the lack of quality or completeness in their socially derived content. So, there is a role for a facilitator. But the type of facilitator required is more like the Jam's facilitator—one you'd more likely find in a mediation session than managing a project budget.

Social media evangelists tend to be allergic to facilitation. One reason is that the traditional facilitative processes associated with collaboration tools (often called "gardening") are more editorial and judging than eliciting. More, they are rarely strategic. Often tucked into the stream of threads, gardening isn't pulling out insights of originators or encouraging the expansion of originators' contextual comments or the clarification questions of the brokers. Another reason for evangelists' aversion to gardening is that social media content isn't always gardenable. It is often transactional (read: having a narrow or unrevealed context) and fleeting. (Imagine gardening Twitter!)

The skilled Knowledge Jam facilitator may very well be the sort of tone-setter and convener needed. The Knowledge Jam facilitator provides two principal services: the *container* (the conditions for the conversation) and *alignment* (getting the right people in the process, to focus on the high-value content). Many forums and blogs would result in more relevant ideas more quickly with someone working to address the container and stimulate business alignment. This would show up in whom the facilitator included, how she introduced topics or topic extensions, and how she made instant connections between people and people or groups.

Brokering Left to Hazard

McAfee's quote in Chapter 5 notes that social media and ESSPs are "largely indifferent" to the various translations he lists, like ERP systems, products, and meetings. That indifference can mean unfettered opportunity. Indeed, I noted that social media and ESSPs are a broker's friend because of their tremendous flexibility. On the other hand, translation left to hazard (broker-free) can limit the impact (or measurability of impact) for an ESSP or social media initiative.

Having some of the brokers identified up-front in the selection of topics, and then having them participate directly in the conversation that occurs during Discover/Capture—such as discussions or microblogging sequences—result in a greater focus on "taking know-how to the bank." The line of sight from investment to value is more direct in a structure when the brokers' responsibility is explicit.

Table 10.1 brings together the ideas of Facilitation, Conversation, and translation as improvements for the social media initiatives. Conversation offers a container "boost," but the shift in planning and translation (knowledge application) is the most dramatic impact that Knowledge Jam can have on the social media experience. You could imagine a similar table for other major organizational change initiatives involving knowledge work. (Many of these, like an ERP rollout, would find the middle column largely empty!)

Seeding E2.0 or Social Media Initiatives with Knowledge Jam

Above we talked about weaving the Knowledge Jam disciplines directly into the strategic planning processes. Another way to use Knowledge

TABLE 10.1. Knowledge Jam Additions to Social Media or E2.0 Initiatives

Discipline	"Naked" Social Media and E2.0	Knowledge Jam Adds
Facilitation	(Not systematic— some "gardening" of content)	Formal subject selection, business case, topic planning with sponsor Container-building and inclusion of originators, brokers, seekers, champions Synthesis
Conversation	Openness component— Model II Cognitive diversity	Openness components—Model II, prepared heart, widened view Cognitive diversity Dialogue
Translation	Translation not explicit, difficult to measure	Formal broker role responsible for translation Reuse measurement

Jam is as a catalyst for transformations. In our social media example (one of the greatest organizational transformations of this decade), Knowledge Jam's laser-sharp focus (Facilitation), its routines of openness, diversity, and dialogue (Conversation), and its formal brokering practices (Translation) could be used to "seed" social media behaviors.

While I was Knowledge Jam facilitator at Intel, the openness we cultivated as part of the Knowledge Jam spilled over into the social media. Consider this example: After a few Knowledge Jams, several Intel consultants started a discussion thread to capture their experiences with an application technology. Their discussion forum was more content-rich, more interactive, and ultimately more reusable than other discussions using the exact same discussion tool. I attributed that to the quality of the rapport that we had built up over a series of Jams and to the fact that the right brokers and originators had self-selected. It was they who were out in the discussion forum exchanging threads.

We could introduce the Knowledge Jam culture into a social media initiative by starting the initiative with Knowledge Jam steps. Specifically, we could ask a sponsor to help select among subjects, formally identifying initial originators, facilitators, and brokers. Then we could work to ensure that named brokers participate through the elicitation of knowledge and into its "post-Jamming" on the social media tools.

Table 10.2 is a quick summary of the important difference between a typical technology-driven social media implementation and a Knowledge Jam "seeded" implementation. Perhaps the social media evangelists "allergic" to facilitation could experience the up-front Knowledge Jam as a welcome antihistamine. Facilitation brings business alignment and momentum. A Knowledge Jam–oriented social media facilitator partners with brokers and originators to practice container-building—igniting, eliciting, traffic-copping, and sense-making. Just what the doctor ordered.

Extrapolating to other business transformations, this social media example teaches us that Knowledge Jam disciplines of Facilitation, Conversation, and Translation can help us to improve our collaborative planning, to ignite our sense-making, and to localize responsibility for

TABLE 10.2. **A Potential "Lift" Comes from Seeding Social Media with Knowledge Jam**

Traditional Introduction of Social Media	Social Media "Seeded" by Knowledge Jam
Get an enlightened sponsor who cares about knowledge transfer.	Get an enlightened sponsor who cares about specific topics and knowledge-transfer.
Build or purchase a tool.	Select subjects with sponsor, and secure initial broker and originator commitment.

(Table 10.2 continued)

Traditional Introduction of Social Media	Social Media "Seeded" by Knowledge Jam
Train people on using the tool (or just communicate that it is there and suggest how it can be used).	Engage committed brokers.
Cultivate champions to play an active discussion role.	From subjects, collectively plan topics. Ensure brokers are prepared to participate and draw out know-how for those topics.
Post guidelines.	Facilitate a real-time Discover/Capture event to seed content and culture. (Ground rules are included.)
Occasionally take down inflammatory or non-secure content.	During a Discover/Capture event, have facilitator, broker, and other participants explicitly model "conversation culture" (posture of openness, pursuit of diversity, practices of dialogue).
Count hits, threads, or content volume.	Brokers re-mix, post, and translate knowledge for expanded online conversation with other brokers, originators, and seekers. Seekers reuse knowledge either from within the social media tool or within other formats, such as processes, product requirements, projects, training. Measure knowledge reuse outcomes and trace to Knowledge Jam components (well-engaged originators, content-rich Discover/Capture event, intentional translation, adept facilitation).

interpreting and internalizing the change. I encourage you to consider using Knowledge Jam as part of your strategic planning and implementation cycle for implementations large and small.

Knowledge Jam, as a set of *steps*, *disciplines,* and a *culture*, can be instrumental in planning and managing change. Knowledge Jam's reach goes beyond typical change management efforts by stepping back into the planning process and setting the stage for better execution by starting with better *knowledge absorption*. Knowledge Jam also may also improve *change absorption* by bringing a greater match-up between sponsors (with strategic imperatives), originators, brokers, and seekers. Routine Knowledge Jamming can set the stage for a more sustainable sharing culture and more persistent sense-making. As we saw in the example when the Intel engineering team effortlessly continued the Jam online after the real-time Jamming ended, extending the Knowledge Jam culture deep into ongoing interactions can come naturally, provided the relationship "container" is developed. Throughout the life of the organization, when we begin to live in Knowledge Jam's culture of intention, openness, and stewardship, our work can be better informed, more productive, and more inspiring.

CHAPTER

AN INVITATION

"An Invitation" considers how current events and collaboration technology developments could mean new uses of Knowledge Jam and new forms of "Jamming." It also issues an invitation to the reader to participate in a community of "Jammers Without Boarders."

"We speak of genius when we speak of leadership, hoping for some of that elusive genius in ourselves, but the word genius in its Latin originality means simply, the spirit of a place. The genius of Galapagos lies in its being unutterably itself; the genius of an individual lies in the inhabitation of their peculiar and particular spirit in conversation with the world. Genius is something that is itself and no other thing."

DAVID WHYTE, CROSSING THE UNKNOWN SEA: WORK AS A PILGRIMAGE OF IDENTITY.* USED WITH PERMISSION.[1]

WHY KNOWLEDGE JAM (AND OTHER FORMS OF KNOWLEDGE ELICITATION) WILL TAKE OFF

In today's complex, ever more interdependent organizations and nations survival requires us to leverage knowledge to do work. Organizations and governments stumble as they delayer, restructure, merge, and lose retirees. They stumble as they try to learn from and coordinate with partners, customers, and far-flung operations. We can't go on letting good know-how walk out the door or descend into a black hole, or go on discouraging would-be learners by missing their needs.

Let's make blind spots, mismatches, and jails a thing of the past. Let's chalk it up as our youthful (though expensive) lesson.

Because Knowledge Jam is rapid and targeted and it intentionally involves collaborative sense-making and translation, it is an efficient means to replace blind spots with boundary-spanning, mismatches with usable insight, and jails with knowledge-put-to-work. Welcome, bespeckled, married, emancipated organizations!

Such was the perspective we took looking back. We also discussed two forward-looking applications of the Knowledge Jam cycle and Knowledge Jam's intention-openness-stewardship culture. These were strategic planning and business transformation:

- Knowledge Jam can structure the planning process, not as one-off knowledge elicitation but as a way of propelling insight, synthesis, and commitment through that process. Over a planning cycle, as in the Shared Insight in Action (SIA) method, successive Knowledge Jams accelerate innovation by helping strategy teams make sense of the hidden insight in the organization, improving the absorption of actionable know-how into planning.

- Knowledge Jam disciplines and culture also improve the absorption of change into the organization or network. Social media integration is likely to be the biggest business change of our decade, a paradigm shift in how we define our organization, interoperate, and innovate. First we saw social media were invaluable for planning Knowledge Jams, storing, extending, and propagating knowledge. Next, we saw that Knowledge Jam, with its intentional focus, participation, and active engagement, was a vital starting point for a social media program. Often insufficiently aligned to business priorities, social media programs need the plan-ful facilitation discipline to come out of the gate on a value message. Often insufficiently aligned to subject-matter experts' priorities, social media programs need the Conversation dimensions of openness, diversity, and dialogue to draw out originators' insights and map those to future contexts. Social media programs are a remarkable test case for leveraging Knowledge Jam to overcome the change management obstacles to such critical business transformations.

■ Because Knowledge Jam's origins, intelligence acquisition, organizational learning, and collaboration are themselves growing and evolving, their evolution will continue to inform the way Knowledge Jams impact any business initiatives involving teams, know-how, and innovation.

YOU HAVE YOUR TOOLKIT

Knowledge Jam, a five-step process, succeeds because it combines business practices of intelligence acquisition, organizational learning, and collaboration technology to help "broker" the found insight into the work of the organization. I hope I have effectively shown you how to start on your Knowledge Jams and that I have made Jams come alive for you though my anecdotes from high-tech, consulting, finance, healthcare, and energy. I encourage you to seek out and practice the Knowledge Jam disciplines:

1. *Facilitation*, critical for creating the structure, *or intention*, for sharing know-how and for creating the container of trust and common curiosity. (Facilitation is a lot more than coordinating events and recording knowledge originators' words.)

2. *Conversation*, engaging the knowledge brokers and originators together throughout the Knowledge Jam process (rather than waiting until after knowledge was captured), creating a climate of openness and diversity, and driving dialogue practices into serendipitous meaning and relationships.

3. *Translation*, leveraging the self-interest of the brokers to get the knowledge into circulation and to put the knowledge to work. Translation is "taking it to the bank." It is helping seekers use knowledge for swifter, less wasteful processes, profitable products, fewer points of failure and employee job satisfaction.

For the table lovers among us, I offer you a tidy summary of the book in five columns in Table 11.1.

TABLE 11.1. A Cheat Sheet for the Table Lovers

Discipline	Thorny Problem Addressed ("Rationale," Chapter 1)	Knowledge Jam Differentiators ("Bespeckled," Chapter 6)	Knowledge Jam Inheritance ("Heritage," Chapter 7)	Knowledge Jam Culture Applicable to Other Business Processes ("Leading Change," Chapter 10)
Facilitation	Knowledge Blind Spots	Boundary Spanning	Intelligence Acquisition	Intention
Conversation	Knowledge Mismatches	Surfacing Usable Insight	Organizational Learning	Openness
Translation	Knowledge Jail	Putting Knowledge to Work	Collaboration Technology	Stewardship

MORE THAN A BUSINESS TOOL

I originally wrote this chapter as Massachusetts recovered from two horrendous rain events in March 2010, with some counties seeing the highest rainfall in recorded history. The National Guard was brought in to sandbag, and parts of Massachusetts and Rhode Island were declared federal states of emergency.

Now, months later, I can say that in the last twenty-four months we have seen violent natural events all over the world—from earthquakes in Szechuan Provence, China, Port-o-Prince, and Central Chile; to floods in Rio de Janeiro and Sind Province, Pakistan; to unprecedented drought in Russia. As if our decade hadn't seen enough with Hurricane Katrina and Indonesia's tsunami. Sharing know-how about managing our infrastructures for safety and economic stability is an international imperative. Rescue workers in Massachusetts could Jam with officials in Rio de Janeiro. Earthquake civil engineers in California could Jam with Haitian aid workers. And the omnipresent Red Cross could teach us all ways of aiding, feeding, and sheltering survivors, preventing worker burnout, and raising funds.

What we need is "Jammers Without Boarders," facilitators who know how to inspire and unite, brokers who can accomplish a speedy translation, and sponsors who understand the idea that conversation, and not documentation alone, yields insight transfer *and* impact.

Ultimately, I hope you take up Knowledge Jam and help grow the capacity for (and appreciation for) Jamming around your office, your school, your community, and your globe. Start with a small team, each of you trying on facilitator, originator, and broker hats. Spring some hidden know-how into action, and see how the Knowledge Jam disciplines (and culture) compare to other ways you innovate and change. Do you hear the music?

I love the quote at the beginning of this chapter. Years ago I spent an entire weekend listening to David Whyte. It was billed as "interpreting our professional calling through the lens of poetry." (David Whyte's poetry, and that of the many other greats who preceded him.) The audience was primarily business professionals, not poets, and at first, we felt a deep sense of inadequacy. I recall listening intently for some sort of mystery revealed. (After all, Whyte is a genius, in the traditional sense of the word.) To our surprise, Whyte urged us to see our own genius-spirit and to "inhabit it." Whyte's gift as originator was the way he took the body of great poetry and contextualized it through his own brilliant poet lens. And he challenged us, as "brokers" to translate that message of "inhabitable genius-spirit" to others.

That must be my life-Jam, as I don't think I'll ever be finished.

With Knowledge Jam, all participants are called upon, as Whyte called us, to inhabit their genius-spirit. We are all originators. We are all brokers. We are all facilitators. And we are all seekers. It's just a matter of context. A Knowledge Jam should be something we create each time we consciously engage "in conversation with the world."

APPENDIX

KNOWLEDGE TYPES

In the body of the book I described how to elicit know-how and its context using tools like subject selection frameworks, Knowledge Jam recording templates, systems thinking maps, and concept maps. But unpacking *how we know what we know* (our "cognition") I've purposely kept at a high level. Exploring cognition could consume several more books!

Nonetheless, I'd like to introduce you to some ideas that can help you to understand how originators know what they know: *scenarios* and *knowledge types*. Scenarios we first encountered in Chapter 3 ("Facilitation") and I'll recap them here. Knowledge types have been studied extensively by my friend, Larry Todd Wilson, managing director of Knowledge Harvesting, Inc.

TOPIC SCENARIOS (FROM THE FACILITATION CHAPTER)

During the Planning step, we saw that, even after choosing the subject, many choices about topics (or agenda items) can be overwhelming. I've successfully used scenarios to take subjects down a notch and to set up the agenda (the "scaffolding") in a manner that helps us to pinpoint where know-how may reside. As we saw in the Institute for Healthcare Improvement "Process versus Content" example (in Chapter 3

["Facilitation"]), working through scenarios during the Planning step can help move the participants onto the same page and improve the efficiency of the Planning step. Here are those scenarios that have helped me to narrow down Knowledge Jam topics:

- *For product knowledge:* Product or product feature change, product upgrade, a change in product interface (to another application, complementary product, data, or partner product). Products could be anything from doorknobs to drug development software.

- *For process (procedure), project, or functional knowledge:* Scaling up or scaling down, cycle time compression, project/process/function scope, stakeholder or team member change, working with outsiders/contractors, working with virtual participants, introducing new measurements, or adapting to new controls or regulations.

- *For competitive or market strategy knowledge:*[1] Anticipating or responding to new entrants, to changes in competitors' features or pricing, to changes in customer or segment preferences, to changes in customer or supplier concentration, to changes in supplier reliability, or to changes in ability to control bargaining (for example, through control of resources or channels).

You can imagine other scaffolding themes outside traditional business contexts—variants of Product, Process, and Market—such as humanitarian services, fund raising, and international trade strategy. In Chapter 3 we saw that the focusing like this continues even into the Discover/Capture event. Facilitation moves like "topic probe" and "context probes" help this.

TYPES OF KNOWLEDGE

These scenarios and "probes" (re)focus the Jam conversation. But to surface *how* the originators know what they know, it may help to frame questions using Larry Todd Wilson's framework of the five " knowledge types":

1. Declarative Knowledge—Support information. "Knowing about."[2]

2. Procedural Knowledge—Guidance. "Knowledge of what to do and how to."

3. Conditional Knowledge—Signals. "Knowing when to and why to."

4. Social Knowledge—Collaborative norms. "Knowing how to work with others."

5. Systemic Knowledge—Big picture, mental model. "Knowing how parts are related."

Larry and I participate in a knowledge-transfer practitioner group called Knowledge Elicitation and Transfer (KEAT). As an overlay to the scenarios, I've found that his framework (Table A.1) helps me and the other Jam participants to more systematically draw out the originators' reasoning.

TABLE A.1. Scenarios and Knowledge Types

Knowledge Type	Sample Questions That Can Be Adjusted to Scenario
Declarative	What *product/process/strategy* do we have today? What are the features, services, target customers?
Procedural	What *product/process/strategy*-planning method or rule of thumb did you use? What are the steps?
Conditional	When would you choose each product/process/strategy option? What triggers you to choose a particular approach?
Social	What about the politics or your networks influenced how you went about this? In general, whom do you engage in *product/process/strategy* direction? Why?
Systemic	What other programs, roles, emotions, processes influenced your *product/process/strategy*-planning, and how? Is there a feedback loop? How does that particular experience size up to others you've done or seen?

For example, annual profitability might be the subject, and we might have decided that the individual products are the topic (considering for each product macro-markets, cost structures, and customer reactions to features). How might we use the knowledge types? I (and the brokers) could use declarative questions like "What products do you have?" and procedural questions like "What product-planning rule of thumb did you use?" and conditional questions like "What triggers you to choose *that* product feature?" Finally, we could raise systemic questions like "What feedbacks do you see? What other programs influenced your product-planning?" Table A.1 provides some sample questions.

While you are planning the Jam, you might consider which knowledge types are going to be important for your brokers (and the seekers they represent), and feed them into your asking kit.

KNOWLEDGE JAM TEMPLATES

*Starter questions are from Forest Bioproducts Research Initiative Jam.

Knowledge Jam Planning Event Template for [Subject]

Step 1: Complete Knowledge Jam information

Knowledge Jam Title:	
Project Manager/Sponsor:	
Knowledge Planning Participants:	
Planning Session Date:	
Last Updated:	

Step 2: Document knowledge planning session(s) in the chart below. [Replace these starter questions with your own.]

Knowledge Topic	Description, Themes, Related Documents, Off-Line Considerations	Jam Event Date	Estimated Time for Topic	Knowledge Originator Names	Knowledge Broker Names
1. How do we build multi-disciplinary organizations effectively? Is there a deliberate process that we can derive from our experience with FBRI?					
2. How do we take advantage of commercialization opportunities? What learning can we take forward?					

Knowledge Topic	Description, Themes, Related Documents, Off-Line Considerations	Jam Event Date	Estimated Time for Topic	Knowledge Originator Names	Knowledge Broker Names
3. Are we pushing the science envelope—new knowledge encourages academic pursuit. How do we know whether it is differentiated enough to be a magnet for researchers and funders?					

Total Estimated Time for Knowledge Jam Events:

Step 3 (after meeting). Generate agenda with start and stop times for topics (facilitators do this offline and transfer to Knowledge Jam capture document).

Introduction/Ground Rules

Topic 1

Topic 2

Topic 3

Topic 4

Etc.

Next Step/Reflections

Knowledge Jam Discover/Capture Event Template

Date:

Revision:

Format: (Conference call, in person, asynchronous collaboration)

Next Meeting:

Scribe:

Distribution: (Participants only or participants, plus who?)

Participants:

Name	Originator	Broker

Table of Contents

Topic 1:

Topic 2:

Topic 3:

Planning Event Background

Program Overview	
Team Composition	
Project Time Frame	
Planning Meeting Notes	

[Subject] Knowledge Jam Template

Topic	Knowledge Jam Participant Comments	Summary/Implications
Topic 1	Name: Comment	
Topic 2	Name: Comment	
Topic 3	Name: Comment	

Parking Lot
(Place topics or questions in here to be addressed after the Discover/Capture event.)

213

APPENDIX

GLOSSARY OF TERMS

(*Note:* The first useful mention of each term is in brackets after the definition.)

BKMs: "Best known method" related to a particular process (also called best practice). [Chapter 3 ("Facilitation")]

Champion: Go-to person for the Knowledge Jam. Plays role of on-the-ground project manager, maintains client attention, manages logistics and communications. Most valuable when the facilitator is an outsider and there is a need for on-the-ground coordination. [Chapter 3 ("Facilitation")]

Collaboration: Co-creation of a knowledge-product, with or without collaboration technology, such as SharePoint, Lotus Notes, or social media. Collaboration is a behavior that can be enabled by these tools, but it is not a technology. [Chapter 5 ("Translation")]

Community of Practice: A group of people who come together, generally crossing organizational boundaries, to build out a shared body of knowledge and to network with each other. Effective communities of practice (CoPs) have strong leadership/facilitation and sponsorship, meaningful working groups to put knowledge to work, good measurement and incentives, and a regular, real-time meeting. (In effect, they share with Knowledge Jam the three disciplines of Facilitation, Conversation, and Translation.) [Chapter 8 ("Comparing")]

Complex Systems: Systems where the behavior we experience is characterized by non-linearity of cause and effect, path dependence, and emergence. Complex Adaptive Systems are Special kinds of complex systems with the capacity to learn and adapt to complexity. Unlike non-adaptive complex systems in which the parts do not learn, such as the molecules of air and water in a weather system, the parts in a complex *adaptive* system contain local memories to which they are able to respond and are capable of learning from their experiences by generating new responses to their local contexts. [Chapter 7 ("Heritage")]

Content Management: Management of content snippets through a classification and storage system so that those snippets can be rendered on a website in accordance with who the seeker is, when he or she is clicking or receiving email, or the content displayed alongside the content in question. [Chapter 1 ("Rationale")]

Context: Knowledge about knowledge improves our ability to comprehend that knowledge and to apply in a new situation. Examples of context include "When this deliverable was used," "Who contributed," "Why the scope was limited," "What the original recipients already knew," or "Whom to contact." [Chapter 1 ("Rationale")]

Conversation: One of the three Knowledge Jam disciplines: A real-time interchange between Knowledge Jam participants that is characterized the dimensions of openness, diversity and dialogue. [Chapter 4 ("Conversation")]

Discover/Capture Event: The event during which brokers, originators, facilitators and other participants come together around a common agenda (or "topics") to surface the hidden know-how of the originators and the context around that know-how. Also called the "Conversation." [Chapter 3 ("Facilitation")]

Enterprise 2.0: Social media program inside the organization's firewall. [Chapter 5 ("Translation")]

Enterprise Social Software Platforms: Web 2.0 tools used in the enterprise, also called ESSPs. (Name introduced by Andrew McAfee, *Enterprise 2.0*, Harvard Business Press, 2010.) [Chapter 5 ("Translation")]

Facilitation: One of the three Knowledge Jam disciplines. The act of adding intention, coordination, and structure to the act of eliciting and transferring knowledge using a group of knower and seeker participants. [Chapter 3 ("Facilitation")]

Facilitator: Knowledge Jam leader who guides the participants through the five steps, Select, Plan, Discover/Capture Broker, and Reuse. The centerpiece of the facilitator's work is facilitating the Discover/Capture event. [Chapter 3 ("Facilitation")]

Innovation Jam: A "wisdom of crowds" approach to knowledge capture and transfer. the Innovation Jam brings the benefits of finding and engaging people at the periphery of the organization. [Chapter 9 ("Building")]

Know-How: Knowledge, insight, learned intelligence. In *Sharing Hidden Know-How*, we use knowledge, insight, and know-how interchangeably. [Chapter 2 ("Basics")]

Knowledge Broker: A type of seeker-representative accountable for surfacing knowledge and helping seekers to put knowledge into processes, training, etc. During Knowledge Jam, knows and represents the knowledge seeker, and after the Discover/Capture event translates appropriate knowledge from the event into downstream use. Promotes and models reuse and extends the relationships with other participants. [Chapter 5 ("Translation")]

Knowledge Jam: A process that includes (1) a facilitated conversation among knowledge originators and knowledge seekers that draws out tacit knowledge and (2) intentional "brokering" of the resulting knowledge to seekers and new formats. ("Putting knowledge to work.") [Introduction]

Knowledge Jam Events: Any real-time, facilitated events in the Knowledge Jam cycle in person or online. Knowledge Jam events are "Planning event" and "Discover/Capture event." [Chapter 2 ("Basics")]

Knowledge Jam "Panel": During the Knowledge Jam event the originating team is in the "panel" for the "audience" to ask questions. The audience is the knowledge brokers, sponsor, champion or observers. The facilitator moderates the discussion through the topics defined during the Planning event. [Chapter 3 ("Facilitation")]

Knowledge Jam Subject: The broad scope of the Knowledge Jam (as opposed to "topic," which is the component in the outline of the Jam). For example, a subject might be "Product X design approach," whereas a topic might be "designing the packaging." [Chapter 3 ("Facilitation")]

Knowledge Jam Topic: A plank in the Knowledge Jam agenda, or an area of discussion within a larger subject. For example, a subject might be "Product X design approach," whereas a topic might be "designing the packaging." Generally, these are defined before the Discover/ Capture event. [Chapter 3 ("Facilitation")]

Knowledge Originator: Subject-matter expert or project veteran (part of a team or individual contributor) who has know-how that may be useful to others. [Chapter 2 ("Basics")]

Knowledge Originating Team: Team of knowledge originators. Members may be formerly of the same team and are Jamming about a shared experience, or may be joining the team in the Jam and have common experiences. [Chapter 2 ("Basics")]

Knowledge Seeker: Anyone looking for knowledge and/or using knowledge surfaced in the Knowledge Jam. A seeker organization is the organization "dispatching" the broker to the Jam. [Chapter 1 ("Rationale")]

Peer Assist: Team-to-team knowledge transfer. Involves a new team drafting a project plan and then a veteran team reviewing that plan in a talk-back. Occasionally facilitated. Mostly bilateral and structured. (Focus stays on the new team's objectives and thereby surfacing only relevant inputs from the veterans.) [Chapter 8 ("Comparing")]

Shared Insight in Action (SIA): A strategic planning process that uses the Knowledge Jam to surface insight and plan at each step of the process. SIA seeks to generate insight and accelerate problem solving by using the disciplines of Facilitation, Conversation, and Translation to add credibility, fit, and engagement to problem solving and to inject a *culture* of intention, openness, and stewardship into planning. [Chapter 10 "Leading Change"]

Social Media: Collaboration tools that enable a variety of contributions to shared content through a web interface, or platform. Often include alerts, cross-linking, and various forms of dialogue. Examples include wikis, blogs, microblogs, social bookmarks, and discussion forums. (Within the organization, social media are called "enterprise social software platforms" (ESSPs) and the tools and collaborative practices together "Enterprise 2.0.") [Chapter 5 ("Translation")]

Sponsor: Leader who selects Knowledge Jam subjects, funds Knowledge Jam, advocates for events, and may advocate for the brokers and brokering activity after the Discover/Capture event. [Chapter 3 ("Facilitation")]

Translation: One of the Knowledge Jam disciplines. Translation is "carrying over" know-how that has surfaced during the Jam into a new application. It generally involves re-mixing and re-contextualizing the ideas. [Chapter 5 ("Translation")]

WIFM: Acronym for "What's in it for me?" A Knowledge Jam is initiated to improve the effectiveness of individuals and the organization. This needs to be obvious throughout the Knowledge Jam. [Chapter 9 ("Building")]

APPENDIX

CASE STUDIES

CASE STUDY: INSTITUTE FOR HEALTHCARE IMPROVEMENT (HEALTHCARE QUALITY IMPROVEMENT NON-PROFIT)

What do you do when you have knowledge spread around the heads of multiple people in multiple organizations—and they themselves don't even consider themselves experts? Here's an example of just that: A community of healthcare quality practitioners with some remarkable successes and some failures, but few seeing what we call the "wider view"—the cause and effect of their teams' success.

The Institute for Healthcare Improvement, a not-for-profit organization dedicated to fostering improvements in healthcare delivery throughout the world, saw the imperative of knowing what made healthcare quality improvement teams successful. Spreading the knowledge could mean life and death for impacted patients. A Knowledge Jam was performed by Katrina Pugh and Nancy Dixon, Common Knowledge Associates, in Spring 2009. Leadership from IHI included Jo Ann Endo, Sara Jackson, Jonathan Small, Marie Schall, Ginna Crowe, and Kiette Tucker.

Cambridge, Massachusetts–based Institute for Healthcare Improvement (IHI) is an independent not-for-profit organization helping to lead the improvement of healthcare throughout the world. Founded in 1991 and based in Cambridge, Massachusetts, IHI works to accelerate improvement by building the will for change, cultivating promising concepts for improving patient care, and helping healthcare systems put those ideas into action.

Situation: One of IHI's most far-reaching products is their IMPACT communities. These are gatherings of hospital teams from all over the United States who want to introduce quality initiatives, adopting IHI's tools and methods while interacting as a distributed community. IMPACT communities have covered such important healthcare quality issues as healthcare-associated infections and improving care in emergency departments and clinical office practices, with improvements in the millions of dollars annually.

In 2009, the multi-hospital "perinatal" IMPACT community of about one hundred doctors, nurses, technicians, administrators, and project managers had been working with IHI for two years to reduce medical errors using IHI's process improvement methods in the labor and delivery care area. IHI knew that it would be launching future improvement communities in other care areas, and IHI believed that they could learn a great deal from this group.

Burning Question: During the planning discussions, IHI leadership felt that there were some remarkable cases of hospital quality teams' coming together to integrate and practice quality tools with a low "time to gel," while other teams took a longer time to form, agree on goals, establish effective communication, and become productive—if they ever did.

> *How do hospitals become ready to consistently adapt IHI's practices?*

> *How do diverse hospital quality team members "gel" into a team that is a force for change within their organizations?*

Select/Plan Before Knowledge Jam Discover/Capture Event: During the four planning months we identified topics and participants,

Healthcare Quality Non-Profit (cont'd): "Gelling" Knowledge Jam Summary

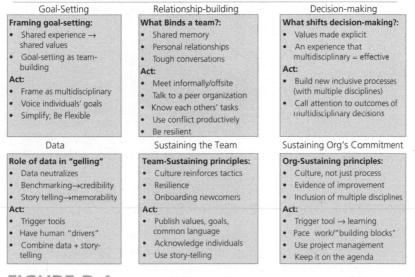

Goal-Setting	Relationship-building	Decision-making
Framing goal-setting: • Shared experience → shared values • Goal-setting as team-building **Act:** • Frame as multidisciplinary • Voice individuals' goals • Simplify; Be Flexible	**What Binds a team?:** • Shared memory • Personal relationships • Tough conversations **Act:** • Meet informally/offsite • Talk to a peer organization • Know each others' tasks • Use conflict productively • Be resilient	**What shifts decision-making?:** • Values made explicit • An experience that multidisciplinary = effective **Act:** • Build new inclusive processes (with multiple disciplines) • Call attention to outcomes of multidisciplinary decisions
Data	**Sustaining the Team**	**Sustaining Org's Commitment**
Role of data in "gelling" • Data neutralizes • Benchmarking→credibility • Story telling→memorability **Act:** • Trigger tools • Have human "drivers" • Combine data + story-telling	**Team-Sustaining principles:** • Culture reinforces tactics • Resilience • Onboarding newcomers **Act:** • Publish values, goals, common language • Acknowledge individuals • Use story-telling	**Org-Sustaining principles:** • Culture, not just process • Evidence of improvement • Inclusion of multiple disciplines **Act:** • Trigger tool → learning • Pace work/"building blocks" • Use project management • Keep it on the agenda

FIGURE D.1. *Summary of Healthcare Improvement Teams' "Gelling" Approaches*

held a planning meeting, and prepared for the Discover/Capture event. We also conducted approximately ten interviews with brokers and originators.

Participants: Nurses, doctors, quality program managers, IHI faculty, and program designers representing six hospitals.

A Big Insight: Effective teams revealed that it is critical to "gel" intentionally (using process, people, and quality methods), but that informal interactions such as storytelling helps them stick together. See Figure D.1 for a high-level summary of the gelling observations.

Result: IHI added "gelling" components to their organization-wide design model called the "driver diagram." The driver diagram was a critical part of the intervention methodology IHI used across all programs touching policy-makers, hospitals, healthcare providers, and healthcare provider organizations.

FIGURE D.2. *Imagining Fuel from Biomass*

CASE STUDY: FOREST BIOPRODUCTS RESEARCH INITIATIVE (NEW ENERGY INSTITUTE)

What do you do when a growing organization is undergoing a significant transition in terms of how it is governed, how it operates, how it makes money, and how it presents itself to the market? Can you glean from the successes and failures that led up to this positive development? This is what Forest Bioproducts Research Initiative's (FBRI) director Hemant Pendse asked in early 2009 as he stood at the threshold transitioning his National Science Foundation (NSF) funded *initiative* into an independent *institute*.

The FBRI Knowledge Jam was performed by Kate Pugh and Nancy Dixon, Common Knowledge Associates, in Spring 2009. Leadership for the FBRI Knowledge Jam included Hemant Pendse, Darrell Donohue, Peter Van Walsum, and Mike Eckhart.

Orono, Maine–based Forest Bioproducts Research Institute aims to transform Maine into a regional, national, and world leader in the transformation of forest resources into a valuable bio-economy. The research goals are to:

- *Promote forest health for a sustainable bio-economy,*
- *Understand and separate wood components, and*
- *Create and commercialize new bio-products, such as fuels and chemicals.*

Situation: After three years operating as a primarily academic, NSF-funded initiative, FBRI was graduating to a larger "institute," with more diverse funding, more diverse partners in industry, government, and academia, and with even more diverse forest-derived products, ranging from jet fuels to fish food. As an "institute," FBRI's complexity would increase. Its expanded footprint would require deepening the research partnerships and expanding channels for commercialization of forest-derived products.

Burning Question: During the planning sessions, FBRI leadership felt that there were pockets of operational cxccllcncc that could be extended into the new partnerships and products. However, there had not been a mechanism for discovering any process successes and spreading them. Their burning question was quite fundamental:

> *"What can we glean from first three years of running the initiative to 'hit the ground running' with the institute? Can we convince the board of our readiness for this next move?"*

Select/Plan Before Knowledge Jam Discover/Capture Event: During the approximately ten weeks of planning, we identified topics and participants, held a planning meeting with representative originators and brokers, and communicated to participants about the timing and format of the Discover/Capture event.

Participants: Participants included approximately twenty-five people: chemical engineers, chemists, statisticians, sociologists, economists, business sponsors, and industry associations who had worked on the FBRI "initiative" during the previous three years.

A Big Insight: A big insight from the FBRI gathering was that the many "thrusts" of the program and the diversity of participants meant that few individuals saw the big picture about how the program fit together. Importantly, some theoretically interdependent groups had been parallel tracking with only infrequent meetings. Take, for example, the forest lifecycle analysis group (who look at the entire trajectory from seed, through harvest, through bio-product) and the bio-refinery researchers. The Lifecycle analysts had not fully understood how important their predictions of forest yield were to the people designing the bio-refinery. Meanwhile, the bio-refinery researchers didn't see how they were holding up the Lifecycle analyst by holding off estimating feedstock demand in various scenarios until they had perfected their refinery processes. These groups stood in stark contrast to a third group, Mix-Alco, which had been making progress in studies with other Maine universities through regular weekly conference calls and extensive document sharing.

The group realized that it wouldn't take too much effort to jointly construct roadmaps representing multiple parallel tracks of work, and to express how inputs from each other (even if only rough estimates of volume and quality, from the Lifecycle and Bio-Refinery teams, respectively) could alleviate guesswork and delays. Participants reasoned that this could be made sustainable by taking a page out of the Mix-Alco group's book.

Below is an excerpt from the Knowledge Jam output. (Notice how Proposal 5 aligns with the "big insight." That is what participants in the Discover/Capture event dubbed the "chicken and egg game.")

Excerpt from Forest Bioproducts Research Initiative Knowledge Jam

Participants *translated* their experiences into several future multidisciplinary institute processes. Moreover, the Knowledge Jam Discover/Capture event spawned *new relationships* and *commitments* to new collaborations.

Proposal 1: Broaden industry/business integration in Institute

Proposal 2: Design explicitly to link across the "themes" and "thrusts"

Proposal 3: Generate a "common language"

Proposal 4: Improve awareness of ongoing work and commitment levels

Proposal 5: Break the "chicken and egg game" with roadmap exercises

Proposal 6: Act on each participants' declared "brokering" intentions (seventeen "commits" and only two "passes")

Result: During the Discover/Capture event, participants agreed that they were more ready to demonstrate FBRI's operational potential as a more complex, multiple work stream "institute." Within weeks of the event, several new cross-team discussions were initiated to improve productivity. The result of the Knowledge Jam was that participants, particularly the leaders of major work streams, were well-prepared to describe the Initiative's operations to board members (and other funders). Within one year of the Jam, FBRI's board and the university chancellorship approved funding for FBRI's new institute status.

APPENDIX

KNOWLEDGE JAM PRACTICE FAQS

Several clients and colleagues have asked me about how to optimize the Knowledge Jam process, expand its benefits, and set up the Knowledge Jam organization for success. I've compiled the most common here as FAQs.

WHAT IS BETTER: AN OUTSIDE OR INSIDE FACILITATOR?

I have been both an insider and an outsider. I found that the benefits of being an outsider were that I didn't need to tiptoe around the "sleeping lions" or "sacred cows" during the Planning and Discover/Capture steps. I also could stand back objectively during the inevitable debates that would occur during the Select and Plan steps. Another advantage was that I could accumulate and share (anonymously) interesting patterns I'd seen with different organizations, say, in bringing the originators into the Jam.

I found that there were equal, although different, benefits of being an insider. One was that I immediately understood most of the concepts, say, about the industry, the function, product line, or operation. I also readily empathized with originators' knowledge hoarding or the over-exuberant brokers dominating, as *I* experienced the information gaps and pressures first-hand. I also knew how people were (or weren't) rewarded for sharing. Often I knew that my originators were sharing because they trusted me and trusted the process, even though they knew that they could be diminishing their subject-matter expert "persona."

I also had another advantage as an insider: I could help brokers translate knowledge and even do some translation of my own. Helping to broker does put time pressure on, as knowledge needs to circulate while it's fresh.

If you're having an impact, your Knowledge Jam facilitator's job never slows down.

- If challenging sacred cows is your goal, and you're an insider, you might use systems thinking tools more heavily (to externalize the undiscussable), or you might collaborate with a neutral facilitator or draw in an unbiased broker from another division.

- If you feel insider-like empathy is needed, you might invest more time up-front getting to know the policies or incentives that constrain or compel your originators and brokers. Or you might lean more heavily on your champion to help navigate and translate.

In sum, both insiders and outsiders can have an impact. The trick is to discern the strengths and weaknesses of each.

CAN A BROKER BE AN ORIGINATOR?

The boundary between originator and broker is permeable. Many times I have had participants introduce themselves, not by stating their titles or geographies, but by stating why they are an originator, a broker, a seeker, etc. I always give them the option to say some sort of "hybrid" originator-broker-observer. This also gives me license early in the Discover/Capture or Planning event to seek out their diverse perspectives. ("You say you are just a broker. I bet you are a closet expert!") The group also appreciates the depth of experience in the room or virtual room, and often originators are delighted to meet up with other originators-cum-brokers, and find that their parallel worlds collide.

In addition to spontaneous cross-over, frequently a member of an originating team intends to start up a new team or program. He sees that the Jam can be a convenient way to bring out insights among his former teammates and to explore how those insights could inform those new projects.

SHOULD I AUDIO-RECORD A KNOWLEDGE JAM?

Many would-be Knowledge Jam facilitators have asked me whether making an audio tape of the Knowledge Jam would be a suitable sub-stitute for note-taking in real time. My answer is that recordings rarely help, occasionally are neutral, and mostly hinder the Knowledge Jam.

Why is this? First, many participants may not feel comfortable being recorded. They fear being quoted out of context. Or they hold back lest they be accused of being non-patriotic when they describe institutional conditions for project failures. In a word, *safety* drops.

Second, transcription is expensive (as much as five person-hours for typing and editing a one-hour script), and a transcription is a difficult read. Pitch, emphasis, and pacing are all lost. One of my knowledge-elicitation colleagues recounted that after several expensive transcrip-tions, she abandoned the practice. For her teams, not only was it a waste of money, but participants didn't feel the recording was a credible common record. They fell back on their individual (and selective) notes, and had to relearn the art of collective note-taking.

Third, during the Planning or Discover/Capture events, when the "transcript" (or soon-to-be-transcript) is sitting inside the recording machine, rarely is there productive real-time reflection on what's being recorded. When we project what is being captured in the front of the room (or virtual room), participants make clarifications, ask to see pre-vious statements, ask questions, re-order concepts, and even contribute to a healthy parking lot of follow-up items. I've found that swiftly taking down ideas that come up ahead or behind their planned agenda slot gives a speaker the confidence that she has not been ignored. We can even back space when emotions get heated or step sideways to "unpack" some phrase projected in front of us. Ultimately, seeing their contributions on the screen contributes to participants' collective owner-ship of Jammed knowledge and how it came together.

In Chapter 3 ("Facilitation") I pointed out that the only situation in which recording may be a helpful supplement to the real-time typing is when the group is very large and the topic complexity is beyond the knowledge of the available brokers or facilitator. In that instance, brokers may need to have others listen with a more informed ear at a later date. This doesn't improve the Jam's safety, cost, or ownership, but it may enable you to capitalize on the limited availability of a knowledge originating team before they disband.

WHAT IF YOU CAN'T JAM IN REAL TIME? (THE WIKI ALTERNATIVE)

I have a few colleagues who are attempting to do asynchronous Knowledge Jams using wiki technology. I submit that the lack of "conversation" in the moment limits the generative quality of the interaction. We interact naturally at the cadence of human conversation. Most of us are biologically programmed to think, respond, and build relationships in real time. Text only, with time lapses and few auditory or visual cues, limits the experience of knowledge emergence, relationship building and trust. Recent research has shown that simply having pictures of participants in the wiki increases participants' motivation to engage. But creative knowledge flow is not guaranteed.

Nonetheless, with vigorous preparation, assertive facilitation, and some strong cultural predispositions, text and asynchronous knowledge transfer via a wiki (a shared web-based document) can be effective. (Effective, even without spending for a full Innovation Jam™!) Here are wiki-able Knowledge Jam ideas I've offered to some of my colleagues. I argue that you should use the disciplines of Facilitation, Conversation, and Translation all the more feverishly to make up for gaps resulting in the real-time to asynchronous shift:

■ *Facilitation:* Facilitators need to be more assertive in pulling in the participants, responding directly to their initiations, encouraging specific individuals to add to a thread, and summarizing. If you can do this using a table format (for example, in Google Docs), use the same three columns we saw in the Discover/Capture Template in Chapter 3 ("Facilitation"). Left-most is the agreed-on topic/agenda item, middle is the comments (for example, using "speaker: comment" syntax—"JD: It took longer than we planned because the client had scheduling issues."), right is for conclusions, summaries, or "pull ups." As facilitator, you need to constantly enforce the need for conclusions. This is because of the change in dynamic from real time. People are generally not as focused or not uniformly focused. In my experience, asynchronous users can be either less motivated to interact (and, therefore, less additive/iterative or attentive to the storyline), or they can come out of the fire hose. There is rarely middle ground.

■ *Conversation:* Facilitators need to convey the ground rules and desired tone explicitly. They also need to model those. Less conversation will happen naturally, unless the group has spent a great deal of time collaborating asynchronously. It's important to get out the dialogue practices of voice, listening, respect, and suspending early in the interaction. (It's helpful to post a sample dialogue example.) Establishing openness and dialogue can take more time and more words in writing than in real time. In real time, you can use pitch, pacing, laughter, and body language that fit best in the moment. As said, another challenge with asynchronous text interaction is that people can grandstand. No one asks them mid-sentence to clarify, to course-correct, to practice respect, etc. So they tend to write longer, more multi-part comments. Such entries are more difficult to build upon than vocal interactions. "At least they are writing," you may think, "so we can all respond to them." In my experience, other potential writers may be scared away. If you have grandstanding, adding conclusions in the table's right column may attract others to skim and jump in.

■ *Translation:* (Although this is last in my list, it merits an early focus.) Translation begins with bringing in brokers who will represent a need from their division or function and who will participate actively in the conversation. They are responsible for really getting out the context. They are also formally responsible for putting the knowledge to work in their setting. They need to step forward and be enthusiastic about the Jam. If brokers are passive (which is harder to detect online than in person or in voice/real time), then the know-how that participants surface will not be helpful, seekers will be reluctant to apply it, and you will not get your return on investment.

Wiki-Jammers are often unable to do real-time Discover/Capture events because everyone is time-constrained. But if the wiki interaction is mired by passivity or grandstanding, you may *waste* the precious time you are allocating to the task! The facilitator needs to be more vigilant to draw originators and brokers out, prod connections they may be missing, and support them in their quest for context.

A final remark: Considering all of the adaptations you will need to adjust for the limitations of wikis or other similar asynchronous web or Enterprise 2.0 tools, you may have a lower return on investment for time spent. However, you might not have been able to do Knowledge Jam *at all* had you waited to have all participants at a real-time Discover/Capture event.

WHERE DOES KNOWLEDGE JAM FIT IN A KM PROGRAM? DOES IT HAVE TO?

Knowledge Jam can be a highly effective addition to a KM program because it can achieve results relatively quickly, the technology investment is low, and it is intentionally directed at mission-critical knowledge. Currently, many KM programs are positioned to focus on content or document volume, collaboration and search tools, and purchased subscriptions. They are not positioned to go after tacit knowledge.

Knowledge Jam raises the caliber of KM'ers and raises the perception of relevancy for KM. For example, at a financial services company, the Knowledge Jam team stepped in to help accelerate the transfer of knowledge during a high-profile office closure and operations transfer. The team was positioned squarely as a change resource for solving the immediate challenge of business continuity. It also engaged multiple divisions. Before that point, the KM program was known within one division.

Knowledge Jam doesn't have to be part of a KM program, and in some organizations optics are better when it is aligned to other departments, such as innovation or quality improvement. Even when there is no KM program or the KM program budget is limited, you can introduce Knowledge Jam with a very low up-front investment. It rides more on process management and facilitation, traditional *management* skill sets, rather than traditional KM skill sets, such as information architecture and document management.

HOW CAN KNOWLEDGE JAM JUMP-START AN ENTERPRISE 2.0 (SOCIAL MEDIA) INITIATIVE?

You can use Knowledge Jam to jump-start or reinvigorate an Enterprise 2.0 (social media) initiative. Frequently, an Enterprise 2.0 initiative wanes in participation and value because the content is not core to the business ("mismatches") or nuggets are lost in a clutter of Yammerings or Tweets (knowledge "jail"). Or the real originators may simply not be online ("blind spots").

Contrast this to the Knowledge Jam. At the outset we are getting a sponsor to approve and advocate for the Knowledge Jam subjects and, as facilitators, we draw in appropriate originators and brokers. In the Discover/Capture event, we are managing the experience to maximize openness, diversity, and dialogue.

Yet, even more business-relevant knowledge may surface, and better knowledge will get into use when enterprise social software platforms (ESSPs) are added to the mix. We can use ESSPs to identify the subjects, to flesh out the agenda (topics), to vet or expand the written Discover/Capture outcomes, and to increase its chances of serendipitous discovery.

Without question, ESSPs can help the Knowledge Jam. But what also happens (as seen in Chapter 10 ["Leading Change"]) is that Knowledge Jam's disciplines of Facilitation, Conversation, and Translation endow an Enterprise 2.0 initiative with higher-impact topics, participation from more appropriate originators and brokers, and a more reflective and intentional "reuse culture." Not only does know-how grow, but it flows more systematically when managers bring in Knowledge Jam disciplines.

NOTES

Introduction

1. We will come back to these three examples in Chapter 10.
2. This term was first introduced by Andrew McAfee, "Enterprise 2.0: The Dawn of Emergent Collaboration," *MIT Sloan Management Review, 47*(3), Spring 2006, 21–28.
3. Reprinted by permission of Harvard Business School Press. From *Enterprise 2.0* by Andrew McAfee. Boston, MA, 2009, page 69. Copyright © 2009 by the Harvard Business School Publishing Corporation; all rights reserved.
4. Aneesh Chopra, Obama's chief technology officer, "Innovation for America: Restoring Growth, Reforming Government, Fixing Health Care, and Expanding Opportunity." Presentation to TiE (The Indus Entrepreneurs, Boston Chapter, December 2, 2009).
5. Intel Solution Services is now part of the Intel Software and Solutions Group.
6. I also call them "originators" and "brokers," for short. The term "broker" may connote "ruthless money-handler" to you, but I encourage you to think of an unselfish networker, seeking to help both giver and receiver. See also Appendix C for a glossary of terms. The terms "originating teams" and "reuse teams" were first used by Nancy Dixon, "Does Your Organization Have an Asking Problem?" *KM Review, 7*(2), May/June 2004.

Chapter 1, "Rationale"

1. *The Family Mark Twain*. New York: Harper & Row, 1972, p. 1110.
2. Laurence Prusak and Al Jacobson, "The Cost of Knowledge," *Harvard Business Review*, November 2006, Reprint F0611H. All excerpts used with permission.
3. Nancy Dixon, *Common Knowledge: How Companies Thrive by Sharing What They Know*. Cambridge, MA: Harvard Business School Press, 2000. All excerpts used with permission.
4. For this reason more companies like PricewaterhouseCoopers are investing in "redacting" documents. Redacting entails asking a battery of questions of the authors, then generating a sanitized document free of confidential client references.
5. I talk about this mixed-incentive pattern between quality and quantity of knowledge assets contributed in Chapter 4 ("Conversation") as I discuss the systems thinking principle of unintended consequences.
6. Katrina Pugh and Nancy Dixon, "Don't Just Capture Knowledge, Put It to Work!" *Harvard Business Review*, May 2008. Reprint F0805C.

7. Chait, Larry, Boston KM forum, Bentley College, Waltham, MA 10/22/09, quoting RoyalRingdom.com (reference updated). http://royal.pingdom.com/2011/01/12/internet-2010-in-numbers/
8. Larry Chait (2009) summarizing www.softpanorama.org/Social/overload.shtml.
9. Margaret Parish. (1963), *Amelia Bedelia*. New York: Harper & Row.

Chapter 2, "Basics"

1. I use the terms "originators" and "originating team" interchangeably and "brokers interchangeably with "brokering team." Typically, a team of individuals (often current or former co-workers) originate, and several teams of individuals broker representing multiple receiving organizations.
2. These costs of Knowledge Jam are detailed in Chapter 9.
3. Occasionally, you will see the term "champion" used to refer to a sponsoring or funding person or entity. I am using the term to describe someone who is responsible "on the ground" and who communicates what's happening, when, and with whom. In this sense, the champion is more tactical than the sponsor. In some organizations the sponsor and the champion are the same person.

Chapter 3, "Facilitation"

1. Quotation from http://thinkexist.com/quotation/a_leader_is_best_when_people_barely_know_he/214091.html.
2. This section refers to elements of Michael Wilkinson's "10 Principles of Facilitation," *The Secrets of Facilitation*. San Francisco: Jossey-Bass, 2004. Reprinted with permission of John Wiley & Sons, Inc.
3. "Organizations as Cognitive Maps: Charting Ways to Success and Failure," Karl Weick and Michel G. Bougon. Chapter 4 in *The Thinking Organization*, edited by Sims and Gioia, published by Jossey-Bass. (Example mine)
4. It is often helpful to check Michael Porter's Industry Structure or Five-Forces model to be sure that you are looking at the correct forces: rivalry, buyer power, supplier power, threat of substitutes, or threat of entrants. Michael Porter, *Competitive Advantage*. New York: The Free Press, 1985, p. 5. Also see, Michael Porter's "The Five Competitive Forces That Shape Strategy," *Harvard Business Review*, January 2008, Reprint R0801E.
5. See Larry Todd Wilson, www.knowledgeharvesting.com. Also see Appendix A for a discussion of five "knowledge types": systemic, conditional, procedural, declarative, and social.
6. Michael Wilkinson, 2004, p. 48.
7. Joel Keller, "Larry King May Have Lobbed Softballs, But He Got Results," *TVSquad.com*, June 30, 2010. www.tvsquad.com/2010/06/30/larry-king-may-have-lobbed-softballs-but-he-got-results.
8. Michael Wilkinson, 2004, p. 175.

Chapter 4, "Conversation"

1. Williams College Board of Trustees, *Williams Alumni Review*, *104*(7), June 2010, p. 4. Used with permission.
2. In 1994 Chris Argyris articulated this idea in "Good Communication That Blocks Meaning." *Harvard Business Review*, July 2001, 1994. Prod. 94401-PDF-ENG

3. Olivia Parr-Rud. *Business Intelligence Success Factors*. Hoboken, NJ: John Wiley & Sons, 2009, p. 152. Used with permission.
4. Scott E. Page. *The Difference: How the Power of Diversity Creates Better Groups, Firms, Schools, and Societies*. New York: Princeton University Press, 2007, p. 10. All excerpts used with permission.
5. For more on the concepts of perspectives, interpretations, heuristics, and predictive models, see Scott E. Page, 2007, p. 7.
6. Scott E. Page, 2007, p. 15.
7. Thomas Gordon, *Origins of the Gordon Model*, on Gordon Training International Site: www.gordontraining.com/about-origins-of-the-gordon-model.html.

Chapter 5, "Translation"

1. R.V. Burgin joined K Company of the 3rd Battalion of the 5th Marines in 1943 and participated in some of the most difficult battles of the Pacific war. He earned a Bronze Star and a Purple Heart on Okinawa and was the inspiration for the character played by Martin McCann in the HBO series, "The Pacific." www.npr.org/templates/story/story.php?storyId=124580077.
2. Rob Cross, Andrew Parker, Laurence Prusak, and Stephen P. Borgatti, "Knowing What We Know: Supporting Knowledge Creation and Sharing in Social Networks." *Organizational Dynamics*, *30*, 2001, 100–120.
3. Amyris Biotechnologies produced a bio-product malaria-treatment drug using a sugar fermentation process. Then they applied the fermentation know-how to ferment sugar cane to produce a unique biofuel intermediate. *Technology Review*, a publication of the Massachusetts Institute of Technology, March-April, 2010.
4. Robert Hoffman credits Rear Admiral Len Hering, speaking to the San Diego Rotary Club in 2008, for this colorful metaphor.
5. Special thanks to Nancy Dixon, Common Knowledge Associates, for an earlier framing of these concepts. These ideas are also explored in Nancy M. Dixon and Kate Pugh, "Harvesting Project Knowledge," *NASA ASK Magazine*, Spring 2008. http://askmagazine.nasa.gov/pdf/pdf_whole/NASA_APPEL_ASK_30_Spring_2008.pdf.
6. J. Rusike, S. Twomlow, H.A. Freeman, and G.M. Heinrich, "Does Farmer Participatory Research Matter for Improved Soil Fertility Technology Development and Dissemination in Southern Africa?" *International Journal of Agricultural Sustainability*, *4*(3), 2006, pp. 176–192, 191. (Copyright Earthscan, 2006.) Used with permission.
7. More on the peer assist and knowledge elicitation interview follows in the comparison of knowledge elicitation approaches in Chapter 8.
8. See Appendix D for the Institute for Healthcare Improvement Knowledge Jam case study.
9. Reprinted by permission of Harvard Business School Press. From *Enterprise 2.0* by Andrew McAfee. Boston, 2000, p. 212. Copyright © 2000 by the Harvard Business School Publishing Corporation; all rights reserved.
10. Nancy Dixon, "If the Army Can Put Its Doctrine Up on a Wiki, You've Got No Excuse." September 23, 2009. www.nancydixonblog.com/2009/09/if-the-army-can-put-its-doctrine-up-on-a-wiki-youve-got-no-excuse.html.
11. Chip Heath and Dan Heath, *Made to Stick: Why Some Ideas Survive and Others Die*. New York: Random House, 2007.

Chapter 6, "Bespeckled"

1. http://allpoetry.com/poem/2822318. From Emancipated Dialogue by BlackRabbit9X. Used with permission.

Chapter 7, "Heritage"

1. Albert Schweitzer, "The Dignity of the Individual," in *Albert Schweitzer: An Anthology,* edited by Charles R. Joy, p. 153, Beacon Press, Boston, 1947. (Albert Schweitzer 1875–1965 was a German medical missionary, theologian, musician, and philosopher who won the 1952 Nobel Peace Prize.)

2. The consensus date for knowledge management's origins is Karl-Eric Sveiby's writing in the Eighties. The first book with the word "knowledge management" in the title was published in 1990 in Sweden by Karl-Erik Sveiby. www.gurteen.com/gurteen/gurteen.nsf/id/karl-erik-sveiby and www.entovation.com/seminars/bios/BioCVSveiby.pdf.

3. Complexity researchers tell us that our modern world is unpredictable because consequences are separated in time and space from causes, and causes interact in non-linear ways to get us the outcomes we see (such as market demand or soggy feet). We often respond to complexity by clinging to what we know (old business models, worn waffle treads), and unintentionally reinforce the very problems we want to fix.

4. William Isaacs, *Dialogue and the Art of Thinking Together.* New York: Currency/Doubleday, 1999, p. 244. All excerpts used with permission.

5. Society for Organizational Learning history can be found at www.solonline.org/aboutsol/history/

6. Chris Argyris and Donald Schön, *Organizational Learning: A Theory of Action Perspective.* Reading, MA: Addison-Wesley, 1978.

7. See the Society for Organizational Learning's history at www.solonline.org/aboutsol/history/

8. See Peter Senge, *The Fifth Discipline.* New York: Doubleday/Currency, 1990.

9. Concept mapping was developed by Joseph D. Novak and his research team at Cornell University in the Seventies. See Joseph D. Novak and Alberto J. Cañas, "The Theory Underlying Concept Maps and How to Construct and Use Them." Institute for Human and Machine Cognition, 2006.

10. There are differences in how the two knowledge-representation tools, concept maps and systems thinking, are used. In my experience, concept maps are helpful renderings of just about all of the elements in a conversation, and they are also therefore very good records. Meanwhile, systems thinking elects to focus on only those "levers" that have a material impact, and non-material (or dominated) impacts are generally left in the "parking lot" to the side of the diagram.

11. Of course, a secondary benefit may have been simply publicity for knowledge contribution as a noble behavior. But at what cost?

12. This spun off of MIT in 2001 and is now the Society for Organizational Learning. www.solonline.org/

13. D. Kantor and N. Heaton Lonstein, "Reframing Team Relationships: How the Principles of 'Structural Dynamics' Can Help Teams Come to Terms with Their Dark Side." In Peter Senge et al. (Eds.), *The Fifth Discipline Fieldbook.* New York: Doubleday, 1994. Referenced with permission. See also Kantor's forthcoming book: *Reading the Room,* to be published by Jossey-Bass in 2011.

14. These diversity practices are also core teachings in William Isaacs, *Dialogue and the Art of Thinking Together*. New York, Currency/Doubleday, 1999, and in the Leadership for Collective Intelligence training program, as well. All excerpts used with permission.

15. William Isaacs, Dialogue and the Art of Thinking Together. New York: Currency/ Doubleday, 1999, p. xvii.

16. Rick Ross and Charlotte Roberts, in Senge et al., *Fifth Discipline Fieldbook*. New York, Doubleday, 1999, p. 253.

17. History of IBM Lotus Notes is at www.ibm.com/developerworks/lotus/library/ ls-NDHistory/

18. Katrina B. Pugh, The World-Wide Web: Implications for Organizational Alignment. MIT Sloan School of Management Master's Thesis, 1996.

19. Ibid, page 34

20. Wanda J. Orlikowski and Debra Hoffman, "An Improvisational Model for Change Management: The Case of Groupware Technologies." *MIT Sloan Management Review* January 15, 1997. http://sloanreview.mit.edu/the-magazine/articles/1997/winter/3821/an-improvisational-model-for-change-management-the-case-of-groupware-technologies/2/ Used with permission.

21. Reprinted by permission of Harvard Business School Press. From *Enterprise 2.0* by Andrew McAfee. Boston, 2009, p. 48. Copyright © 2009 by the Harvard Business School Publishing Corporation; all rights reserved.

22. Mary Clare Jalonick, "Sherrod Gets Biggest 'I'm sorry'—from Obama." *Yahoo News*, Thursday, July 22, 2010. http://news.yahoo.com/s/ap/20100722/ap_on_go_pr_wh/us_ usda_racism_resignation

23. Gil Yehuda, The Blogger's Transformation, January 2011. www.gilyehuda.com/2011/01/ 03/the-bloggers-transformation.

Chapter 8, "Comparing"

1. Nancy Dixon, *Common Knowledge*. Boston, MA: Harvard Business School Press, 2000, p. 22. Copyright © 2000 by the Harvard Business School Publishing Corporation; all rights reserved.

2. Diane Piktialis and Kent A. Greenes, "Bridging the Gaps: How to Transfer Knowledge in Today's Multigenerational Workplace." Conference Board research report, 2008, R-1428–08-RR.

3. "Knowledge Harvesting" is a trademark of Knowledge Harvesting, Inc., under Larry Todd Wilson. www.knowledgeharvesting.com.

Chapter 9, "Building"

1. Occasionally, facilitators have typing assistance during the Discover/Capture event. I rarely split the facilitator job like this because I value the facilitative opportunity in clarifying what I'm writing as I write.

2. IBM Press Release 14 November 2006. www-03.ibm.com/press/us/en/pressrelease/20605 .wss.

3. Gartner Fellows interview with Nicholas Donofrio. www.gartner.com/research/fellows/ asset_185385_1176.jsp.

4. Jim Kouzes and Barry Posner, *The Leadership Challenge* (4th ed.). San Francisco: Jossey-Bass, 2008.

Chapter 10, "Leading Change"

1. This is well described by Robert A. Nieman in *Execution Plain and Simple: Twelve Steps to Achieving Any Goal on Time and on Budget*. New York: McGraw-Hill, 2004.
2. Euan Semple, British Broadcasting System ESSP manager, puts this nicely: "Having context in the question, context in the answer, and the collective memory of your corporate meat-space, empowered by the mighty hyper-link, in between [are] hard to beat." www .fastforwardblog.com/2007/01/08/survey-proves-90-of-managers-are-clueless/ (as quoted in *Enterprise 2.0* Andy McAfee, 2009, page 113).
3. Reprinted by permission of Harvard Business School Press. From *Enterprise 2.0* by Andrew McAfee. Boston, 2009, p. 207. Copyright © 2009 by the Harvard Business School Publishing Corporation; all rights reserved.
4. Ibid, p. 208.

Chapter 11, "An Invitation"

1. Printed with permission from Riverhead Books, www.davidwhyte.com David Whyte, *Crossing the Unknown Sea: Work as a Pilgrimage of Identity*, Riverhead Books, 2001, p. 61.

Appendix A

1. See Michael Porter, *Competitive Advantage*. New York: The Free Press, 1985, p. 5.
2. See Larry Todd Wilson, 2008, www.KnowledgeHarvesting.com.

ACKNOWLEDGMENTS

Many people contributed to the ideas and writing of *Sharing Hidden Know-How*—and to the emotional well-being of its over-caffeinated first-time author.

First, I'd like to thank people who helped shape the Knowledge Jam. Its roots go way back to my childhood, when my mom, Julie Pugh, the consummate broker, brokered ideas from car pools to career paths. My dad, Alexander (Jack) Pugh, also instructed me in system dynamics and systems thinking, encouraging me to invite my fellow originators or brokers to stand back and see feedback loops. MIT Professor Wanda Orlikowski nurtured my initial interest in the Jam back in the mid-1990s with her pioneering research into collaboration technologies and with her support for my master's thesis on how these influence our organizations. Then *Working Knowledge* author, friend, and KM pioneer Larry Prusak showed that knowledge-transaction costs drop precipitously when people actually get together. (Larry is the consummate "talk trumps technology" guy.) Meanwhile, my friend, Knowledge Jam co-facilitator and mentor Nancy Dixon (Common Knowledge Associates), showed that harmonizing technology and knowledge-sharing behaviors has real promise, that is, when you do it with curiosity and intention.

Leadership Strategies Managing Director Michael Wilkinson shared a framework of facilitation structure and facilitator "fitness." Knowledge Harvesting™ Director Larry Todd Wilson and Pam Holloway (About People) shared an appreciation for the facilitation intensity required to surface *how we know*, not just *what we know*. Bill Isaacs (Dialogos, Inc.), Scott Page (University of Michigan), and Carl Gaertner (State Farm Insurance) inspired the Conversation discipline's dialogue, diversity, and heart-preparedness, respectively. And Andrew McAfee (MIT) made the link between Conversation and Translation by calling on managers to link "Model II" with "Enterprise 2"—a form of listening that makes know-how grow and flow.

Other contributors to the Knowledge Jam were the patient Jammers who helped to validate Knowledge Jam's substance and structure. Intel colleagues Brett Collingwood, Marlyn Haslund, Laurie Jones, Dave Knight, Oliver Mark, Rahul Ravel, Pam Tenorio, and Vince Sheetz (and

Intel clients like Asklepios and Caltrain, and Intel's legal expert, Helen Martin) helped demonstrate the value of real-time Jamming between states and continents. Fidelity Investments India IT operations vice president Neeraj Wadhera sponsored Knowledge Jams between software developers. Forest Bioproducts Research Institute Director Hemant Pendse and Professor Darrell Donahue piloted the large-format Jam as a vehicle for business transformation. Institute for Healthcare Improvement staffers Sarah Jackson, Jo Ann Endo, and Kiette Tucker helped show Knowledge Jam's potential as a vehicle for discerning different hospitals' new process-adoption strategies. Concord Academy volunteer coordinator Brendan Shepherd helped test the "expert Jam" with twenty-five-year Harvard fund-raising veteran Nancy Couch. Finally, Frederic Deriot (Darwin Ecosystem) endured about fifteen brokers at once, while playing the originator in a mock-Jam with MIT Sloan master's students.

Many people helped shape the writing of the book—in both content and form. David Creelman (Creelman Research), my development editor, showed tremendous vision as he helped me to refine the overall arc of the book. He also taught me life lessons about communicating (what he called "taking pebbles out of the reader's path"). Astute and careful reviewers included Tilia Klebenov Jacobs (Worcester Fencing), Alex Brodsky (Travelers Insurance), Anil Paranjpe (FreedomforaPrayer), Michelle Ransom (ShiftChange), Terry Porter (University of Maine Business School), and Gil Yehuda (Yahoo! executive and blogger). Tilia went well beyond the call of duty, presenting me with a full notebook of minute editing marks—cover to cover.

Over the last year I learned that publishing a book is a major business undertaking. I'm grateful to Jossey-Bass Senior Editor Kathe Sweeney, legal advisor Debbie Notkin, Senior Production Manager Dawn Kilgore, Rebecca Taff, editor, editorial program coordinators Rob Brandt and Dani Scoville, and the whole Jossey-Bass team for educating me on the process and raising my appreciation for many of the commercial activities of a leading publisher. Special thanks to Kathe, for her warmth, tireless enthusiasm, and candor.

Finally, I owe a immeasurable thanks to Peter Van Walsum (University of Maine Biological and Chemical Engineering), my Canadian fiancé, who believed in the Knowledge Jam (even doing one!), and sacrificed countless nights and weekends. (He sits across from me even now as I write this, on an enticingly sunny August Saturday.) Peter, let's see whether facilitation, conversation, and translation make good marital disciplines, eh?

THE AUTHOR

Katrina (Kate) Pugh is president of AlignConsulting, specializing in business planning and knowledge-based transformation. She has sixteen years of consulting and seven years of industry experience in the health care sciences, energy, information technology, and financial services sectors. She consults and lectures widely and facilitates both Knowledge Jams and Knowledge Jam training workshops.

Kate consulted with Monitor Group, Oliver Wyman (formerly Mercer Management Consulting), PwC Consulting/IBM, and Dialogos, Inc. She is currently a Lead Benchmarker with Intranet Benchmarking Forum. Among Kate's clients are Cubist Pharmaceuticals, Eli Lilly, Institute for Healthcare Improvement, Jobs for the Future, Mitokine Bioscience, and the World Bank. She co-founded and launched the Knowledge Management (KM) strategy practice with PricewaterhouseCoopers/IBM and led or co-led dozens of KM strategy initiatives.

Kate held leadership positions in industry with Intel Corporation, JPMorganChase, and Fidelity Investments. She launched and ran Fidelity's Personal and Workplace Investments KM program, helped manage Intel Solution Services' Knowledge and Process Management Group, and initiated and ran JPMorganChase's finance portal program. She has also helped launch and/or run more than twenty communities of practice, including Intel's award-winning Enterprise Architects' community. Kate has designed and launched numerous social media, collaboration, and document management initiatives.

Kate has published in the *Harvard Business Review*, *NASA Ask Magazine*, *The European American Business Journal*, and *InPharmation*. She has lectured or workshopped at NASA, MIT Sloan School of

Management, Babson University, Boston University, Center for Business Intelligence, and CPSquare.

Kate has an MS/MBA from the MIT Sloan School of Management, a BA in economics from Williams College, and certificates in Dialogue, Facilitation, Mediation, Project Management, and LEAN Six Sigma. Kate is a member of SIKM Leaders (International and Boston Chapters), Boston Facilitators' Roundtable, and Boston KM Forum.

When not Jamming, Kate can often be found jamming with family and friends on the flute or vocals around New England.

INDEX

Page references followed by *fig* indicate an illustrated figure; followed by *t* indicate a table; followed by *e* indicates an exhibit.

243